"*Virtuous Persuasion* is the most important work on moral theology and missions that currently exists. It should be in the hands of everyone—scholar, clergy or lay—involved in missions. It offers a judicious, generous, and profound diagnosis of the limits of mission understood as growth or dialogue. The remedy set forth through virtuous practices, parsing the complexity of divine and human agency, is marvelous. Everyone engaged in moral theology should be reading this book."

D. Stephen Long, Cary M. Maguire University Professor
of Ethics, Southern Methodist University

"In this compelling first book, Niebauer offers an important corrective to standard accounts of Christian evangelism in favor of an understanding of mission as a virtuous practice that aligns with New Testament accounts of the nature and purpose of mission, particularly that laid out in the book of Acts. Niebauer argues that drawing a stronger connection between mission and the field of theological ethics, particularly virtue ethics and the work of Alasdair MacIntyre, overcomes limitations that arise in dogmatic and anthropological approaches to mission. He develops a constructive view of mission understood in the specific formative activities of proclamation and gathering, drawing on historical and contemporary Catholic and Protestant theologians as well as scholarship in rhetoric and communication. While Niebauer's primary goal is to equip missionaries to understand their work faithfully and effectively, his book also contributes to conversations important to Christian theology more broadly: the interplay of divine grace and human agency, the nature of conversion, the meaning and significance of prayer, and the role that sacraments and liturgy play in moral and spiritual formation."

Elizabeth Agnew Cochran, professor of theology, Duquesne University

"I've watched Michael Niebauer on mission for more than twenty years. He brings theology and practice together in ways rarely seen among pastors, especially church planters. So I'm eager to see how *Virtuous Persuasion* will shape the next generation of church leaders who have been called to proclaim the good news of the risen and glorified Christ."

Collin Hansen, editor in chief and vice president of content
for The Gospel Coalition; host of t

T0385690

"While many works have focused on the centrality of mission in biblical and theological perspective and the dynamics of intercultural theology, much less attention has been given to the lived realities and tensions of those engaged in ongoing missionary encounters. In this volume, Michael Niebauer addresses this lacuna by offering a theology of Christian mission rooted in theological ethics and virtue that addresses these lived realities, providing both critical and constructive reflection on longstanding and recurring issues in mission studies. In so doing, it makes an important and interdisciplinary contribution to the literatures of mission, theology, and ethics."

John R. Franke, Second Presbyterian Church, Indianapolis; general coordinator of the Gospel and Our Culture Network

"Michael Niebauer has written an important book. By locating mission within Christian ethics, Niebauer is able to demonstrate not only the importance of virtue for an understanding of what mission should be but also the importance of proclamation and gathering for determining what virtue actually is for Christian missionaries. Niebauer draws on a deep well of sources—Aquinas, Barth, MacIntyre, for example—and grounds his observations in the text of the New Testament itself. This book should be read by anyone interested in thinking well about Christian mission."

C. Kavin Rowe, George Washington Ivey Distinguished Professor of New Testament, Duke Divinity School

"I highly recommend this book. Niebauer offers tremendous resources for the missionary trying to be faithful to God's mission while being ethically virtuous within the complexities of contemporary life. He begins by problematizing some of the leading models of mission and then leverages resources found within theological ethics to help the missionary find more faithful, virtuous forms of mission within the world. If missiology flourishes when it drinks from fresh streams of other disciplinary flows while being faithful to Scripture and God's mission, this book nourishes missiology with the life-giving tributaries found in theological ethics. It caused me to think about God's mission and the life of the missionary in helpful, impactful ways."

Greg Okesson, provost and senior vice president for academic affairs, Asbury Theological Seminary

"This is an outstanding book on a tremendously important theme—Christian mission. Pastor-theologian Michael Niebauer does what every good pastor-theologian is called to do. He utilizes the best biblical and theological reflection to shed fresh light on an issue of profound significance for the life and ministry of the church. *Virtuous Persuasion* offers a compelling vision of Christian mission informed by theological ethics and grounded in virtuous practice. Take and read—and live—the vision of this book. Highly recommended!"

Todd Wilson, cofounder and president,
Center for Pastor Theologians

"Here Michael Niebauer offers a genuinely fresh theological perspective on mission. This book, which I expected to read dutifully out of loyalty to a former student, quickly became captivating instead. Niebauer enriched my thinking and sometimes even changed my mind. His framework deserves deep and wide reflection."

Daniel J. Treier, Knoedler Professor of Theology, Wheaton College

"*Virtuous Persuasion* delves deep into the most basic questions of mission. It refuses to separate what we know of God from the life we live with God. In so doing, it upends any easy formulas for mission. Read this book and allow Michael Niebauer's careful scholarship, real life experience, and serious attention to Scripture to connect *missio Dei* to the life you live.

David Fitch, Lindner Chair of Evangelical Theology,
Northern Seminary; author of *Faithful Presence*

"This book offers a rich and rewarding understanding of mission as virtuous practice as it demonstrates the goodness of missional proclamation and the Spirit-promotion of joy, hope, and love through faithful witness. Be prepared to draw closer to God and experience the reward of seeing the Lord as you read this volume that deals with the ethics of Christian mission grounded in Scripture and virtue."

Robert L. Gallagher, professor emeritus of intercultural studies,
Wheaton College Graduate School Chicago

"Michael Niebauer's *Virtuous Persuasion* is one of those rare texts that brings different fields of study into a mutual conversation: systematic theology, missiology, Christian ethics/moral theology, missiology, biblical theology, and communications theory. Niebauer argues that each one of the three dominant contemporary theories of mission—*missio Dei*, church growth/church planting, and dialogue—fails to provide an adequate account of human moral agency. As a corrective, he draws on the field of virtue ethics to provide an account of mission as 'virtuous practice' characterized by proclamation and gathering. Along the way, there are discussions of prayer, worship, evangelism, ecclesiology, and pastoral ministry, among other topics. *Virtuous Persuasion* not only introduces a new theological account of church mission. It is a book of wisdom and spiritual guidance that should be read not only by those interested in mission, but by systematic theologians, Christian ethicists, and anyone who is involved in or cares about pastoral ministry."

William Witt, associate professor of systematic
theology and ethics, Trinity School for Ministry

"In a Christian world filled with books commending strategies and techniques for making Christianity effective in the modern world, Michael Niebauer offers a refreshingly theological foundation for Christian mission today. Born of his years as a pastor theologian, Niebauer takes us to the heart of the church's task in the early twenty-first century, proposing a virtuous Christianity that draws on resources from across the history of the church to focus on theological ethics as the center of Christian mission. Niebauer offers a thoughtful and pastorally motivated account of Christian mission rooted in the practices of the proclaiming and gathering church, whose formation into the character of Christ is her primary missional influence. As the twenty-first-century church faces a more complex world, we need able pastors who can guide us back to the theological resources we need to be faithful followers of Jesus. Niebauer is among this company, and this book is a valuable resource for the church's witness to Christ today."

Joel Lawrence, executive director,
Center for Pastor Theologians

VIRTUOUS PERSUASION

A Theology of Christian Mission

STUDIES IN HISTORICAL & SYSTEMATIC THEOLOGY

SHST

H
S ✛ S
T

VIRTUOUS PERSUASION

A Theology of Christian Mission

MICHAEL NIEBAUER

STUDIES IN HISTORICAL AND SYSTEMATIC THEOLOGY

LEXHAM
ACADEMIC

Virtuous Persuasion: A Theology of Christian Mission
Studies in Historical and Systematic Theology

Lexham Academic, an imprint of Lexham Press
1313 Commercial St., Bellingham, WA 98225
LexhamPress.com

Print ISBN 9781683595052
Digital ISBN 9781683595069
Library of Congress Control Number 2022933802

Lexham Editorial: Elliot Ritzema, Elizabeth Vince, Abigail Stocker, Danielle Thevenaz,
    Mandi Newell
Cover Design: Brittany Schrock
Typesetting: Fanny Palacios

CONTENTS

PREFACE

—

This book is about the underlying and inevitable challenges faced by those who embark on the practices of mission and a call for those so engaged to morally reflect on their actions. The roots of this project can be traced as far back as 2005, when I had the extremely good fortune of starting a new church on the campus of Northwestern University with the help of William Beasley and Steve Long. In William I found someone who followed the Holy Spirit and was confident that the Holy Spirit would work in all faithful missional endeavors, no matter what the material outcome. From Steve I learned the value of consistent intellectual and moral reflection on such endeavors. This work is in many ways the confluence of these influences.

While taking Elizabeth Cochran's class on virtue ethics at Duquesne University, I underlined a passage in Alasdair MacIntyre's *After Virtue* concerning his critique of bureaucratic managers. In the margin I wrote "church planting?" That note birthed a term paper for the class, which I then turned into a dissertation with Dr. Cochran's guidance. That dissertation laid the foundations for this work. I could not have asked for a better adviser, as Elizabeth provided much-needed direction, insight, and critique without being obtrusive. Several other professors at Duquesne introduced me to theologians and areas of thought that have been instrumental in shaping this work. I am grateful particularly for William Wright, Darlene Weaver, Marinus Iwuchukwu, Radu Bordeianu, and Bogdan Bucur.

Numerous friends also provided (mostly willing) sounding boards for many of the ideas in this work, including Jens Notstad, Alex Wilgus, and Kerby Goff. In addition, Michael Moore provided much-needed late-stage feedback.

I am grateful for the opportunity to have this work published. Jesse Myers with Lexham Press has been instrumental in this project seeing the light of day and has been a fantastic to work with. I am thankful for Robert Hunt and Darrell Whiteman with the American Society of Missiology for including this book in their series. Ryan Peterson offered vital counsel in regard to the content and scope of this book.

In writing a book on the virtues, I must also thank my parents, John and Diane, who instilled in me a multitude of virtues that made this work possible, most notably the virtue of fortitude. When dealing with dead ends, rejections, and setbacks, I was continually reminded of the paucity of these trials when compared to the sacrifices they have made for our family.

Finally, I am greatly indebted to my extraordinary wife, Allison Morris Niebauer, for her patient endurance through numerous unplanned verbal processing sessions. In Allison I have been blessed with a spouse who is both a well of encouragement and an erudite intellectual sparring partner. Her advice regarding the rhetorical sections of this book has been invaluable, and this work would not have been finished without her love and companionship.

THE AMERICAN SOCIETY OF MISSIOLOGY SERIES PREFACE

—

The purpose of the American Society of Missiology Series is to promote—without regard for disciplinary, national, or denominational boundaries—scholarly works of high quality and wide interest on missiological themes from the entire spectrum of scholarly pursuits relevant to Christian mission.

By mission is meant the effort to effect passage over the boundary between faith in Jesus Christ and its absence. In this understanding of mission, the basic functions of Christian proclamation, dialogue, witness, service, worship, liberation, and nurture are of special concern. And in that context questions arise, including how does the transition from one cultural context to another influence the shape and interaction between these dynamic functions, especially in regard to the cultural and religious plurality that comprises the global context of Christian life and mission.

Monographs in the American Society of Missiology Series reflect the opinions of their authors. They are not understood to represent the position of the American Society of Missiology. Selection is guided by such criteria as intrinsic worth, readability, coherence, and accessibility to a range of interested persons and not merely to experts or specialists.

The American Society of Missiology Series promotes scholarly works of high merit and wide interest on numerous aspects of missiology. Able presentations on new and creative approaches to the practice and understanding of mission will receive close attention.

INTRODUCTION

—

Two contrasting narratives paint a complex and seemingly paradoxical picture of Christian mission in the book of Acts. First there is Peter's speech in Jerusalem immediately following the pouring out of the Holy Spirit at Pentecost. The speech is characterized by brilliant exegesis, exquisite testimony to the resurrected Christ, and a powerful and persuasive exhortation to repent and believe. The response of the crowd is consonant with Peter's Spirit-filled eloquence: three thousand repent and are baptized and gathered into the new worshiping community.

A few chapters later, Luke depicts a similar narrative with the speech of Stephen before the high priest in Jerusalem. Stephen's exegesis is equally insightful, giving a persuasive appeal to acknowledge Jesus as the "Righteous One" (Acts 7:52) and fulfillment of Old Testament hope. Stephen's speech ends with a powerful rebuke of those who have rejected Jesus, but the response of his interlocutors does not mirror the response of Peter's. Instead, the crowd apprehends and stones him.

Modern conceptions of mission have much to commend concerning Peter's actions but have little room for the story of Stephen. Peter's missional proclamation is a story of superb contextualization, eloquent speech, and astonishing numerical results. Stephen's story is one of equally astute contextualization and persuasiveness, but it is ultimately one characterized by hostility and worldly ineffectiveness. By modern standards, Stephen could be noted principally for his lack of tact and the failure of his words to achieve missional success. And yet, Stephen receives the greater reward: the glory of God and a vision of Jesus standing at the right hand of the Father.

MISSION GROUNDED IN VIRTUE

Contemporary practitioners of mission are beset with a host of tensions: the desire to grow one's mission without being fixated on numbers, the desire to proclaim the gospel while respecting the beliefs of the religious other, and the discernment of which actions constitute mission. While the codification of mission as participation in the mission of God (*missio Dei*) has advocated effectively for the centrality of mission in biblical and dogmatic theology, and anthropological approaches to mission have had a profound effect on understanding the dynamics of intercultural theology, little has been written to address these underlying tensions which the missionary encounters daily. What is missing in these emerging theologies is a robust examination of the day-to-day actions of missionaries and the host of challenges that are concomitant with these actions.

This project alleviates these tensions by proposing a theology of Christian mission rooted in theological ethics. It uses the tools of ethics to critique various conceptions of mission and assess the recurring issues prevalent within the field of missiology. Then, it uses theological ethics as a foundation for constructing a theology of mission grounded in virtue.

The genesis of this project is my own background in mission and ministry, particularly my fifteen years spent as a church planter in North America. The perpetual challenges faced within this work presented a host of questions regarding missions and the role of the missionary, and I found in the field of missiology that such questions were frequently asked but inadequately answered. Theological ethics and moral philosophy provide an essential grammar for articulating these critiques and constructing a way forward for mission that more adequately answers these questions.

The first section of this book involves a critical assessment of three major models of mission, identifying three major problems within the study of mission as a whole. In addition to elucidating the major theological and philosophical underpinnings of these issues, it also demonstrates how these issues affect the day-to-day challenges and anxieties of missionaries. These three problems I identify as *distinction, agency,* and *persuasion*:

1. *Distinction*—Which actions constitute mission? Is mission about evangelism, church planting, development, or all of the above? This is not an otiose debate over semantic range. If mission is the entirety of all Christian actions, then the missionary will continually struggle with prioritizing some activities, such as evangelism or social works, over others.

2. *Agency*—Can human beings contribute at all to God's mission? How does one grow their mission without turning people into statistics? If growth is the ultimate goal of mission, then the missionary will subvert ethical claims to the desire to master human behavior with scientific precision, denying human agency at the behest of mechanistic processes.

3. *Persuasion*—How does one persuade another to convert to Christianity without being manipulative? An enterprise whose goal is the invitation to change one's worldview must wrestle with the often-blurry frontier between persuasion and coercion. If intentional persuasion is inherently manipulative, mission would seem to be rendered inert.

The second section of this project answers these problems by moving from dogmatic and anthropological approaches to mission to an approach centered on ethics. Specifically, mission is construed as two specific activities (proclamation and gathering) that develop virtue in their practitioners and further them toward their goal of partaking in the glory of God. It proceeds with a framing of mission in ethical theories of virtue, drawing substantially from classical sources such as Gregory of Nyssa and Thomas Aquinas, as well as contemporary sources including Alasdair MacIntyre and Oliver O'Donovan. This paves the way for a thorough examination of the practices of proclamation and gathering, revealing how this conception of mission both addresses the aforementioned problems and accords best with the practices of mission in the book of Acts.

WHY THEOLOGICAL ETHICS?

Part of the goal of the ensuing critique section of this book is to demonstrate that ethics is a more appropriate field through which to examine Christian mission. While chapter four will take up this apologia more thoroughly, a few preliminary remarks are in order.

My use of the term "ethics" in this work is different from the way in which ethics is often construed, which is as simply the schema for demarcating right actions from wrong ones. Although the discernment of right from wrong action is a part of ethics, I would argue that this is not its primary purpose. Instead, I take my cues from a definition of ethics outlined by Herbert McCabe in *What Is Ethics All About?*: that ethics is "the quest of less and less trivial modes of human relatedness."[1] For McCabe, in the pursuit of ethics, one probes the depths of human behavior in search of its deeper significance. In doing so, one can "enjoy life more by responding to it more sensitively."[2] Such a pursuit will involve the discerning of right from wrong, but it will also include the demarcation of certain activities as more trivial than others. McCabe draws a parallel between ethics and literary criticism: the point of criticism is not simply to separate good poetry from bad poetry, but rather to probe the significance of poetry. Such a pursuit done well will identify poetry that is not very significant (bad poetry) as well as those poems that, because they are exquisite, lend themselves to inexhaustible analysis.

To this end, the point of my critical chapters is not to identify three bad forms of mission, paving the way for one good conception of mission. Rather, it is to probe the depths of the significance of mission and search for forms of mission that are more and more significant. Such probing is inexhaustible, and, as such, this book makes no claims to be the final word on mission.

This book is not only a work of ethics but specifically a work of "theological ethics," a term that is used synonymously with "Christian ethics" and "Christian moral theology." That this is a work of theological ethics can be gleaned from the discussion concerning the authority of Scripture in chapter four. To state that Scripture is authoritative is already to describe some of the limits of moral inquiry. Though Christian ethics can be used as both a critical and constructive tool, this book presumes that it cannot be used to contradict Scripture.

While this work is based in theological ethics, it is not limited to this field. A broad study of Christian mission necessarily touches on a whole host of topics: the relationship between human mission and Trinitarian missions, biblical approaches to mission, cross-cultural communication, and the practical activities of missionaries. In order to adequately address these topics as they arise, this book draws on the various fields of study that undergird these issues. These fields, what we might call minor interdisciplinary partners, are listed here in order of their importance to this study: communication studies

---

1. Herbert McCabe, *What Is Ethics All About?* (Washington: Corpus Books, 1969), 99.
2. McCabe, *What Is Ethics?*, 95.

and rhetoric, dogmatics,[3] anthropology, interfaith theology, and management/organizational theory. The reason for the selection of these particular partners is twofold: First, in the critical section of the work, I will examine specific construals of mission that are based in part on theories that draw from these fields. In order to adequately critique these models of mission, to "cut to their core," so to speak, it is thus imperative to engage with their related academic disciplines. Second, my constructive construal of mission as virtuous practice touches on topics that can be more fully understood only by examining these related fields.[4] The most important application of this methodological approach will be my use of rhetoric and communication in crafting a conception of the missional practice of proclamation.

In grounding mission in ethics, this book aims to substantially contribute to each of these disciplines: mission affords a practical context to explore particular and recurrent issues in moral theology, and ethics provides a grammar through which one can morally reflect on the specific activities that constitute mission. In addition, this project offers encouragement to pastors, laity, and missionaries who engage regularly in the practices of mission. The concluding chapter spells out some of the practical implications for my conception of mission and is meant to show that, though a calling to Christian mission might be difficult at times, it does not have to be overly complicated. Becoming a skilled missionary is linked more with one's ability to follow Christ than it is in the disembodied mastering of techniques. The pursuit of the mastery of the craft of mission is ultimately a holy pursuit whose gains are the growth of virtue, sanctification, and the partaking in the glory of God. The proclamations of the gospel by Peter and Stephen in the book of Acts testify to this claim, and at the minimum, I hope that my

---

3. Listing dogmatics as an interdisciplinary partner is perhaps creating too great a distinction between this field and theological ethics. For example, one cannot completely extricate the ethics of Karl Barth or Thomas Aquinas from their dogmatic assertions regarding the Trinity and the incarnation. However, these dogmatic assertions do get discussed on their own apart from ethics, and one can give these issues closer scrutiny while also acknowledging that there will be necessary implications for human action as a result. Chapters two and five will examine this issue in fuller detail.

4. The risk of such an approach is to craft a book that quickly becomes unwieldy, as each of these disciplines has their own historical trajectories and seemingly interminable debates. For this work to fit an appropriate scale and length, I have attempted to engage with these disciplines to address specific issues only when those issues arise in the course of my arguments, using extensive footnotes to engage in some of the broader issues in each of these fields. The use of footnotes in this way is meant to help maintain greater coherence within the work as a whole.

conception of mission sheds light on the seemingly paradoxical story of a deacon's eloquent and persuasive words met with both violent rejection and a vision of Jesus standing at the right hand of the Father.

AN OVERVIEW OF THIS BOOK

PART I—THE CRITICAL TASK: THREE MODELS, THREE PROBLEMS

The first section of this book will examine three models of mission (mission as *missio Dei*, mission as growth, and mission as dialogue), in the process identifying three perpetual problems within the field of mission. Each of these chapters is devoted first to an examination and critique of one of these models of mission, followed by an extended discussion of one particular problem that emerges through this critique, a problem that remains persistent within the study of Christian mission as a whole. These three issues I have labeled the problems of *distinction, agency*, and *persuasion*. These issues, while being highlighted within an analysis of specific models of mission, are not necessarily limited to these models, but in many ways they characterize many of the challenges within the study of Christian mission as a whole. In the following synopses, I will briefly describe these models of mission and their corresponding problems, as well as highlight some of the interdisciplinary partners that will aid in this task.

Chapter 1: Mission as Missio Dei and the Problem of Distinction

The first way of construing mission comes out of the field of missiology. It conceives of mission as the participation in and witness to the mission of God (*missio Dei*). Mission as *missio Dei* construes election as a call to witness rather than a statement on eternal judgment and sees mission within a communal context that is beyond simply personal conversion.

While the emergence of *missio Dei* as a preeminent missiological concept has provided a welcome and corrective voice to conceptions of mission that explicitly emphasized the winning of souls and implicitly viewed Western cultural dispersal as intertwined with the Christian message, there remain challenges as a result of its ascendance. A principal challenge is the problem of *distinction*. In placing mission at the heart of theology, there is a danger of mission losing its distinctive character. Mission becomes simply all Christian

activity, which makes it difficult to assess both the moral and practical implications of specific missional activities.

The conception of mission as *missio Dei* is grounded in both the fields
of missiology and dogmatics, particularly the work of Karl Barth. For this
reason, the chapter will also serve as an introduction to the field of missiology as a whole and engage in the work and theological reception of Karl
Barth, particularly his conceptions of mission and agency.

Chapter 2: Mission as Growth and the Problem of Agency

Mission as growth construes the goal of mission as the numerical increase
in both the number of converts to Christianity and in the numerical attendance of church gatherings. This model addresses the problem of distinction
that characterized mission as *missio Dei*. It emphasizes active participation in
mission work: the missionary can get better at their job, and such improvement can yield tangible results. However, mission as growth carries with it
several weaknesses related to the problem of *agency*. If growth is the ultimate goal, the missionary will subvert ethical claims to the desire to master
human behavior with scientific precision; missional growth models attempt
to control human behavior in an attempt to maximize numerical success,
leaving the morality of missional actions unquestioned. This would appear
to rob individuals of their ability to meaningfully choose to adhere (or not
adhere) to Christianity.

Because adherents to the mission as growth paradigm draw substantially from the social sciences, as well as management and organizational
theory, this chapter will also engage in substantial critiques related to these
specific fields.

Chapter 3: Mission as Dialogue and the Problem of Persuasion

Mission as dialogue attempts to answer the problem of persuasion in mission
by characterizing mission as the distinct practice of interreligious dialogue,
with the goal simply stated as the knowledge of the other. Here, the ability
for individuals to be persuaded of the validity of the Christian message is
rejected under the auspices that such persuasion is inherently manipulative. However, such construals of mission deny the intrinsic persuasiveness of ideas, falsely assert a coherence of the self that is incapable of being

persuaded, and ignore the multitude of persuasive missional acts present in holy Scripture. We can characterize these issues as the problem of *persuasion*. Mission as dialogue ultimately denies the ability of individuals to choose whether to accept, modify, or reject invitations to reassess their current religious and moral worldviews.

Because the mission as dialogue paradigm has been prominent amongst theologians who hold some form of the pluralistic account of religions, and because the focus on dialogue places communication as the central missional activity, this section will draw extensively from the fields of communication and rhetorical studies, as well as engage in some of the debates concerning theologies of religious pluralism.

PART II—THE CONSTRUCTIVE TASK: MISSION, VIRTUE, AND
THE PRACTICES OF PROCLAMATION AND GATHERING

The remainder of this project is devoted to constructing a theory of mission based on virtue. The thesis posited is this: Christian mission is best construed as specific activities (proclamation and gathering) that develop virtue in its practitioners, moving them toward their ultimate goal of partaking in the glory of God. The rest of the book will be spent unpacking this statement. This conception of mission carries with it three major goals: First, that it addresses the aforementioned problems of distinction, agency, and persuasion. Second, that it fits with the New Testament accounts of mission. And third, that it enables moral reflection on the practical performance of mission activities. These three goals will be further explained in the beginning of chapter four, and the concluding paragraphs of the remaining chapters will summarize the ways these chapters have sufficiently met these goals.

Chapter 4: Mission as Virtuous Practice

Chapter four will be devoted to casting Christian mission in the framework of Aquinas's moral theology. This will involve first an explanation of Aquinas's articulation of the relationship between God and creation, human action, and virtue, followed by an explanation of how fitting mission within this framework might solve many of the aforementioned issues surrounding distinction and agency. Within this framework, mission will be construed as two virtuous practices: proclamation and gathering. The next part of chapter four will be devoted to elucidating Alasdair MacIntyre's concept of a virtuous practice

and demonstrating how conceiving of proclamation and gathering as virtuous practices best addresses the aforementioned issues in Christian mission.

Chapter 5: The Practice of Proclamation

Chapter five examines in detail the missional practice of proclamation. The
goal of this chapter is to show how this conception of proclamation as a
virtuous practice coheres with MacIntyre's conception of a practice, how it
helps to explain the actual practices of Christian proclamation in the book
of Acts, and how it enables moral and practical reflection on the task of proclamation itself. Because the proximate goal of proclamation is conversion,
and because the problem of persuasion is a significant issue in the study of
Christian mission, an extended treatment of Christian conversion is also
offered at the beginning of this chapter.

Chapter 6: The Practice of Gathering

This chapter elucidates the virtuous practice of gathering. It begins by first
drawing the necessary connections between the proclamation of the gospel
and the assembling for worship of those who assent to this message. It continues by describing the three major activities involved in the practice of
gathering: the translation of the contents of the Christian faith, the inculturation of Christian worship into local contexts, and, finally, the delegation
of authority to indigenous leadership.

Chapter 7: Entering into the Craft of Mission—
Tragedy, Tradition, and Telos

The final chapter will place the practices of proclamation and gathering
within the broader context of the craft of mission as a whole. This will involve
an examination of the dynamics between those who are teachers of mission
and those who wish to become experts in the practice of mission. It will also
discuss how the practice of mission may be performed by both vocational
missionaries as well as those who do not practice mission as a career. Finally,
I will attempt to place the practices of mission within the overall context of
a life lived well. The practice of mission is one of numerous practices that
are open to the Christian, and part of living a life holy and pleasing to God is
learning how to order a whole host of these practices. This includes the possibility of tragedy: that practitioners of mission may have points in their life

where the conflicting duties of the Christian—to church, to family, to those in need—necessitate a scaling back of the practice of mission.

Conclusion

The book concludes by briefly exploring three passages from Scripture that both summarize and illustrate the core concepts of mission as virtuous practice, offering warrant and inspiration for all those who wish to enter into the craft of mission.

Part I

—

THE CRITICAL TASK: THREE MODELS, THREE PROBLEMS

1

MISSION AND THE *MISSIO DEI*

The field of missiology has been dominated by two major perspectives rooted in different methodologies. At the one end of the spectrum, biblical and dogmatic theology provide a starting point for an understanding of the mission of God as it is revealed in history, with the hope that such an understanding will help the church interpret its task as intrinsically caught up in this divine activity. At the other end, anthropology and history provide a starting point to help better comprehend the ways in which the Christian message is made intelligible in new contexts. The establishment of these approaches as complementary partners within missiology is well justified. As Bevans and Schroeder famously summarize, "Christian mission … must preserve, defend, and proclaim the *constants* of the church's traditions; at the same time it must respond creatively and boldly to the *contexts* in which it finds itself."[1] Biblical and dogmatic theology help one understand the constants of mission, while anthropology and history help one understand the contexts of mission. These partnerships have borne much fruit, from David Bosch's dogmatic treatise *Transforming Mission*[2] to Lamin Sanneh's *Translating the Message*.[3]

Despite these achievements, significant gaps and tensions remain between these two perspectives, what Darrell Guder describes as tensions "between Theo and Christocentric approaches on the one hand and the anthropocentric cluster of approaches on the other."[4] In what follows, I will trace the development of missiology by describing the emergence of the term

---

1. Stephen B. Bevans and Roger Schroeder, *Constants in Context: A Theology of Mission for Today* (Maryknoll, NY: Orbis Books, 2004), 1.

2. David J. Bosch, *Transforming Mission: Paradigm Shifts in Theology of Mission* (Maryknoll, NY: Orbis Books, 1991).

3. Lamin O. Sanneh, *Translating the Message: The Missionary Impact on Culture* (Maryknoll, NY: Orbis Books, 1989).

4. Darrell L. Guder, *Called to Witness: Doing Missional Theology* (Grand Rapids: Eerdmans, 2015), 35.

missio Dei as the term par excellence of dogmatic mission theology and by identifying two of the concerns raised by this emergence, with an ensuing section focusing specifically on the problem of distinction.

HISTORICAL BACKGROUND

Darrell Guder describes the emergence of what he calls "the *missio Dei* consensus" as a distinct shift in mission studies out of practical theology and into the very heart of dogmatics. Prior to its emergence in the twentieth century, the term "mission" either referred in a very limited way to the movements within the Triune God (Trinitarian missions)[5] or to practical issues faced by missionaries. Thus, mission studies focused primarily on evangelistic methods and catechetical best practices, with anthropology being the primary interdisciplinary partner: missiology was primarily the Christian attempt to understand other cultures in order to better proclaim the gospel.[6] As such, there was little interplay between dogmatic theology and mission: the former described theory, the latter practice.[7] This began to change primarily through the work of Karl Barth, whose arguments regarding the intrinsic missionary nature of the church sparked a movement toward situating mission within the context of biblical and dogmatic theology. For Barth, the calling of the individual to Jesus Christ intrinsically unites the individual to both Jesus Christ and all called by Christ. To be a Christian is to witness to the salvific activity of Jesus Christ and to be united to all those who do the same:

> But in his ministry of witness—and it is this essentially which makes him a Christian—he is from the very outset, by his very ordination to

---

5. Gilles Emery summarizes a traditional understanding of Trinitarian missions: God has revealed God's self as Trinitarian through the sending of the Son and the Holy Spirit, and this sending invites Christians to enter into Trinitarian faith. This sending is a concrete revelation in history and reveals the very person of God. This ensures that the source of our understanding remains dependent upon the gift of God, and that such understanding is meant to bring us into intimacy with God. Hence the mission of God both reveals God as Trinitarian and enables salvation for humankind. See Gilles Emery, *The Trinity: An Introduction to Catholic Doctrine on the Triune God* (Washington, DC: Catholic University of America Press, 2011).

6. The dominance of anthropology in mission theology during the mid-twentieth century is perhaps best evidenced by the popularity of the journal *Popular Anthropology*, which was renamed as *Missiology* in 1973.

7. Guder, *Called*, 4. See also Gerald H. Anderson, "The Theology of Mission among Protestants in the Twentieth Century," in *The Theology of the Christian Mission*, ed. Gerald H. Anderson (New York: McGraw-Hill, 1965).

it, united not only with some or many, but—whether or not he knows them and their particular situation—with all those who are charged with his ministry. He is united to them by the simple fact that, since there is only one work as the Word of God and only one Mediator between God and man self-declared in His activity, the content of his witness cannot be other than that of theirs, nor the content of theirs other than that of his.[8]

Thus, for Barth, bearing witness to Christ is not a separate or additional activity for the Christian but is intrinsically part of one's existence. As the church is defined *as* the people united in their witnessing to the Triune, salvific mission of God, part of the individual life of the Christian includes such witnessing actions.[9] The term "*missio Dei*," though not mentioned by Barth, began to connote the understanding of the mission of the church as an extension of the Triune mission of God and as a witness to God's salvific activity in human history.

The apex of the emergence of the term "*missio Dei*" comes in David Bosch's 1991 work *Transforming Mission*, which remains arguably the most influential missiological text produced in the past fifty years. Bosch traces the history of Christian mission and demonstrates how theories of mission have changed based on the particular historical epoch they inhabited. Bosch sees with the end of the Enlightenment era the advent of a postmodern era that must also usher in a new way of thinking about mission.[10] The concept of *missio Dei* is key in the development of this postmodern missiological paradigm. Bosch characterizes the term "*missio Dei*," drawing upon the work of Johannes Aagaard, as follows: "In the new image mission is not primarily an activity of the church, but an attribute of God. ... Mission is thereby seen as a

---

8. Karl Barth, *Church Dogmatics*, vol. IV/3, trans. G. W. Bromiley (Edinburgh: T&T Clark, 1961), 682–83.

9. John Webster sees this rooted in Barth's description of the prophetic office of Jesus. The church does not establish Jesus Christ on earth but shares in the prophetic office of Jesus by pointing to his already sufficient salvific work. The community of the church is not defined principally by its activity, but by its prophetic pointing to Jesus: "Perhaps the most radical extension of what Barth is arguing concerns the understanding of the mission of the church. In essence, speaking of Jesus as prophet shifts the primary locus of activity away from the community of believers on to Jesus himself, who is the agent of his own realization. Thereby the church is redefined as a community whose task is not that of making effective Jesus' reality but of attesting its inherent effectiveness." John Webster, *Barth* (London: Continuum, 2000), 135.

10. Bosch, *Transforming*, 349.

movement from God to the world; the church is viewed as an instrument for
that mission ... to participate in mission is to participate in the movement of
God's love toward people, since God is a fountain of sending of love."[11]

KEY ASPECTS OF THE MISSION
AS *MISSIO DEI* MODEL

There are three key aspects to the conception of mission as *missio Dei* that are
pertinent for this study. First, the movement places mission at the heart of
Christian theology. By folding the very nature of the church into the mission
of God, mission becomes the lens through which the church should perform
its theological task. The church's mission is directly related to the Triune missions. Francis Oborji summarizes this development, which is rooted in Barth:

> Mission was to be understood in the context of the Trinitarian theol-
> ogy's classical doctrine of the *missio Dei* as God the Father sending the
> Son, and God the Father and the Son sending the Holy Spirit. Barth
> correctly expanded this to include the Father, Son, and Holy Spirit
> sending the church into the world.[12]

If theology's goal is to aid the church in deepening its understanding of God,
and if the church is defined by its witness to God's mission, then theology
must flow out of the church's participation in God's missional activity. Bosch
summarizes the implications of this for missiology:

> Just as the church ceases to be church if it is not missionary, theology
> ceases to be theology if it loses its missionary character. The crucial
> question, then, is not simply or only or largely what church is or what
> mission is, it is also what theology is and is about. We are in need of a
> missiological agenda for theology rather than just a theological agenda
> for mission; for theology, rightly understood, has no reason to exist
> other than critically to accompany the *missio Dei*.[13]

---

11. Bosch, *Transforming*, 390. See also Johannes Aagaard's summary of mission as participation in the *missio Dei* in Johannes Aagaard, "Trends in Missiological Thinking during the Sixties,"
International Review of Mission 62, no. 245 (1973), 8–25.

12. Francis Anekwe Oborji, *Concepts of Mission: The Evolution of Contemporary Missiology*
(Maryknoll, NY: Orbis Books, 2006), 146.

13. Bosch, *Transforming*, 494.

The second aspect is related to this first point. Since mission is wrapped up in the Trinitarian missions, mission is ultimately the prerogative of God. Mission is not limited to the activities of the church, and even more so it is not limited to specific missionaries and missionary agencies. Mission is the *activity of God*,[14] and the church's mission is simply one of "service to the reign of God's universal *shalom*."[15] Such assertions lead to both a broadening of the activities that constitute mission and an emphasis on history as the arena through which God's mission is accomplished. The role of the church is to witness to this redemption and point to a hope in the future eschaton and the establishment of God's kingdom.

Third, an understanding of the church as witness to the *missio Dei* presented a welcome critique of the paternalistic aspects of the missionary past. The emphasis on God's salvific mission and the characterization of the church as a witness to, rather than creator of, this salvation presented a corrective voice to missionary work that explicitly emphasized the winning of souls and implicitly viewed Western cultural dispersal as intertwined with the Christian message.[16] The *missio Dei* consensus construes election as a call to witness rather than a statement on eternal judgment and sees mission within a communal context that is beyond simply personal conversion. Guder thus sees *missio Dei* as a massive critique of Western Christendom:

> In its [Western Christendom's] tendency to reduce the gospel to individual salvation, it fails to confess the fullness of the message of the

---

14. Oborji, *Concepts*, 134.

15. Oborji, *Concepts*, 136.

16. It should be noted that critiques of pre-twentieth-century missionary activities codified under the auspices of "Western Christendom" are admittedly overly broad. The relationships between missionaries and colonial governments, for instance, run the spectrum from overt collusion to overt hostility. In regard to cultural dispersal, perhaps the most charitable read on history is that the conflation of Western cultural values with the gospel was not a conscious decision on the part of many missionaries but appeared as an unnecessary and harmful conflation only in hindsight. See Andrew F. Walls, *The Cross-Cultural Process in Christian History: Studies in the Transmission and Appropriation of Faith* (Maryknoll, NY: Orbis Books, 2002), 49–71. Guder is right, however, in pointing to moments throughout the history of Christian mission where specific missional practices unduly tied conversion to Christianity with conversion to Western culture. One of the most glaring examples would be the practice of sending African leaders to Europe in order to mold them into European Christians. Such leaders were then sent back to Africa in order to become ecclesiastical, and sometimes political, leaders. Scott Sunquist charts how such a practice became common for various European missions, both Roman Catholic and Protestant. See Scott W. Sunquist, *Understanding Christian Mission: Participation in Suffering and Glory* (Grand Rapids: Baker Publishing Group, 2013), 52.

inbreaking reign of God in Jesus Christ. In its tendency to make the church into the institution that administers that individual salvation, it fails to confess the fullness of the church's vocation to be, do, and say the witness to that reign of God breaking in now in Jesus Christ.[17]

We can trace in all three of these aspects a common thread of *expansion*. Mission has grown out of the confines of practical theology; it has been expanded to include the very activity of God, and, as such, it enables a critique of previous theologies of the mission that narrowly focused on the evangelistic activities of certain churches or individuals.

A CRITICAL EVALUATION OF MISSION AS *MISSIO DEI*

While the emergence of *missio Dei* as a preeminent missiological concept has provided a welcome and corrective voice, there remain challenges as a result of its ascendance. In many ways these challenges reflect the perpetual difficulties within the study and practice of mission as a whole. The first critiques center on the ways in which the *missio Dei* consensus gives rise to a problematic account of moral agency in human beings. This account reflects greater challenges emerging from the relationship between nature and grace in Barth's thought. These issues then lead to perhaps the biggest problem with *missio Dei*, which I identify as the problem of distinction. As such, the problem of distinction will be treated in extended detail in a separate section.

The conception of mission as *missio Dei* makes human agency problematic in two ways. First, it renders the exercise of agency by those engaged in missionary activity superfluous vis-à-vis the activity of God. Second, it denies the ability of those who are the recipients of missionary endeavors to exercise their agency in rejecting the claims of their interlocutors. What follows will be a treatment of both of these issues, showing how they are in part predicated on a particular reading of Karl Barth's view of nature and grace.

---

17. Guder, *Called*, 24.

DIMINISHED MISSIONARY AGENCY

A conception of mission as participation in the *missio Dei* emphasizes the missional activity of the Triune God in a manner that risks minimizing the individual agency of the missionary and the church as a human institution. To some degree, the reduced emphasis on human agency within the *missio Dei* consensus was intentional—a welcome corrective to the perceived excesses of Western approaches to mission collectively labeled under the banner of Christendom. Here, the emphasis on personal and individual conversion, and the church as the sole bearer and guarantor of salvation, seemed to deny the action of God in bringing about the reconciliation of the world, as well as to render missionaries both the agents of salvation and the final judge over who is or who isn't saved. In challenging this discourse, those advocating for mission as the *missio Dei* argued that election is not primarily about divining foreknowledge of St. Peter's list, but instead about the call placed on those elected to witness to the work of God in Christ. As Guder puts it, this "engenders great modesty with regard to the claims that the Christian community makes about itself, but at the same time deep conviction about the utter reliability of God's mighty acts and certain promises."[18]

A conception of mission that emphasizes God as principal actor is meant to counter the prideful habituation of professional missionaries, a pride that often manifested itself in collusion with Western colonialism and the promulgation of Western civilization as essential to Christianity. Mission became construed as a practical task, separate from theology and left to a handful of professional missionaries. The conception of mission as primarily practical led to the leveraging of colonial advantages for pragmatic missionary gains, as evidenced in the 1842 treaty that ended the First Opium War, in which China was "forced open for trade and for missionaries by foreign gunships."[19] A mission separated from God and stripped of theological depth also led to the undue conflation of Western civilization as Christianity, as in the case of

---

18. Guder, *Called*, 25.

19. Sunquist, *Understanding Christian Mission*, 94. It is perhaps best to view the interplay between missionaries and Western colonialism under this pragmatic lens. Missionaries would leverage colonial power whenever it suited their needs but would often circumvent political channels if such channels restricted access to foreign countries. "It is tempting, therefore, to see missionary work as riding on the coattails of Western colonialism. While missionaries are not imperialists, they are often pragmatists. When it seemed difficult to move farther, to go to new regions, or to reach new peoples, missionaries would find a way" (Sunquist, *Understanding*, 95).

missionaries shipping African church leaders back to Europe to be properly enculturated in Christian (i.e., European) values before returning to lead,[20] or the insistence of British missionaries on pairing mission work with a proper British education.[21]

We see in these critiques of mission's colonial past a prideful conflation of the missionary's effort with God's effort. Missionaries developed habits aimed at the efficient conversion of the heathens in the belief that they were learning to further God's mission. The problem is that such an over-corrective leaves little room for real participation amongst human beings in the missionary effort. If mission is everything, and mission is the work of God, then what is left for the missionary to do?

Issues regarding human agency that result from a codification of mission as *missio Dei* are in part due to its heavy reliance on the dogmatic theology of Karl Barth. The minimization of human agency in the *missio Dei* consensus reflects the problematic status of human agency within Barth's theology, and, for this reason, it is important to briefly trace the development of agency within Barth's thought. Barth's theological trajectory was defined in large part by his struggle to create space for a genuine human knowledge of God that does not render God an idolatrous projection of the human mind. This struggle leads Barth away from a sharp dichotomy between God and humankind (which renders knowledge of God nearly impossible)[22] and toward a grounding of human knowledge solely in the reconciliatory work of Jesus Christ.[23] This reconciliation is already won for humankind prior to

---

20. Sunquist, *Understanding*, 52. See footnote above.

21. Kevin Ward, "Africa," in *A World History of Christianity*, ed. Adrian Hastings (Grand Rapids: Eerdmans, 2000), 218.

22. Keith L. Johnson, "A Reappraisal of Karl Barth's Theological Development and His Dialogue with Catholicism," *International Journal of Systematic Theology* 14, no. 1 (2012): 7.

23. While Barthian scholars acknowledge a shift in Barth's theology away from the dialectics of *Commentary on Romans* and toward a knowledge of God grounded in the doctrine of reconciliation, there is significant disagreement concerning how this shift should be interpreted. D. Stephen Long argues that this difference is between those who interpret Barth as claiming that the Triune hypostases constitute election, and vice versa (170). While the details of these disagreements are beyond this work, I would agree with Long that an interpretation of Barth that stresses the preeminence of election over the Triune hypostases creates a host of problems that places Barth well outside of the mainstream, and "his work will have little ability to garner ecumenical attention outside a narrow tradition of Reformed theology committed to doing theology under the conditions of modernity" (183). See D. Stephen Long, "From the Hidden God to the God of Glory: Barth, Balthasar, and Nominalism," *Pro Ecclesia* 20, no. 2 (2011).

their existence, and it establishes the grounds through which any and all knowledge of God might be found.[24]

In his desire to create a genuine space for human knowledge of God, Barth grounds human participation in the prior work of Jesus Christ. The reconciliation of man to God is intrinsic to Christ's existence—humankind is created both sinful and redeemed.[25] Such an assertion has a tremendous impact on a notion of human agency, as it would appear to render human participation in actual history as little more than a façade. Such suspicions are in part confirmed by Barth's implicit universalism: since Christ is the reconciler of all of humankind by his very nature, all of humankind will eventually be saved.[26]

It is easy to see how the inevitable eventuality of salvation for all would seem to diminish the individual efforts of missionaries. Since all of humanity will eventually be (or is already) saved by Jesus Christ, the work of the missionary is simply one of hastening the inevitable. We see this in Barth's view of the particular act of Christian witness. John Webster characterizes Barth's view of mission as one of herald, or "passive witness." The goal of the church is not to bring about the presence of Christ, but simply to witness, or "transmit knowledge" of, the presence and work of Christ. According to Barth, the church

> is not commanded to represent, introduce, bring into play or even in a sense accomplish again in its being, speech, and action either reconciliation, the covenant, the kingdom or the new world reality. ... It lives its true prophecy by the fact that it remains distinct from His, that it is subject to it, that it does not try to replace it, but that with supreme power and yet with the deepest humility it points to the work of God accomplished in Him and the Word of God spoken in

24. "It is not that He [God] first wills and works the being of the world and man, and then ordains it for salvation. But God creates, preserves and over-rules man for this prior end and with this prior purpose, that there may be a being distinct from Himself ordained for salvation, for perfect being, for participation in his own being." Barth, *Church Dogmatics*, IV/1 :9. See Johnson, "A Reappraisal."

25. Barth, *Church Dogmatics* IV/1: 9.

26. "On the basis of the eternal will of God we have to think of every human being, even the oddest, most villainous or miserable, as one to whom Jesus Christ is Brother and God is Father; and we have to deal with him on this assumption. If the other person knows that already, then we have to strengthen him in the knowledge. If he does not know it yet or no longer knows it, our business is to transmit this knowledge to him." Karl Barth, *The Humanity of God*, trans. John Newton Thomas (Richmond, VA: John Knox Press, 1960), 53.

Him, inviting to gratitude for this work and the hearing of this Word,
but not pretending to be claimed for more than this indication and
invitation, nor to be capable of anything more.[27]

Barth's view of witness is too passive and neglects the active and participa-
tory nature of Christian mission. Webster gives a sympathetic reading of
Barth in this regard, believing that he is simply placing dogmatic concerns
above ethical ones, yet even Webster concedes that Barth's account of human
action is "opaque."[28] For Barth, human action does not *make* history, it only
attests to a history that is already made.

The emphasis on mission as entirely the work of God places in question
the role of human beings as active participants in this mission. Guder codifies these criticisms as stemming from an interpretation of the *missio Dei*
"in ways that ultimately render the visible and organized church marginal, if
not a questionable deviation from God's actual mission in the world."[29] The
logical conclusion of Barth's account of mission and agency renders the role
of the missionary as something akin to a newspaper striving for a scoop: the
goal is simply to be the *first* to present information that will eventually be
given by another.

DIMINISHED AGENCY OF THE RECIPIENT

The problem of agency in Barth's thought not only affects the missionary,
but also the missionary's interlocutors. If the codification of mission is the
mission of God's salvific actions throughout history, particularly in the reconciliation of all of humanity to God through Jesus Christ, this would seem
to greatly diminish the humanity of those with opposing religious views.
If the task of Christian mission is to inform the villainous person that they
have simply failed to recognize what they will eventually recognize—that
Jesus has and will bring about their salvation—then one is in effect limiting

---

27. Barth, *Church Dogmatics*, IV/3:836.

28. Webster, *Barth*, 161. Gerald McKenny takes a similar view, asserting that Barth's theology
affirms human moral action while acknowledging "liabilities" in Barth's thought, particularly in
regard to how such human participation occurs and the role of the Holy Spirit in such actions.
McKenny rejects an interpretation of Barth's moral action as representational, arguing instead
that it is expressive. See also Gerald P. McKenny, *The Analogy of Grace: Karl Barth's Moral Theology*
(Oxford: Oxford University Press, 2013), 223.

29. Guder, *Called*, 26.

the decision-making capacities of the "other."[30] The non-Christian is denied the freedom to deny Christ. While one can critique the issue of agency from the side of the missionary—if mission is simply the attestation to what God has already done, then this seems to diminish the necessity of the missionary—one can also critique agency from the side of the non-Christian. Here, what is denied in the *missio Dei* consensus is the agency of those who do not know, or want to know, Christ.

What we find in Barth's soteriology is a God who seems to be coercive: all of history is already accomplished in God's salvific activity. God "over-rules" the human prior to their creation. Thus, while the proponents of the *missio Dei* consensus believe that they are correcting against the coercive activities on the part of missionaries, one could argue that they are in fact bolstering mission's coercive aspects. Coercion is not necessarily curtailed by the acquisition of divine foresight, as one can coerce in the name of hastening the inevitable. One can forcibly baptize either to save one from damnation or to enact in history the reality to which they will inevitably adhere. A Puritan eschatology does not necessarily lead to passivity but can also lead to manifest destiny—the elect are called to establish the new Israel in history, which includes the "civilization" of indigenous populations.[31]

A dogmatic emphasis on the centrality of mission as the work of God simply does not address the problem of coercion head on. In order to properly address the problem of coercion, one must look not just to the doctrinal

---

30. Related to this problem are issues regarding divine and human agency dating back at least to Augustine's writings in regard to the Pelagian controversy. Augustine is criticized for a theology of grace that strips free will, creating a determinism similar to Barth's, albeit a determinism that does not end in universal salvation, but rather a separation between the saved and the eternally damned. These issues will be addressed further below, where I will argue that such debates are in part due to a false equivalence between the functioning of human and divine agency. What is important to stress here is the problem with the presumption of universal salvation and the effects of its promulgation for those who claim such foreknowledge. According to Wetzel, Augustine's claims to predestination are meant to establish what Augustine sees as the biblical assertion that faith is ultimately a working of God, "but the implications of having to give up the beginning of faith as a human initiative are left largely to the reader to work out." James Wetzel, *Augustine and the Limits of Virtue* (New York: Cambridge University Press, 2008), 167. The intention is to establish a rule that faith is a gift from God, not to give a comprehensive and definitive view of the extent to which this gift is given (or not given) to humanity. My point is simple: we cannot know the extent of salvation, and claims to such knowledge, even claims to a universal salvation, do not lead to the kind of logical or moral consistency that their advocates desire. To state that God will save all through Christ does not necessarily render God as more loving, since such salvation may appear to come through the exercise of coercion.

31. Bevans and Schroeder, *Constants*, 207.

assumptions of missionaries and the ways these assumptions may affect their actions, but also to the morality of those actions *as such*. Proleptically, this is precisely what this work hopes to address by viewing mission through the lens of Christian ethics.

Issues surrounding persuasion and coercion remain important—perhaps the most important—issues in the study of missiology. A discipline that emerged out of the work of individuals attempting to convince other individuals to make significant changes to their religious, moral, and social worldviews will always face the critique that such attempts are coercive. The conception of mission as witness to the *missio Dei* fails to adequately redress these critiques.

NATURE AND GRACE

We have seen in the above criticisms how a missiology that is wedded to Karl Barth is imbued with the very same problems regarding human agency which persist in his thought. Here, it seems the agency of both the missionary and their interlocutors are placed in jeopardy. The work of mission is one of passive witness rather than real participation, and the ability of individuals to reject this witness is rendered ultimately and eschatologically futile.

Hans Urs von Balthasar identified the problematic status of agency in Barth, associating it with Barth's radical distinction between nature and grace, seen most vividly in his early commentary on *Romans*. Barth's insistence on the necessity of grace to free theology from the "secular misery" of Schleiermacher forced him to drive too far a wedge between nature and grace, making nature a "pure nature" that was intrinsically sinful and distant from God. While this safeguarded humanity's need for grace, it came at the expense of human agency: "For Barth ... the only authority for the church is God, and no human participates in this authority. The church was merely a conduit through which God works."[32] Balthasar labels this Barth's philosophical actualism:

> Actualism, with its constant, relentless reduction of all activity to God the *actus purus*, leaves no room for any other center of activity outside of God. In relation to God, there can only be passivity. ... Once

---

32. D. Stephen Long, *Saving Karl Barth: Hans Urs von Balthasar's Preoccupation* (Minneapolis, MN: Fortress Press, 2014), 74.

more everything collapses into the unholy dualism of *Romans*: viewed from above, the Church completely coincides with God's Word: but, viewed from below, all her attempts to give expression to this Word are radically fallible.[33]

As will be discussed in the next section, this actualism can be seen as the result of a breakdown of the careful distinctions between creator and creature throughout patristic and medieval theology. These distinctions posited a relationship between God and humanity that was nevertheless different from and lower than the relationships within the Triune life of God. The loss of these distinctions led to a radical separation between God and creation that must be fully overcome by God through the reconciled work of Christ. Human nature is here conceived of as radically separate from God and must be radically repaired through grace. Grace becomes everything, solely subsuming human nature and human activity, including missionary activity.[34] The missionary thus labors toward that to which they cannot contribute, since salvation is the work solely of God's grace: grace will, or will not, do everything in the lives of their interlocutors. The work of the missionary is ultimately insignificant.

For Balthasar, the way through this impasse was to recover Aquinas's subtle relationship between nature and grace, which both affirms the preeminence of grace and leaves room for real human participation.[35] Chapter four

---

33. Hans Urs von Balthasar, *The Theology of Karl Barth: Exposition and Interpretation* (San Francisco, CA: Ignatius Press, 1992), 105. Referenced in Long, *Saving*, 74–75.

34. In his assessment of Balthasar and Barth, D. Stephen Long summarizes the challenges with a radical separation between nature and grace, one that has plagued both Protestantism and Counter-Reformation Catholicism. The result of this separation is that "Protestantism lost any natural ethical and theological agency by annulling it and lifting nature up solely into grace. This occurred primarily in double predestination where the human being's fate is decided by an absolute decree prior to the Trinitarian economy. Grace does, or does not do, everything. Election becomes the singular doctrine within which everything gets conceived. Nature is no longer intelligible, but in practice it still exists, so whatever it might still be, it is left to its own devices." Long, *Saving*, 60.

35. My use of Balthasar to critique Barth's conception of nature and grace, a conception that leads to his implicit universalism, may seem odd given Balthasar's own seeming advocacy of a type of universal salvation. It should be noted that there are important differences. First, Balthasar does not believe that the portions of Scripture that point to eternal judgment can be set aside nor simply held in dialectical tension, but must be affirmed (Balthasar, *The Theology*, 372). For this reason, Balthasar explicitly rejects any construal of his thought that would make him a promoter of "universal salvation." Hans Urs von Balthasar, *Dare We Hope "That All Men Be Saved"?: With a Short Discourse of Hell* (San Francisco, CA: Ignatius Press, 1996), 166. Second, as

will further examine the implications of such an understanding of nature for Christian mission and propose a turn away from Barth, dogmatics, and the *missio Dei* and a return to Aquinas's understanding of virtue, grace, and moral agency.

THE PROBLEM OF DISTINCTION

While ruminations on nature, grace, and agency may not be ever-present on the minds of those engaged in mission on the ground level, these aforementioned issues do manifest themselves in the problem of distinction: What constitutes mission, and what doesn't constitute mission? As D. Stephen Long states, the false dichotomy between nature and grace means that "grace does, or does not do, everything."[36] If God's grace accomplishes everything or nothing, mission as it witnesses to this grace either does everything or nothing. If God does everything in salvation, and the church is merely the passive witness to the entirety of this work, then this would seem to render the individual practices of the missionary questionable at best. Missiology is no longer related to soteriology: the missionary is free to leave everything to God or claim that every type of action they perform is actually the work of God.

"If mission is everything, nothing is mission."[37] Stephen Neill's famous quotation from half a century ago remains the most persistent and prominent critique of the *missio Dei*. When mission is placed at the heart of theology and the heart of the church, mission is in danger of losing its distinctive character. This is evidenced most visibly in David Bosch's aforementioned *Transforming Mission*. Bosch's own approach to mission includes thirteen distinct characteristics, and he describes mission as "a multifaceted ministry, in respect of witness, service, justice, healing, reconciliation, liberation, peace, evangelism, fellowship, church planting, contextualization, and

---

a consequence, Christians may (and should) hope for the salvation of all, but they cannot ever claim to know one way or another since such knowledge would be an attempt by the human to limit divine freedom. For Balthasar, we all stand under divine judgment, without knowledge of the extent of hell's population. Third, Balthasar's understanding of nature and grace does not lead logically and necessarily to universal election, as it appears to do with Barth. This may mean that Balthasar's peculiar eschatology does not disqualify him from critiquing Barth, but it is not an endorsement of it. I believe Balthasar's eschatological hope for universal salvation to still be somewhat at odds with biblical eschatology, most explicitly in Paul's statement of hope for the resurrection of the righteous *and the unrighteous* (Acts 24:15).

36. Long, *Saving Karl Barth*, 60.

37. Stephen Neill, *Creative Tension* (London: Edinburgh House Press, 1959), 81.

much more."[38] With such a comprehensive definition of mission, it becomes difficult to see what is still distinctive in regard to the term. Bosch himself was aware of this danger but insisted that preference should be given to the flexibility of the term, lest we attempt to limit the infinite God.[39]

Critiques surrounding the distinctiveness of the term *missio Dei* are not simply arguments about semantic range. The problem with a multivocal term is not just that it is indistinct, but also that this lack of distinction enables the user of the term to preselect a meaning to suit their needs. Here, every work of human hands can be justified as participation in the mission of God. "In this way, all secular activities can get a kind of divine sanction—and support—again indiscriminately and unqualifiedly."[40] The problem of definition thus has moral implications: if one cannot define mission adequately, then one cannot define what mission is not, and one cannot discern good from bad missional acts.

It is important to note one prominent attempt to remedy this particular issue of the construal of mission as the *missio Dei*: John Flett's work *The Witness of God*. Flett gives perhaps the best articulation of the problem of the lack of distinctiveness of the term *missio Dei*, summarizing a superb history of the concept with his assertion that "*Missio Dei* is a Rorschach test. It encourages projection, revealing our own predilections rather than informing and directing our responses."[41] Flett argues that this lack of distinction is due to a failure to understand mission as the work of the Triune God.[42] Mission that lacks any connection to the Trinitarian missions of the Father sending the Son and the Father and Son sending the Holy Spirit will strip mission of its doctrinal content, turning concepts such as "mission'" and "sending" into placeholders for any activity of which one can conceive.[43]

---

38. Bosch, *Transforming*, 512.

39. Bosch, *Transforming*, 512.

40. Johannes Aagaard, "Mission after Uppsala 1968," in *Critical Issues in Mission Today* (Grand Rapids: Eerdmans, 1974), 17.

41. John G. Flett, *The Witness of God: The Trinity, Missio Dei, Karl Barth, and the Nature of Christian Community* (Grand Rapids: Eerdmans, 2010), 76.

42. Flett argues that this lack of a Trinitarian foundation is in part due to the failure of mission theologians to adequately engage in Barth's work, particularly *Church Dogmatics*. Flett, *The Witness*, 11–17.

43. Flett, *The Witness*, 49.

Flett's solution is to reconstruct a notion of the *missio Dei* centered upon the Trinity and a close re-reading of Barth. For Barth, there can be no separation between God's being and God's revelation: "It is as the personal triune God that He is self-existent. And although the converse is certainly true, it is only because we must first say that it is as the personal triune God that He is self-existent."[44] Flett grounds his notion of Christian mission in this assertion: the revelation of God as Father, Son, and Holy Spirit occurs in time and in the context of mission. The immanent Trinity is discovered by humanity through the economic Trinity in the context of the church on mission. God is by his nature missionary—his being is his becoming—and as such the church's mission is one of accompaniment of this mission in history.[45]

While Flett's work helps to address the ways in which missiology neglects the Trinitarian foundations of God's mission, it is difficult to see how Flett addresses the issue of lack of distinctiveness within a concept of the *missio Dei*.[46] This is because his desire to see mission at the heart of dogmatics undermines his desire to better define the *missio Dei*. Flett's preoccupation is with the role of mission vis-à-vis dogmatic theology; hence, some of his strongest practical exhortations concern the need to fully incorporate missiology into all levels of theological training.[47] However, he fails to describe with any degree of clarity what exactly constitutes missionary activity. In his quest to prove that "mission is necessarily, and must become, a central concern of dogmatic theology,"[48] Flett *adds* to the list of actions that mission encompasses, including worship, fellowship, and community.

For Flett, worship, fellowship, witness, joy, and reconciliation all encompass the missionary act. Any attempt to define mission with any further

---

44. Karl Barth, *Church Dogmatics*, vol. II/1, ed. G. W. Bromiley and Thomas F. Torrance (Edinburgh: T&T Clark, 1957), 350.

45. "Mission is not a second step in addition to some other more proper being of the church, because, as the living one, God's relations to the world belongs to his eternal being. The Christian community is, as such, a missionary community, or she is not a community that lives in fellowship with the triune God as he lives his own proper life." Flett, *The Witness*, 34.

46. As will be discussed below, this problem of distinction is also not remedied due to a lack of sufficient understanding of the differences between God and creation, as well as human and divine agency.

47. "If the missionary act is the concrete form of divine and human fellowship here and now, then the lack of reference to mission at every level of the teaching ministry of the church is a frightful abrogation of theological responsibility." Flett, *The Witness*, 296.

48. Flett, *The Witness*, 296.

distinctiveness is an attempt to make mission's "programmatic forms," its temporal activities, normative for the whole of mission.[49] Instead, the church itself is completely free to contextualize its mission in any way it sees fit. The following quotation, in the last pages of *The Witness of God*, is an apt summary:

> Since creation possesses no inherent capacity to facilitate or retard the communication of the gospel, the community is totally free with regard to the particular forms the community's witness takes in the world, not with regard to her definite service of witness. In other words, within the limits established by the divine and human fellowship, the community is free as she exercises her freedom; that is, missionary forms develop through the process of intentional engaged movement into the world.[50]

This passage encapsulates the problem of distinction (and the connection of this issue to the problematic relationship between nature and grace in Barth) which haunts the conception of mission as participation in the *missio Dei*. Because creation does not do anything to advance mission, it is free to take up whatever forms it desires in embodying this mission. Because human beings do not do anything, they are free to do everything. Mission becomes simply "engaged movement into the world." Mission is *all* activity which is done within the divine and human fellowship. Thus, Flett comes full circle—he begins by calling *missio Dei* a Rorschach test, but his reconstructed definition of *missio Dei* actually renders *missio Dei more*, not less, multivocal.

If mission is everything, then mission is nothing. If one sees God, the church, the world through mission-colored glasses, then there becomes no way of defining what constitutes mission and what doesn't. The broadness of the term means that those engaged in radically different, even contradictory, approaches to mission can still claim to be faithfully witnessing to the *missio Dei*. David Bosch highlights how the concept of *missio Dei* was used by Hartenstein to "protect mission against secularization," as well as by Hoekendijk to emphasize the *exclusion* of the church from missionary involvement altogether.[51]

---

49. Flett, *The Witness*, 294.

50. Flett, *The Witness*, 294–95.

51. Bosch, *Transforming*, 392.

This lack of definition also comes with significant practical implications for missionaries and the practice of mission itself. If there are no standards to define what constitutes mission, there are no standards for discerning good from poor missional practices. One can declare any action they perform as an act of participation in the *missio Dei*, with immunity from criticism. The caustic street preacher, the musical worship leader, the holy war soldier, and the public aid worker are all doing mission and are free from whatever burdens that the Great Commission may impose on both what the missionary must do and how they should go about doing it.

The aforementioned issues regarding human agency and distinction vis-à-vis the *missio Dei* consensus will be addressed in chapter four of this book. There I will argue more fully that a recovery of Aquinas's nuanced account of nature and grace provides resources that effectively remedy Barth's problematic account of nature, grace, and agency. Proleptically, these issues can be adequately addressed through an emphasis on Aquinas's theory of virtue and Alasdair MacIntyre's notion of a virtuous practice. MacIntyre defines a practice as an action whose goods are internal to it, goods that "can only be identified and recognized by the experience of participating in the practice in question."[52] Applying this notion to mission enables one to discern which actions are necessarily constitutive of mission and those actions whose goods may be obtained through non-missional endeavors.

TRINITARIAN DISTINCTIONS, *MISSIO DEI* CONFUSIONS

There is another way of approaching these aforementioned issues of agency and distinction that sees their emergence as part of a larger loss of distinctive ways of speaking about God. Kathryn Tanner's *God and Creation in Christian Theology* is helpful for charting this loss. Tanner sees throughout the Christian theological tradition the exercise of ruled language when it comes to speaking about God's transcendence and God's agency. Tanner lists two rules: "First, a rule for speaking of God as transcendent vis-à-vis the world: avoid both a simple univocal attribution of predicates to God and world and a simple contrast of divine and non-divine predicates. ... The second rule is as follows: avoid in talk about God's creative agency all suggestions of limitation

---

52. Alasdair C. MacIntyre, *After Virtue: A Study in Moral Theory*, 2nd ed. (Notre Dame, IN: University of Notre Dame Press, 1984), 189.

in scope or manner. The second rule prescribes talk of God's creative agency as immediate and universally extended."[53] These rules are meant to govern core Christian claims of God's radical transcendence and radical immanence.

Tanner sees in the history of Christian discourse concerning God the adaptation and importation by theologians of non-theological language that is nevertheless governed by the aforementioned rules concerning God, creation, and agency. Theologians work within these rules and the given theological and non-theological language of their milieu to engage in talk of God. The reason that theologians import non-theological language is to make their work more intelligible, as the language being imported already contains a context for its use and its own history of interpretation. This also lends a greater rhetorical force, as this language also carries its own argumentative weight. Theologians can thus play "on the linguistic expectations of an audience."[54] What I believe Tanner is getting at in this statement is something akin to the use of an enthymeme in rhetoric: a way of speaking, usually in truncated syllogisms, that draws upon the unspoken premises of the audience, enabling the speaker to argue more succinctly, directly, and effectively with their audience.

There is thus in Christian discourse regarding the nature and activity of God both the importation of non-theological language in order to make such discourse intelligible and rhetorically effective, and, at the same time, an implicit adherence to linguistic rules that ensure that such discourse affirms the Christian assertion of God's radical transcendence and radical immanence.

One can diagnose the problems of agency and distinction within *missio Dei* thought as rooted in an abrogation of Tanner's ruled language concerning God's transcendence and immanence. First, there is a tendency to conflate the distinctions between the divine relations and the divine-human relationship. There is a strain of modern theology, following a particular reading of Barth,[55] that attempts to abolish the distinction between the Trinitarian rela-

---

53. Kathryn Tanner, *God and Creation in Christian Theology: Tyranny or Empowerment* (Minneapolis, MN: Fortress Press, 2005), 47.

54. Tanner, *God and Creation*, 54.

55. It is important to stress that what is being critiqued is a strain of thought from both systematic theologians and mission theologians that is indebted to a particular reading of Barth, a reading that remains disputed. Tanner sees in Barth one who maintains this ruled language of God (see Tanner, *God and Creation*, 77–80). Gerald McKenny believes Barth to have sufficiently

tionships and the divine-human relationship. This strain of theology is reacting against a perceived overly hellenized metaphysics within the tradition,
which defined God first in abstract, platonic terms (simplicity, perfection,
etc.) and then added the description of God as Triune. In response, there is
an emphasis on beginning theological discourse with the economic Trinity
and God's revelation in history: it is only from the revelation of God in history as Father, Son, and Holy Spirit that we can begin to speak of his divine
attributes. Here, God's being is God's becoming, or God is an event in history.
Long sees this trajectory in a wide range of theologians, including Eberhard
Jungel, Robert Jenson, Jurgen Moltmann, and Greg Boyd.[56]

While such an emphasis was meant to counter perceived over-stoic conceptions of God, what emerges from this view is a God who is tied to, and a
certain degree dependent upon, creation. This is manifest most visibly in the
doctrine of the incarnation. Here, God commits himself to the salvation of
humanity through the incarnate Son by virtue of his decision to create. The
adoption of the *missio Dei* in many ways reflects this development. It is seen
as a reaction against a hellenized Christendom, which featured a remote and
distant God who gives the sole authority of mission to the church, giving a
blank check to missionaries to do whatever they saw fit in the name of Christ.
Darrell Guder's own historiography of the development of the *missio Dei* consensus in many ways parallels the theological history of Moltmann, Jenson,
and Jungel. What is adopted by both is a specific historical narrative—about
the rise of Christendom and the concomitant infection of Christian theology
by Hellenistic philosophy that rendered God distant, remote, and abstract.

---

buttressed both human and divine action. Long sees in Barth an attempt to correct an undue
separation between *de deo uno and de deo trino* (D. Stephen Long, *The Perfectly Simple Triune God:
Aquinas and His Legacy* [Minneapolis, MN: Fortress Press, 2016], 320). This correction quickly
leads to a historicizing of God—God's being is an event in history. Whether Barth approved
of such a step is debated. However, evidence for such an approval is documented by Long in
Barth's approval of Robert Jenson's dissertation on Barth, which asserts the temporality of God
(Long, *The Perfectly*, 338). In can be stated at the minimum that Barth's work was part of a highly
influential trajectory in modern theology that rejects such ruled language concerning God, a
trajectory that has also significantly influenced theologians who have developed the conception
of mission as *missio Dei*. Whether Barth's theology in toto violates traditional understandings
of God and creation is a debate best left to Barthian scholars. I would simply state that his rendering of agency, nature, and grace, particularly in regard to mission, is deeply problematic
for the various reasons already stated in this chapter. In addition, the large influence of such
renderings on the conception of mission as *missio Dei* has contributed substantially to its flaws.

56. Long, *Triune God*, 321–25.

God and creation become unduly separated. Guder sees in the development of Western doctrine a "continuing pattern of separating the theologically inseparable: separating the church and its mission, separating ethics and witness … separating Christ as moral example from Christ as the basis of salvation. Such dichotomies are a deeply engrained problem in Western Christendom."[57] Pulling creation closer to God, which for Guder comes through a recovery of Christology, enables mission theologians to view the practice of mission as something in which God was more intimately involved. Flett, drawing on Barth, Jungel, and Jenson, identifies a similar gap between God and creation, insisting that the formulation of *missio Dei* needs to further shore up this weakness by eliminating an undue distinction between the essential and economic Trinity. Hence, there is a need to pull God and creation closer together through the incarnation as the event of reconciliation in history: God's being is his becoming, and the church is taken up into real relationship with God through the event of Christ's reconciliation.[58]

I have already stated above one of the unfortunate side effects of this position in regard to a theology of mission: if creation is already and entirely redeemed by Christ, the mission of the church simply becomes one of passive witness. We may add to these issues the loss of distinctive language to speak about God and creation. Since the distinctions between God and creation are abolished, there is, to use Tanner's words, a univocal attribution of predicates to God and world. One can no longer speak of the workings of God and the workings of human beings as distinct yet related. In terms of language concerning mission, creation is so tied up with God that mission becomes the sole prerogative of God.

The conception of *missio Dei* also bears the collapse of the distinction between human and divine agency. As the distinctiveness between God and creation is lost, so is the principle of analogy. One loses the ability to see how God works in different ways from human beings. With this loss of distinction, there is a tendency to use human concepts of freedom and agency as the basis for construing divine agency. One begins with an understanding of human agency and freedom and works backward to God. Here, God's agency is rendered as something that is simply human agency multiplied by a large

---

57. Guder, *Called*, 52.
58. Flett, *The Witness*, 211–12.

number, pushing matter into form and structuring it with mechanistic efficiency. Because God's agency is of the same type as human agency, the workings of God and humanity become competitive.

When such a conception of agency is imported into mission, it inaugurates an interminable debate over the role of the church vis-à-vis the mission of God. Mission, like other activities performed by both God and human
beings, is construed, in Tanner's words, as competitive and contrastive. The
missional activities of God are the same type of missional activities performed by the church, simply done on a larger scale. Human beings either
compete with God for space to perform mission, or cede their agency to the
workings of God, with their role being one of passive witness.

This can be seen in one of the primary works on the *missio Dei*, George
Vicedom's *The Mission of God*. Vicedom begins with a critique similar to that
of Guder—that previous conceptions of mission construe it as something
secondary to God, done purely under the auspices of a church intending
to spread Christian culture. The *missio Dei*, in response, sees mission as the
prerogative of God:

> The church and its missions cannot be conceived apart from God and
> can therefore be understood only from the viewpoint of the existence
> of God and His mission. The former are nothing more than an instru-
> ment, a work-schedule of God in relation to his creatures, a gathering
> of those who permit themselves to be called to Him through God's
> definite sending.[59]

What we see here is a loss of the careful distinction between God's mission and human mission. There is no difference between the two—there is
only God's mission, God's sending, and human beings who have the ability to
become instruments of this sending. The subsuming of all mission under the
auspices of the *missio Dei* leads to what Tanner calls theological occasionalism.
Here, the occasionalist is one "that refuses to the creature the ability to act or
produce effect by its own proper power, in order to ensure the sovereignty of
divine agency. ... What the creature does is simply the occasion for God's own
creative action in bringing to be what happens next. The creature becomes

---

59. Georg F. Vicedom, *The Mission of God: An Introduction to a Theology of Mission*, trans.
Gilbert A. Thiele and Dennis Hilgendorf (Saint Louis, MO: Concordia Publishing House, 1965), 47.

the empty shell for an exercise of divine power."[60] When there is a loss of the distinctions between divine mission and divine agency, and human mission and human agency, all are subsumed under the universal agency of God's mission. The missionary is simply an empty shell, providing an occasion for the *missio Dei* to happen in history.

What has emerged in the *missio Dei* consensus is a type of missiological grammar stripped of distinctiveness. Mission is the mission of God; the church does not act on its own but participates in this mission, with no discussion regarding how the workings of human beings may differ from the workings of God. The way in which the church participates, and how such participation may differ, is simply not addressed.

It is helpful here to retrace the development of the *missio Dei* consensus. We can discern four key steps, articulated most visibly in Bosch's *Transforming Mission*: (1) a critique of ecclesiocentric views of mission that placed too much power and autonomy in the hands of the church and individuals; (2) the emergence of the term "*missio Dei*," an image of mission that is "not primarily an activity of the church, but an attribute of God. ... To participate in mission is to participate in the movement of God's love toward people"; (3) a widening of the scope of the term and an ongoing tension concerning the role of the church in mission vis-à-vis the mission of God; and (4) the assertion that, despite these disputes, the emergence of the term remains a "crucial breakthrough," since it has successfully broken mission out of its ecclesiocentric confines and helped to articulate the conviction that "neither the church nor any other human agent can ever be considered the author or bearer of mission."[61]

My assertion is that the critical flaw in the *missio Dei* lies in step two, which abrogates the careful ruled language theologians have used to speak about God and creation. There is little to no awareness that such an abrogation has occurred. The sending of the church in mission is simply caught up in the sending of the Triune God, without acknowledging the possibility that the ways in which created beings are sent differs from the way God can send of himself, and without acknowledging that human beings are speaking

---

60. Tanner, *God and Creation*, 86.
61. Bosch, *Transforming*, 392.

analogously in the ways in which they speak of God's sending.[62] This loss of ruled language creates the problems articulated in step three, which places into question whether the gains articulated in step four are worth the appropriation of such flawed terminology.

The inability to speak distinctively about human sending and the sending of God also creates a situation in which the *missio Dei* cannot be abandoned, for all its acknowledged flaws. To abandon it would be to turn back to a model of mission that is human centered and ecclesiocentric: "The Copernican turn of *missio Dei* is not something from which the Christian community can depart. Any other conception of the ground, motive, and goal of mission apart from *missio Dei's* Trinitarian location risks investing authority in historical accident and human capacity."[63] Once the distinction between human agency and divine agency, between divine missions and human missions, is abolished, there is only zero-sum gain. Human beings can either witness to the *missio Dei* or attempt mission on their own as a rival to God.

LACK OF SEMANTIC DISTINCTION, LACK OF RHETORICAL FORCE

While the collapse of distinction between creator and creation, and between divine and human agency, affect how one views these concepts vis-à-vis mission, the final collapse comes directly within the term *missio Dei* itself. The final critique levied against *missio Dei* is that, in part due to the novelty of the term and the lack of consensus on its precise meaning, the term itself lacks semantic intelligibility and rhetorical force, and, thus, as a linguistic concept, the term *missio Dei* fails to say anything distinct about mission. First, the technical nature of the term has rendered its use unintelligible. For Tanner, the force of much theological language comes precisely from the way in which such language is adopted from non-theological language and adapted to speak of God in a way that affirms God's radical transcendence and immanence.[64]

---

62. Tanner sees in modern theology a tendency to break this ruled language in a way that is to an extent unintentional—the modern context itself has a tendency to push divine sovereignty and human freedom to extreme and incompatible directions. This context creates a scenario in which the theologian may affirm traditional claims about God while implicitly breaking rules concerning God's transcendence and God's agency. Tanner, *God and Creation*, 122. For instance, in Vicedom there remains an assertion of the traditional understanding of God and creation in the midst of a conception of mission that erodes the distinction between human and divine agency. See Vicedom, *The Mission*, 15–17.

63. Flett, *The Witness*, 9.

64. Tanner, *God and Creation*, 32–34.

The adoption of terminology from outside of theology gives such terminology a sort of ready-made intelligibility and a concomitant rhetorical force. The use of novel terminology has none of these advantages, and the intelligibility of such novel terms is entirely intramural within the hyper-specific disciplines within which they emerge. Hence, the intelligibility of the novel term *missio Dei* is left entirely in the hands of a specific wing of mission theology, and the term bears little intelligibility outside of this discipline. H. H. Rosin documents how the term *missio Dei* has been plagued by the problem of distinction nearly from its inception: "Thus even before the term '*missio Dei*' was put into circulation, the process of its interpretation and modification was in full swing."[65] Rosin documents how, in 1963, only eleven years after the term was coined, the international missionary conference in Mexico City reached an impasse regarding the relationship between God's action in all of creation and the church's specific activity.[66]

We can say, in Wittgensteinian terms, that there is an incessant language game being played over the meaning of the term. The lack of a clear-cut winner in its definition renders the term unintelligible. The fact that this game is only being played by a small community of missiologists means that the term will have little resonance within a larger community.

Second, the term *missio Dei* has been adopted with unanimity, but not perspicuity. It has been for many missiologists simply a technical term that stresses the importance of mission,[67] both as a practical and theological endeavor, while the term itself is rarely examined. Flett highlights the relationship between this and the term's lack of coherence: "Few authors reflect on the underlying theological issues. Most introduce the concept by citing from the few seminal texts but, apart from these oft-repeated forms, little substantive development has occurred."[68] This lack of critical reflection creates a situation in which the language the term employs is not examined for nuance or clarity. The result is what in the field of psychology is called "concept creep." Nick Haslam describes this as the process through which

---

65. H. H. Rosin, *"Missio Dei": An Examination of the Origin, Contents and Function of the Term in Protestant Missiological Discussion* (Leiden: Interuniversity Institute for Missiological and Ecumenical Research, Department of Missiology, 1972), 25.

66. Rosin, *"Missio Dei,"* 26.

67. Oborji, *Concepts*, 138.

68. Flett, *The Witness*, 35.

the semantic range of a concept is expanded both vertically and horizontally. Vertical expansion occurs when the definition of a term becomes less stringent. Horizontal expansion occurs when a concept is applied to a new class of phenomena.[69] The result is a semantic inflation that waters down the meaning of concepts.

The historical trajectory of the term *missio Dei* is one of vertical and horizontal expansion. The term has grown horizontally to encompass not only the missional activities of the church, but also all missional works performed by God outside of the church. In addition, it has grown vertically in the degree to which activities great and small all constitute mission. The term *missio Dei* has grown from encompassing specific activities, such as evangelism and church planting, to encompass all forms of human activity, including for Flett communal life and the disposition of joy.

If we take both aforementioned linguistic weaknesses of the term *missio Dei* together, a picture emerges of a term whose popular use is so broad so as to encompass nearly every activity, while simultaneously its precise definition is interminably debated within the specific and sometimes idiosyncratic field of missiology. The conclusion reached is simply that the term *missio Dei* has no rhetorical force. It means very little and conveys very little to its audience. For all of these reasons, one must look to other ways of articulating God's mission in ways that are less problematic, more distinct, and more effective.[70]

While the conception of mission as *missio Dei* does represent, as Bosch affirms, a "crucial breakthrough" in freeing mission from its ecclesiocentric confines,[71] it has replaced a narrow conception of mission with a conception that is broad enough to make it largely unusable. Perhaps it is best to acknowledge the gains it has brought—the emergence of mission as a serious and important aspect of theology, the relationship between the sending of God and the sending of the church, and the belief in the intrinsic

---

69. Nick Haslam, "Concept Creep: Psychology's Expanding Concepts of Harm and Pathology," *Psychological Inquiry* 27, no. 1 (2016): 2.

70. A step in the direction of distinction has begun to emerge with schools of thought labeled "Intercultural and Contextual Theology," which tend to distinguish between the acts of missionaries and the theological ramifications of mission's cross-cultural interactions. As will be shown later, this work would welcome such a distinction, and my conception of mission will focus particularly on an examination of specific missionary activities.

71. Bosch, *Transforming*, 393.

missional nature of the church—while also affirming that a sole reliance on dogmatics may not be the direction best taken for mission theology moving forward. Chapter four will situate mission within Aquinas's moral theology and virtue ethics, with the goal of remedying these problems of distinction and agency through recovering traditional language concerning the relationship between God and creation and human and divine agency, as well as providing a framework for understanding how human beings might exercise this agency in a way that glorifies God. In addition, this framework will provide a way of speaking of mission that integrates both doctrine and practice. Missiology does not have to choose, as Scott Sunquist avers, between dogmatic conceptions of mission and mission's practical implications.[72] Theological ethics, particularly Thomistic virtue ethics, provides an integral way of speaking of both. While *missio Dei* theology has helped to develop a better understanding of how the mission of the church is inseparable from the salvific work of God the Father, Son, and Holy Spirit, virtue ethics can help to clarify this relationship as well as clarify how the specific missional actions of the church can best reflect this reality.

CONCLUSION

Through this brief introduction to the *missio Dei* consensus, one can see the perpetual challenges facing the field of missiology. Issues surrounding the definition and composition of mission activities, the role and agency of the missionary, and the problem of persuasion are all issues that are addressed by the concept of *missio Dei* yet are still present despite its consensus. Before addressing these concerns through a model of mission based upon virtue, it is imperative to first examine two other anthropological models of mission that offer remedies to the aforementioned issues, one which I will label "mission as growth" and the other "mission as dialogue." Both of these construals of mission have their own historical trajectories and luminaries. Both offer approaches to mission that appear to be more concrete and distinct when compared to mission as *missio Dei*. However, both have their own set of unique challenges.

The next two chapters will be devoted to understanding and critiquing models of mission centered upon growth and dialogue. The extensive

---

72. Sunquist, *Understanding Christian Mission*, 8.

discussion of these models will help to develop greater understanding of the unique challenges facing the development of mission as a distinctive enterprise. In addition, selective discussions within theological ethics will be used to aid in the assessment of these models, demonstrating its potential to speak constructively to the concerns of missiology. Consistent themes will emerge that will be addressed in greater depth: the motivation for mission activities, the ethics of persuasion and conversion, and the placement of such activities within a conception of a life lived well. Such questions will pave the way for a conception of mission that draws from the disciplines of moral theology, moral philosophy, and virtue ethics.

2
—
MISSION AS GROWTH

The construal of mission as the attempt to numerically grow the church through conversions and the planting of new congregations is one that, for some missionaries, seems self-evident. The gospel is "good news," and one can infer logically that the more people who receive this message approvingly, the better. Most missionaries would prefer that twenty people become Christians as a result of their efforts as opposed to ten. While the association of mission with numerical increases is rarer in the New Testament than one might presume, there are nevertheless instances of rejoicing in light of mass conversions (Acts 2:41; 6:7). A conception of mission as growth has become particularly dominant amongst evangelical Protestant churches in the West. Its development can be traced from the church growth movement pioneered by Donald McGavran in the 1950s and into the church planting movement of the 1990s to the present time. Such movements have spawned vast networks of organizations, websites, and resources, as well as thousands of published books. Yet, despite this expansive network, there remain several issues with the movement, ranging from ethical dilemmas that have resulted from an overemphasis on numerical growth, to questions as to whether such numerical success has actually occurred.

This chapter will begin by charting the development of the modern construal of mission as growth, focusing particularly on the work of Donald McGavran and Alan Hirsch. McGavran's domestic importation of missionary principles into North America inaugurated the church growth movement. Many of its core principles were then adapted by Alan Hirsch and others and applied outward to the expansion of the church through the planting of new congregations.

Following this brief history, I will use the tools of theological ethics to critique the construal of mission as growth, focusing primarily on Alasdair MacIntyre's assessment of the social sciences in *After Virtue*. Here, I will show how MacIntyre's critique of the social sciences bears striking parallels to the current moral issues surrounding the church planting movement. After this critique will be an extended discussion of the problem of agency in mission and how the mission as growth model significantly diminishes both the agency of the missionary and the recipient of the missionary's message.

DONALD MCGAVRAN AND HIS LEGACY

Mission as growth, and its contemporary manifestation in church planting literature, draws directly from the theology and research pioneered by missiologist Donald McGavran in the 1950s through the 1990s. McGavran's intention was to develop an understanding of the mission of the church as something that does not merely impact individuals but has the possibility of transforming entire social groups. McGavran was reacting against what he perceived was an undue emphasis on personal conversion that necessitated the severing of converts from cultural and communal ties.[1]

In response, McGavran developed a concept of church growth centered upon the conversion of social groups to the gospel. This approach sought to gain a better understanding of specific people groups through a variety of sociological and behavioral science research methods with the goal of tailoring the gospel message to these targeted groups for the maximum number of conversions. Here, the move was to narrow an individual congregation's focus in order to maximize the potential to reach non-believers. The assumption was that people feel the most comfortable around those who are like them, so churches wishing to attract outsiders should not shy away from focusing on reaching those who are the most like them.[2] Much like a business that cuts

---

1. According to George Hunter, McGavran "saw that the usual mission practice, based on the individualism paradigm rather than the group-consciousness paradigm, produced tragic social dislocation in the lives of many converts, as Christianized individuals were rejected by their people and cut off from them." George Hunter, "The Legacy of Donald A. McGavran," *International Bulletin of Missionary Research* 16, no. 4 (1992): 159.

2. "Loose the Churches and let them go! At present Churches in many lands are tied hand and foot. In evangelism they are heard to propose: Leave your ethnic unit and join ours. On biblical grounds, they must make sure that they are heard to propose: Believe on Jesus Christ, be baptized, form congregations of Bible-obeying Christians, while as far as possible remaining in cultural harmony with your own ethnic and cultural units. This basic shift in presentation, will help the tide of redemption to flow strongly throughout many tribes and tongues and kindreds and nations to their enormous benefit in this world and the next." Donald Anderson McGavran, "Loose the Churches: Let Them Go! An Essential Issue in Indian Evangelism," *Missiology* 1, no. 2 (1973): 94.

its losses on a dying market to focus resources on potentially stronger ones, a congregation must focus on the one group of people they can best reach, diverting all of their resources toward reaching that group.

McGavran advocated the development of monoethnic congregations in order to enable a more contextually appropriate and comfortable environment for sharing the gospel—an environment proven by analytical research to increase conversion: "Churches tend to grow when men becoming Christian join others of their own race—tribe, sub-tribe, caste, or clan. When becoming Christian means joining a different 'breed' of men, church growth is always slowed down."[3] The broader unity of the church became secondary to the desire to see the gospel take root in new cultures.

ALAN HIRSCH AND THE CHURCH PLANTING MOVEMENT

The church planting movement is an extension of the church growth movement pioneered by Donald McGavran. McGavran applied his missiological research first to the planting of new overseas congregations, with his research quickly being appropriated for existing congregations in North America to increase existing attendance.[4] The church planting movement developed as an extension of church growth through the starting of new congregations within the North American context. It is best seen as the domestic application of church growth techniques to the starting of new congregations in North America.[5]

The church planting movement shares much of the same hallmarks as McGavran's church growth ethos. It involves a general critique of the ways in which mission has been done in the past, a calling to return to a biblical

---

3. Victor E. W. Hayward and Donald McGavran, "Without Crossing Barriers: One in Christ vs. Discipling Diverse Cultures," *Missiology* 2, no. 2 (1974): 206.

4. George G. Hunter, "The Legacy of Donald A. McGavran," *International Bulletin of Missionary Research* 16, no. 4 (1992): 158.

5. Following an extensive statistical history of missiological terms, Kenneth Nehrbass remarks on the relationship between church growth terminology and church planting terminology: "Church Growth is a missiological sub-discipline that seems to have had a definite half-life. ... Some church growth specialists would say this is a worrisome sign. But it doesn't mean missiologists are thinking less about church growth. ... What is more likely is that we're now talking about church planting movements and church multiplication, partnerships, or insider movements." Kenneth Nehrbass, "The Half-Life of Missiological Facts," *Missiology* 42, no. 3 (2014): 290–91.

approach to mission through the planting of new congregations, and the use of extensive sociological research to better understand the demographics of the church plant's targeted area.

The work of missiologist Alan Hirsch is perhaps the best-known proponent of this type of church planting movement. Hirsch imports and modifies McGavran's growth paradigm for a Western context. Similar to McGavran, Hirsch begins with a critique of the church for its neglect of mission. For Hirsch, the early church was the missional church par excellence, while Christendom ushered in an era in which the institutional church calcified mission for organizational purposes: "For the most part, the Christendom church obscured the need for a full-fledged missional leadership system, because the self-understanding of the church became fundamentally non-missional."[6] McGavran cited institutional overreach as a major cause of unsuccessful mission abroad: missionaries set up too many organizations to do too many things, forgetting their calling to evangelize and grow churches. Hirsch applies this critique to the church in the West. Here, over-institutionalization has clouded its calling to rapidly expand through the promulgation of the gospel and the forming of new worship communities.

McGavran moves from critique to a "recovery" of biblical mission, with the parable of the harvest being central for his characterization of mission as growth. Hirsch calls for a similar recovery of a biblical notion of mission, this time using the structures of the church in the book of Acts as paradigmatic. The name of Hirsch's most prominent work, *The Forgotten Ways: Reactivating the Missional Church*, highlights this notion: the church has "forgotten" the missional ethos and missional structures of the early church. What is needed for the post-Christendom West is a reactivation of this missional ethos.

After critiquing mission practices and calling for a return to a biblical view of mission, McGavran proceeds to use the tools of the social sciences, particularly statistical research and analysis, to better enable church growth.[7]

---

6. Alan Hirsch, *The Forgotten Ways: Reactivating the Missional Church* (Grand Rapids: Brazos Press, 2006), 169.

7. One of the ensuing critiques of McGavran will be that his adoption of the social sciences is done without moral or critical reflection. McGavran does not advocate for a particular statistical theory but simply uses statistical data and analysis as a tool that helps identify where churches are growing. For his data, McGavran uses statistics gleaned from *The World Christian Handbook*, which is itself an amalgamation of reports from various mission agencies. While such data is used for broad assessments of mission, McGavran also advocated for new approaches to the

The focus of McGavran's research is primarily on the target populations of missionaries. The goal is to discover which people groups are most receptive to the gospel so that the missionary may better appropriate their resources. With a focus on a Western context and upon the notion of church planting, Hirsch similarly uses the social sciences but turns their attention to the missionaries rather than the missionary targets. Hirsch uses many of the tools of organizational behavior (as used in popular business texts) to break down the apostolic church into a simple form that can be easily understood and applied.[8] For instance, Hirsch uses extensive diagrams and charts to map out how to plant churches that will have the "missional DNA" (mDNA) to plant additional churches. One of his most well-known charts maps out what he calls the APEPT (apostles, prophets, evangelists, pastors, teachers) leadership team, which divvies up the work of the church into various teams that perform specific tasks (prophetic team performs social justice, pastoral

---

gathering of statistical data on the part of the missionary. The missionary must select, document, and chart over time those statistics that most directly relate to the growth of churches. This includes documenting field totals (simply the number of Christians in a particular area), as well as the totals for specific homogenous units, which are sections of society in which the people all share some common characteristic (85). From here, the missionary should document the sources of change in these statistics, whether the increase or decrease is due to biological growth, transfer growth, or conversion growth (88–89). The task of the researcher is then to identify the homogenous units that have exhibited significant growth and attempt to discern how such growth occurred. Of particular interest are any new practices implemented by the missionary (123–45). Donald A. McGavran, *Understanding Church Growth* (Grand Rapids: Eerdmans, 1970).

8.   Hirsch is particularly interested in the field of organizational behavior as it relates to business management. His model for a successful and growing church is the successful and growing business, and the successful growing business includes leaders who are able to facilitate an environment that fosters creativity and growth. Jim Collins's *Good to Great* is a paradigmatic example of the kinds of organizational behavioral methods that Hirsch adapts for use in church mission. The book identifies companies whose growth far exceeded that of their competitors and attempts to discern the types of leadership and organizational cultures that foster such success, with the hope that such factors can help leaders develop more successful companies. The goal is to discern and describe the attributes of business success in order to help leaders replicate such success. For Hirsch, these attributes are transferable, without modification, to the church. The leadership principles that foster business growth are akin to the successful apostolic leadership of growing church movements, and the culture of a successful business is akin to the culture of a church that is growing. For a detailed example of Hirsch's use of business management texts, see Hirsch, *Forgotten Ways: Missional*, 159–66. Prominent business management sources for Hirsch include Jim Collins, *Good to Great: Why Some Companies Make the Leap … And Others Don't* (London: Random House, 2009); Margaret J. Wheatley, *Leadership and the New Science: Discovering Order in a Chaotic World* (San Francisco, CA: Berrett-Koehler Publishers, 1999); Thomas J. Peters, *Thriving on Chaos: Handbook for a Management Revolution* (New York: Knopf, 1987).

team performs pastoral care, etc.). The adoption of such structures promises results for those that implement it effectively:

> There seems to be a wonderful "ecology" for healthy ministry at work in a fully functioning APEPT system. It provides us with a theologically rich and organically consistent understanding to help leaders and organizations become more missional and agile. In fact it would be hard *not* to be missional if one intentionally develops this into the life of God's people at the local and/or regional levels.[9]

In addition, Hirsch adapts modern psychological profiling theories in order to help potential church planters identify whether they will be successful in their future missional endeavors. Hirsch has developed his own variant, the APEPT test, which helps the assessor find out which of the five ministry orders they fit into. This is but one example of the so-called "Church-Planter Assessments" that have become commonplace amongst many North American church planting organizations, with various assessments being based upon self-assessment tools of psychology.[10] The multitude of pop-psychology evaluations such as the Myers-Briggs test and StrengthsFinder have their spiritual and missional equivalents in the North American church planting world, of which Hirsch stands as one of its most prominent figures.

KEY ASPECTS OF THE MISSION
AS GROWTH MODEL

The impact of Donald McGavran on both North American and world missions should not be understated. In practical terms, his work at Fuller Seminary influenced generations of missionaries and church planters. His pioneering efforts of using statistical and social scientific research is widely adopted even among his critics. Hirsch, likewise, has been highly influential among North American mission practitioners. In what follows I will summarize three key components of the mission as growth model.

---

9. Hirsch, *Forgotten Ways: Missional*, 177. Hirsch is here appropriating Richard Pascale's theories of business management and leadership in Richard T. Pascale, *Managing on the Edge: How Successful Companies Use Conflict to Stay Ahead* (New York: Penguin Books, 1991).

10. See, for instance, "Stadia's Church Planting Assessment Center," Stadia Church Planting, https://stadiachurchplanting.org/plant/assessment/; "General Assessments," Church Multiplication Network, https://churchmultiplication.net/assessment/; and "Church Planter Candidate Assessment," Church Planter, http://churchplanter.lifeway.com/.

First, growth is the goal of mission. While other mission activities—such as the development of education systems, the advocating of changes to social structures, and relief to the poor—are important, they must not obfuscate the preeminent purpose of missions: the salvation of the lost. McGavran writes, "In mission today many tasks must be carried on together; yet the multiplicity of good activities must contribute to, and not crowd out, maximum reconciliation of men to God in the Church of Jesus Christ."[11] The purpose of mission is the numerical increase of the church, and all methods and research should be coordinated toward this end. Hirsch assumes that the goal of mission is growth—his models of mission are the explosive growth of the early church and the contemporary Chinese church—but couples this with an insistence that such growth will come about primarily through the starting of new congregations, rather than simply the growth of current congregations.[12]

A second feature of the mission as growth model is that *such growth can be predicted.* McGavran is explicit in what he means by growth: it is the numerical increase of Christian converts, and as such it is quantifiable and predictable. Such an assertion is not for McGavran simply pragmatic but is itself a theological principle: "The lost are always persons. They always have countable bodies. ... Our Lord would have rejected the thought that the number of those found has no bearing on the direction of the search."[13] For McGavran, mission is a purposeful effort to reconcile men and women to God; the more that are reconciled the better, and thus the counting of those saved both drives mission strategy and keeps the missionary accountable. As McMahon states in a forum on McGavran's legacy:

> One of the things that strikes you about McGavran is his real emphasis on accountability. That's part of the inconvenient questions that he asked, right? ... You know, we measure growth by counting people in a fellowship of believers. You can tell us you are doing mission stuff out there, but where is the accountability in it? Did he get blowback? I know he did because people said it was all about numbers.

11. McGavran, *Understanding Church Growth,* 51.

12. Michael Frost and Alan Hirsch, *The Shaping of Things to Come: Innovation and Mission for the 21st-Century Church* (Peabody, MA: Hendrickson, 2003), x.

13. McGavran, *Understanding Church Growth,* 43.

That's one of the big criticisms, but it comes out of that emphasis on accountability.[14]

McGavran's emphasis on counting and accountability presumes that the pathway to the numerical increase of the church is predictable, and as such missionaries should be held accountable as to whether their works are moving them toward this goal. McGavran was reacting against what he perceived was a weakening of missionary energies in the West. He believed that the rising indifference to mission in the West, coupled with a rise in religious relativism, had led missionaries to conclude that their job was simply to proclaim the gospel, help the poor, and be content with whatever results would emerge. McGavran calls this a "neutralist" position.[15] Such a position not only weakens missionary efforts but is contradictory to the biblical mission mandate: "At base, the trouble is that mere search, detached witness—without the deep wish to convert, without wholehearted persuasion, and with what amounts to a fear of the numerical increase of Christians—is not biblically justified."[16]

For Hirsch, the growth of the church can be predicted through an analysis of the leadership and organizational structures of individual congregations and whether such structures sufficiently replicate what he believes is the proper structure of the biblical church. Like McGavran, for Hirsch such assertions are as much theological principles as pragmatic ones, as Scripture contains the organizational principles necessary to unlock church growth.[17]

That growth is the priority of mission, and that such growth is predictable, leads to a third hallmark of the mission as growth model: the tools of the social sciences should be used to discern the most effective way to proceed in mission to maximize the numerical growth of the church. *Missions should be strategic*, and better research aids in better strategy. Again, such an assertion is not for McGavran purely pragmatic, but also theological. For biblical support McGavran construes the parable of the harvest as a

---

14. Vern Middleton et al., "The Legacy of Donald McGavran: A Forum," *International Journal of Frontier Missiology* 31, no. 2 (2014): 68.

15. McGavran, *Understanding Church Growth*, 38.

16. McGavran, *Understanding Church Growth*, 40.

17. On Hirsch's use of Scripture, see below.

command from Jesus to think strategically: one should discover the people groups who are ripe for the harvest and shift resources toward these groups in order to maximize growth. The use of quantitative research helps identify which fields are ripe for the harvest and aids in discovering which methods yield the best reaping of that harvest.[18] In short, statistical research helps to identify what methods work best for planting and growing churches in specific cultures. This research should be used by the missionary to purposefully plan church planting efforts. "[The missionary's] goal is to devise an intelligent plan for establishing churches—one which fits his population, is similar to plans which have multiplied churches in other populations of this sort, and can be carried out with the resources which God has put into his hand."[19]

For Hirsch, the tools of organizational behavior help elucidate the leadership qualities and organizational culture that best yield success, qualities that are present as well in the leadership abilities of the apostles and in the missional structure of the early church. The tools of organizational behavior help to unlock the leadership and structural secrets of the New Testament.

When compared to conceptions of mission as *missio Dei* and mission as dialogue, the mission as growth model offers the best solution to the problem of *distinction*. As mentioned in the previous chapter, the term "mission" is often so broadly construed that it allows one to apply the term to any activity, eliminating the possibility of discerning the difference between missional acts that are performed well or poorly. McGavran explicitly viewed his emphasis on growth as a counter to broader conceptions of mission that he believed obscured the need for effective evangelism.[20] Service to the poor, the development of Christian education, or political advocacy are important,

---

18. As an example, McGavran includes a graph showing the rapid increase of baptized membership in the Church of Christ in the Sudan from 1930-1963. The graph charts both the membership of the church as well as the number of people enrolled in missionary-led schools. Since the rise of both over thirty-three years appears to follow a similar trajectory, McGavran presumes that school enrollment is the principal cause for growth in the Sudan, and missionaries should employ this tactic in the future in order to continue to bolster church growth in Sudan. Following the homogenous unit principle also means that such a tactic may only apply to the situation of the Sudan; in other countries, school enrollment may not correlate to church growth. McGavran, *Understanding*, 120–21.

19. McGavran, *Understanding Church Growth*, 360.

20. Donald Anderson McGavran, "My Pilgrimage in Mission," *International Bulletin of Missionary Research* 10, no. 2 (1986): 54.

but such activities are not at the heart of what McGavran saw as the biblical missional mandate, which is the conversion of the lost. McGavran, Hirsch, and their disciples are offering a conception of mission that is concrete and distinct: mission is about converting the lost and forming new churches out of the numerical increase of these conversions. It provides a clearly defined goal and an assertion that such a goal can be obtained and that there are resources and skills which can help the missionary in such a pursuit. For this reason, it offers the missionary the opportunity to hone their skills: the missionary can get better at their tasks of proclaiming the gospel and establishing churches. The nebulousness of *missio Dei* obscures such advancement—the missionary could at any time focus on a myriad of other missional activities, with little to no tools for assessing whether such activities are being performed well.

A CRITICAL EVALUATION OF
MISSION AS GROWTH

The tools of moral philosophy and theological ethics can help promote better understanding of this conception of mission as well as identify its flaws. It is not a coincidence that the mission as growth paradigm emerged as a distinct enterprise in the modern era. Just as the concept of a fact, the emergence of social sciences, and the notion of empirical research are all modern phenomena, so too are the missiological fact and empirical missiological research. The modernist underpinnings of the growth paradigm have been largely unrecognized by its adherents, a fact that is revealed particularly in its use of Scripture to support its undertakings. Missiologists like McGavran and Hirsch claim to be heralding a return to the missional dynamics of the New Testament while advocating the essential use of scientific and psychological methods completely foreign to any first-century society. For Hirsch in particular, the book of Acts is a model for Christian mission, but a model that is coded; psychological resources and scientific diagrams must be used to help crack its code.

But perhaps this is speaking proleptically. A fuller critique of the mission as growth paradigm begins by situating it within its modern context. In what follows, I will show how the paradigm fits well into Alasdair MacIntyre's critique of the social sciences and of modern management.

OUGHT, IS, AND THE MYTH OF MORAL NEUTRALITY

MacIntyre's critique of the social sciences is situated within his broader critique of modernity and modern morality in *After Virtue*. His critique of modernity is shared in part by a number of moral philosophers and theologians, notably Charles Taylor and Colin Gunton. MacIntyre's assertion is that one of the most profound changes that emerges in the wake of the Enlightenment is the severing of the link between "ought" and "is." This break had its roots in voluntarism and in portions of Reformation Protestant and post-Reformation Catholic thought, which stressed that Christian morality was linked primarily with the divine will and the divine command and not embedded in God's created order.[21] Enlightenment thinkers, most notably David Hume, brought this to its fuller secular conclusion: the rationality of descriptions of human nature is in no way related to human morality. With this comes the emergence of the historical novelty of the fact/value distinction: the tools of science provide value-neutral facts that are rationally discernable, while values are inherently irrational and distinct, coming from some other place (for most, religion).[22]

A key presumption of this view is the belief that the descriptions of human nature are value-neutral. Just as a microscope can be used to understand the

---

21. It is perhaps not a coincidence that the mission as growth paradigm has its roots in American evangelicalism, to the degree in which this movement is indebted to the radical elements of the Protestant Reformation. While in *After Virtue*, MacIntyre highlights Hume's distinction between "ought" and "is" as paradigmatic of the Enlightenment break with Aristotelian notions of telos, in *A Short History of Ethics*, MacIntyre is quick to point out how such a break is earlier evident in the work of Luther and Calvin. According to MacIntyre, Luther splits the individual from the community, emphasizes obedience to the divine will over the rationality of the created order, and affirms the absolute sovereignty of the political order. "It is, therefore, not just that Aquinas' Christian Aristotelianism and Luther's Christian fideism are based on alternative and competing metaphysical schemes; it is also the case that they are providing an analysis of and insight into different moral vocabularies" (125). See Alasdair C. MacIntyre, *A Short History of Ethics: A History of Moral Philosophy from the Homeric Age to the Twentieth Century* (New York: Macmillan, 1966), 121–27.

22. Charles Taylor charts a similar course in his depiction of the rise of modernity in *A Secular Age*. For Taylor, Hume's thought is paradigmatic of the rise of the modern disengagement of the mind from both the body and the rest of the created world. Taylor's keen observation is to chart the ways in which such disengagement correlates as well to what he calls the "buffered self," which offers the "attached sense of freedom, control, invulnerability, and hence dignity" (285). According to Taylor, this trajectory leads to an expressive individualism, a term that coheres with MacIntyre's assessment of modern morality as emotivism. See Charles Taylor, *A Secular Age* (Cambridge, MA: Harvard University Press, 2007).

structure, function, and movement of an organism, the tools of the social sciences can be used to understand the functions of human beings, and such descriptions are just as neutral. "The explanation of action is increasingly held to be a matter of laying bare the physiological and physical mechanisms which underlie action."[23]

For MacIntyre, this Enlightenment rendering of value neutrality renders morality unintelligible due to the severing of the intrinsic link between human nature and human ends. MacIntyre codifies this link, prevalent in Aristotle and pre-Reformation Christian thought, as a threefold schema: (1) human nature as it is (in its untutored state), (2) the goal of human beings (their telos), and (3) the principles and virtues that enable a human being to reach their goal (ethics).[24] To describe a human being is to speak in some way, implicitly or explicitly, of all three. Descriptions of human beings are thus intrinsically value-laden. For instance, to describe a person who compulsively lies, cheats, steals, and commits violence is to describe a bad or deficient person, in the same way that a description of a watch that fails to accurately keep time is a description of a bad watch. To describe what something "is" in its essence is also to describe in part what it "ought" to be if it reached its telos. An Enlightenment rejection of this link between "ought" and "is" operates under a moral fiction: that human behavior can be understood with scientific precision, and that such understandings have no moral implications.

It is with this that we can see how a conception of mission as growth emerges. Here, the tools of the behavioral sciences are used to predict with precision the behavior of missionary targets. For McGavran, statistics can help better show the gospel acceptance rate amongst differing people groups, and such statistical methods are value neutral: "The numerical approach is essential to understanding church growth. The Church is made up of countable people and there is *nothing particularly spiritual in not counting them*."[25] McGavran goes on to show how counting occurs in the Bible in both negative and positive ways—to show the number of people accepting the gospel and

---

23. MacIntyre, *After Virtue*, 82.

24. MacIntyre, *After Virtue*, 52–53.

25. McGavran, *Understanding Church Growth*, 83. Emphasis mine.

the number of people unfaithful to God.[26] This demonstrates that the use of statistical research is morally neutral.

For Hirsch, psychological profiles and organizational behavior research are predictive of church planting success. The primary tool developed by Hirsch is his APEST test,[27] which is used to assess the giftings of ministers. Such a test is unabashedly derivative of modern business practices, with Hirsch drawing corollaries to organizational behavior assessments:

The Apostle is the entrepreneur: Innovator and cultural architect who initiates a new product, or service, and develops the organization.

The Prophet is the questioner: Provocateur who probes awareness and fosters questioning of current programming leading to organizational learning.

The Evangelist is the communicator: Recruiter to the organization who markets the idea or product and gains loyalty to a brand or cause.

The Shepherd is the humanizer: People-oriented motivator who fosters a healthy relational environment through the management of meaning.

The Teacher is the philosopher: Systems-thinker who is able to clearly articulate the organizational ideology in a way as to advance corporate learning.[28]

According to Hirsch, the test "measures an individual's current ministry motivation and expression in ministry settings. As a result, APEST leads one to new areas of learning and integration for increased ministry engagement.

---

26. McGavran, *Understanding Church Growth*, 83.

27. APEST is an adaptation of Hirsch's APEPT abbreviation. The second P, "Pastors," is replaced by S, "Shepherds."

28. "Frequently Asked Questions for APEST & mPULSE," Alan Hirsch, http://www.alan-hirsch.org/faq. Hirsch gives a more detailed account of the relationship between the APEPT system and business management theory in *The Shaping of Things to Come* (with Michael Frost). Unfortunately, Hirsch does not cite specific sources for the corollaries between management theory and APEPT, stating instead that this correlation is "affirmed by the current best practice in leadership and management theory and practice" (173). It should be noted that, for Hirsch, leadership and management theory are simply reflecting the best leadership practices present in Scripture and articulated by St. Paul: "Current secular leadership theory yearns for the synergistic, creative, dynamic, interactive community proposed by Paul" (175). See Frost and Hirsch, *Shaping*, 173–75.

APEST provides a quantified result to identify one's current place for influence within a larger community."[29]

There is no moral reflection on the use of such tests, as Hirsch believes that the application of these tests is to help missionaries uncover the appropriate biblical model for mission and growth. The belief that what is gained by the application of the social sciences is a better understanding of the missional church as portrayed in Scripture is used to insulate the use of such methods from critique. Even though *The Forgotten Ways* reads as an organizational behavior manual, its use of modern technical approaches to mission are justified because they reveal what is more biblical, and hence more "natural."

However, the counting of people for the sake of maximizing church growth, and the use of psychological and organizational behavior research to predict successful church planting movements, are not morally neutral. Most significantly, McGavran's work has been severely criticized for creating a kind of cultural siloing that perpetuates racial biases for the sake of church growth. One of McGavran's key sociological discoveries, the homogenous unit principle, states that churches grow more quickly when they are generally made up of people from the same culture. Hence, the missionary should be free to focus on a particular people group, starting homogenous churches for the sake of quicker growth.

While McGavran's intention was not to create segregated churches, but to ascertain mission principles based on the observed fact of tribal and cultural distinction overseas,[30] his observations were used as tools in the West to exacerbate distinctions for the sake of numerical growth. Rene Padilla asserts that the adoption of McGavran's strategies in the American suburbs perpetuates and condones the cultural sins present there. For Padilla, McGavran's missiology is "tailor made for churches and institutions whose main function in society is to reinforce the status quo. What can this missiology say to a church in an American suburb, where the bourgeois is comfortable but remains enslaved to the materialism of a consumer society and blind to the

---

29. "The APEST Assessment," Alan Hirsch, http://www.alanhirsch.org/tests/.

30. McGavran, *Understanding Church Growth*, 213–14.

needs of the poor?"[31] In order to maximize growth, the missionary (perhaps unintentionally) downplays specific embedded cultural sins.

Particularly in its adaptation to the West, mission as growth faces another unintended consequence due to its perceived moral neutrality: that growth can occur due to the transferring of Christians from one church to another. William Chadwick documents the ways in which the unreflective use of the social sciences[32] from the church growth movement in part led to an exorbitant increase in the number of people moving from one church to another. Chadwick describes the growth of churches based primarily on this movement as stealing sheep. According to Chadwick, there is a fatal flaw in McGavran's program: statistical research determines the most highly efficient ways to numerically grow churches, yet the most efficient way to grow churches is *not* through evangelism, but by appealing to Christians dissatisfied with their current church. By unreflectively adopting these methods, McGavran actually helped to divert missional resources away from evangelism and toward the transferring of Christians between churches.[33]

If the telos of mission is growth, defined as the numerical increase of persons in a local congregation, then the fastest way to obtain such growth is often by appealing to existing Christians. McGavran may not have been able to foresee such unintended consequences, but this is in part due to the belief that his statistical methods were value-free. The goal of mission from the outset is numerical growth, and the methods used for assessing such growth were considered morally neutral.

Mission thus proceeds under the auspices that the acceptance of the gospel and the numerical success of mission can be predicted, and that the use of social scientific methods to enable better church growth is morally neutral. Criticisms of this approach stem from this assertion. MacIntyre's critique of the social sciences is that they are both manipulative and, ultimately, ironically, ineffective. The same critique holds for the mission as growth model as well.

---

31. Rene Padilla, "The Unity of the Church and the Homogenous Unit Principle," in *Landmark Essays in Mission and World Christianity*, ed. Robert Gallagher and Paul Hertig (Maryknoll, NY: Orbis Books, 2009), 91.

32. Chadwick describes this lack of reflectiveness as a failure on the part of the missionary to engage in inner examination. William Chadwick, *Stealing Sheep: The Church's Hidden Problem with Transfer Growth* (Downers Grove, IL: InterVarsity Press, 2001), 94.

33. Chadwick, *Stealing Sheep*, 90–99.

MANIPULATION AND MISSIONAL CONTRIVANCE

If human behavior can be studied, analyzed, and predicted with scientific precision, human beings can be manipulated in order to achieve predetermined outcomes. Human beings can be manipulated and controlled in a way similar to laboratory rats.[34] Colin Gunton characterizes this aspect of modernity as instrumentalization: "We use the other as an instrument, as the mere means for realizing our will, and not as in some way integral to our being."[35]

In turn, if human beings are predictable, then the power to manipulate lies in the hands of those who can discern such predictability. MacIntyre summarizes this connection between predictability and manipulation:

> It is clear that the Enlightenment's mechanistic account of human action included both a thesis about the predictability of human behavior and a thesis about the appropriate ways to manipulate human behavior. As an observer, if I know the relevant laws governing the behavior of others, I can whenever I observe that the antecedent conditions have been fulfilled predict the outcome. As an agent, if I know these laws, I can whenever I can contrive the fulfillment of the same antecedent conditions produce the outcome.[36]

If a given set of social conditions will consistently lead to specific and predictable human behaviors, then one can seek to create such social conditions in order to bring about these predictable behavioral outcomes. Thus

---

34. It is no coincidence that animals are used in experiments to help understand and predict human behavior, and the use of animals in many cases comes only after it is determined, retroactively, that human beings should not be put through such lab experiments.

35. Colin E. Gunton, *The One, the Three, and the Many: God, Creation, and the Culture of Modernity* (Cambridge: Cambridge University Press, 1993), 14. According to Gunton, the Cartesian detachment and disengagement of the individual mind renders all of nature, including other human beings, as instruments for realizing the will. Such instrumentalization affects both the environment and human relationships.

36. MacIntyre, *After Virtue*, 84. Cf. Marx's Third Thesis on Feuerbach: "The materialist doctrine concerning the changing of circumstances and upbringing forgets that circumstances are changed by men and that it is essential to educate the educator himself. This doctrine must, therefore, divide society into two parts, one of which is superior to society." Commenting on these theses, MacIntyre believes that Marx demonstrates that such a split in society drives the social theorist to believe that their theories grant them a degree of autonomy over their non-autonomous subjects: social theorists "understand those who are the subjects of their enquiries. They understand those whose actions and experiences are to be explained by their theory as the wholly determined products of circumstance and upbringing. ... By contrast such theorists understand themselves as rational agents, able to and aspiring to embody their intentions in the natural and social world" (229–30).

a conception of mission grounded in the ability to predict, with scientific precision, the antecedent social conditions necessary for numerical growth can attempt to contrive those same antecedent conditions to necessarily cause numerical growth.

The church growth/church planting publishing industry deals primarily with the business of contrivance. It is about discovering the conditions that lead to church growth, describing those conditions, and inviting missionaries to replicate such conditions. Here, Hirsch's statement of "cracking the code" of New Testament growth is telling—the ability to convert non-believers, to get those believers to attend a church, is one that is achieved mainly through solving the code. The New Testament church was the first to experience seismic missional growth because the early Christians were the first to crack this code.

Because the social and psychological tools used to predict human behavior are value-neutral, the possibility that such contrivances are manipulative is simply never raised. The question is always "what actions can create the environment for church growth," and never "what are actions that create church growth, but are morally questionable." This is a problem when the goal of mission becomes numerical growth. If the goal is numerical growth, then the actions that lead toward growth are good, or at the minimum morally neutral.

MacIntyre believes that the implementers of the social sciences, the modern-day bureaucratic managers, are often unaware of the manipulative undertones of much of their work. Effectiveness becomes the veiling term for manipulation:

> Managers themselves and most writers of management conceive of themselves as morally neutral characters whose skills enable them to devise the most efficient means of achieving whatever end is proposed. Whether a given manager is effective or not is on the dominant view a quite different question from that of the morality of the ends which his effectiveness serves or fails to serve.[37]

In a similar way, modern mission contrivers veil their manipulation under the auspices of growth, success, and effectiveness. Efficiency is a

---

37. MacIntyre, *After Virtue*, 74.

prominent value in McGavran's missiology—the use of statistical research
is meant to help cater missional resources to those areas in which the largest
number of converts is possible: "Since many aspects and activities have very
little to do with reproduction, the student of church growth concentrates on
those most directly responsible for propagating the Christian religion. The
facts he selects are relevant to bringing the nations to faith and obedience."[38]
Similarly for Hirsch, the goal is to develop the ideal church structures that
replicate the missional dynamics of the early church and will thus replicate
its numerical successes. If one can replicate these right conditions, "meta-
bolic growth and impact *are* catalyzed."[39]

Now, to this argument one could reply: "These missionaries are not
amoral, they are, after all, Christians!" It is true that those engaged in this
model of mission are for the most part aiming to form churches with a particular moral worldview. The hope of many of these missionaries is that those
who are the product of their growth strategies live lives that are good and in
accordance with some conception of biblical morality. McGavran does not
believe that mission is a purely sociological enterprise—the faith of missionaries is important.[40] Hirsch lists a robust confession of Jesus as Lord as one of
the six fundamentals of his mDNA. The issue is that, since success is defined
as growth, missionaries should leverage all resources necessary toward this
goal. As a result, the particular *missional actions* related to church growth—
the systems put in place, the advertising, market research, partitioning of
resources, etc.—are not considered *moral actions*. There is not, in this scheme,
a discussion of actions that could lead to church growth but should not be
partaken in. Faithfulness in both Hirsch and McGavran becomes one of many
components of church growth, listed for Hirsch amongst other essentials
such as "Organic Systems."[41] Faithfulness here is an essential part of the
life of the missionary not only because it is part of being a Christian, but
also because it is one of the many components that help bring about church
growth: the confession of Jesus as Lord becomes instrumentalized toward
the goal of growth.

---

38. McGavran, *Understanding Church Growth*, 98.
39. Hirsch, *Forgotten Ways: Missional*, 76. Emphasis added.
40. McGavran, *Understanding Church Growth*, 16.
41. Hirsch, *Forgotten Ways: Missional*, 79.

We see this particularly manifest in the ways in which mission in the Bible is construed. Here, I am adapting a notion from David Kelsey that the uses of Scripture in modern theology, the ways in which the Bible is construed, are partially determined by pre-textual judgments.[42] For theology, one's imaginative judgment of God's presence amongst his people determines not only which Scripture passages are highlighted, but also how those Scriptures are construed (as concepts, or judgments, etc.). I would assert the same for missiology: our imaginative judgments about the purpose of God's mission help to determine which biblical texts related to mission are highlighted, as well as the way we construe such texts.[43] For the mission as growth paradigm, the controlling image is the advancement of God's kingdom through the increase of the number of Christians to the ends of the earth. This exerts a control over the types of Scriptures used (parable of the sower, Peter's speech in Acts 2) and also how such missiological texts are construed. Here, because the goal of mission is the increase of converts and churches, and such goals are advanced through an understanding of the mechanics of human nature, biblical texts related to mission are construed as missional contrivances—they provide replicable models for how to produce effective mission.

Alan Hirsch's interpretation of Ephesians 4:4 is a vivid example. This passage becomes for Hirsch the foundation of his APEPT system. According to Hirsch, Paul is giving instructions on how to create a system that will grow the church. The church's recovery of this system is key to "unlocking the real power of Pauline teaching."[44] Such a recovery can be bolstered by the behavioral sciences—minsters can take personality profiles to discover which of the fivefold gifts they have and which ones they need in order to fully unlock the fivefold power Paul describes.[45] The relationship of Ephesians 4:4 to the rest of the epistle—particularly its relationship to the unity of the church

---

42. David H. Kelsey, *The Uses of Scripture in Recent Theology* (Philadelphia, PA: Fortress Press, 1975), 170. Kelsey's approach is similar to that of George Lindbeck, who asserts the ways in which church doctrine can function as a hermeneutical grammar. George A. Lindbeck, *The Nature of Doctrine: Religion and Theology in a Postliberal Age* (London: SPCK, 1984), 81.

43. Hirsch is explicit in his appeal to a reading of Scripture that stems from an imaginative prejudgment. The second edition of *The Forgotten Ways* asserts that the book "is written to appeal to the imagination and to direct the church to embrace the more dynamic movement-based paradigm evidenced in the New Testament." Alan Hirsch, *The Forgotten Ways: Reactivating Apostolic Movements* (Grand Rapids: Brazos Press, 2016), xxvi.

44. Hirsch, *Forgotten Ways: Missional*, 171.

45. Hirsch, *Forgotten Ways: Missional*, 172.

and the ascent and descent of Jesus—is ignored. The passage is instead construed as providing a prescriptive model for church growth. Hirsch sees his
task as that of biblical decoder—using scientific tools to unlock the model
for growth hidden throughout the New Testament:

> We need a comprehensive mental model of movement that makes
> sense of New Testament ecclesiology as well as unlocks the logjam
> of thinking that has resulted from twenty centuries of Christianity
> in Western settings. What this book proposes is just that: a synthe-
> sized, integrated model that does justice to the primary codes of Jesus's
> church and provides us with a viable way forward.[46]

When the business of mission is growth, its currency will be contrivances.
The goal of McGavran and Hirsch is to manipulate mission strategies and
church structures in order to bring forth a numerical increase of Christianity,
with Scripture providing the key strategies. The problem is that such success is predicated on the belief that individuals can be manipulated in such a
way that their conversion to Christianity is partially predetermined by such
strategies. The conversion of the unbeliever is not the result of a free decision
by the individual as much as it is the product of the strategic effectiveness
of the missionary. The grounding of these strategies in dubious scriptural
warrants inoculates the missionary from the self-reflection necessary to
realize the ethical issues associated with their schemas.

IRONICALLY INEFFECTIVE

According to MacIntyre, managerial effectiveness and efficiency will always
be proved to be a farce. Though the manager may possess a limited, short-
run capacity to manipulate circumstances to achieve desired outcomes, their
methods and tactics will ultimately be undone by the interminable unpredictability of human beings, characterized by Machiavelli as the goddess
Fortuna: "What I want to emphasize is Machiavelli's belief that, given the
best possible stock of generalizations, we may on the day be defeated by an
unpredicted and unpredictable counter-example—and yet still see no way to

---

46. Hirsch, *Forgotten Ways: Apostolic*, xxiv.

improve upon our generalizations and still have no reason to abandon them or even to reformulate them."[47]

Such unpredictability can derive from a sort of uncontrollable feedback loop: our interactions with other people necessarily change the circumstances by which future interactions are premised. In addition, the ability to exert control over human beings will always be limited, as both the manager and the customer exist within an infinitely complex web of other relationships that exert their own influence on them. There is also the simple fact of contingency. Something as simple as the common cold could change the course of key events in human history.[48]

Human beings cannot be manipulated as inert objects, and hence the use of scientific means to manipulate human beings will be doomed to eventual failure: "The dominance of the manipulative mode in our culture is not and cannot be accompanied by very much actual success in manipulation."[49] Managerial effectiveness is a fiction, and hence the manager must devise a way to prop up such a fiction, which is done through the equally mythical notion of bureaucratic expertise. The manager becomes involved in a masquerade: they must present themselves as experts of human behavior in a world in which such experts cannot exist. They must engage in a type of social performance—displaying their credentials, success, expertise, and continually adjusting means to suit their ends. Such a social performance is most evident in the literary genre of the business success book. Such books begin with a display of business success, an analysis of why such business

---

47. MacIntyre, *After Virtue*, 93.

48. MacIntyre, *After Virtue*, 100.

49. MacIntyre, *After Virtue*, 107. Public policy theorists William Dunn and David Miller come to a similar conclusion through their assessment of the New Public Management theory of administration and its major rival, the Neo-Weberian State. They see in both of these theories similar deficiencies to those outlined by MacIntyre in that they are unable to overcome instrumental rationality, nor are they able to provide the kind of efficiency they promise: "Both perspectives are also abstract, sweeping, and often ambiguous, leaving much to the imagination. Both tend to ignore the mixed or plainly ineffective results of organizations that have historically been governed by their principles. Both embody a techno-utilitarian perspective that in most respects resembles the kind of instrumental rationality that Max Weber exposed, criticized, and feared." William N. Dunn and David Y. Miller, "A Critique of the New Public Management and the Neo-Weberian State: Advancing a Critical Theory of Administrative Reform," *Public Organization Review* 7, no. 4 (2007): 353.

succeeds, and a practical application for the reader.[50] Of course, if the application of the insights displayed in such texts strongly predicted business success, they would be perpetual bestsellers. However, most of these books are quickly forgotten, since few such success stories exist. On occasion, the failure to predicate success is followed up by a kind of doubling down by the author—the reasons for this lack of success are on the part of the implementer, who has failed to fully implement their system.

Mission as growth attempts to develop law-like generalizations that predict mission outcomes but have ultimately been shown to have little to no predictive power. The goddess *Fortuna* is as much at work in the mission manager as their counterpart in business. This is because the missionary cannot account for the immense and infinitely complex web of social relationships that exist in their particular locale. The conversations that missionaries have with others do not take place in a vacuum. Previous relationships and conversations influence their interlocutor's view of Christianity—positively, negatively, or both. The people with whom they communicate have other responsibilities that limit the amount of time they allot for church-related activities.

There is also the sheer contingency of mission. For all of the strategizing, for all of the careful analysis of human tendencies, for all of the growth secrets allegedly divined from Scripture, at the end of the day, someone may catch a cold. That cold may prevent the next Billy Graham from attending a church service or strategy meeting. Perhaps the next week they attend some other church or begin a new activity that prevents them from attending. Difficult people may begin attending the church plant, driving away other potential attendees. Contingency is perhaps even more of a factor in missions than it is in business—church gatherings are often public events in which random strangers may attend, strangers who defy demographic datum. The church planter typically does not have the same luxury of hiring and firing their parishioners as the business manager has with their employees.

---

50. There are numerous examples of such books. One of the most popular over the past twenty years is Jim Collins's *Good to Great*, which analyzes several companies that superbly outperformed their particular markets and discerned the organizational principles common to these companies, with the hope that such principles can then be applied by the reader. Tom Peters's *Thriving on Chaos* is structured first around key management principles, with examples from successful businesses used to highlight the effectiveness of these principles if applied by the aspiring business manager.

The contingencies of working with human beings, as opposed to atoms, severely limits the effectiveness of the modern manager. Their ability to successfully manipulate human beings is short lived and capricious, and because of this fact, they must engage in an elaborate charade, adjusting means to ends and social customs that certify their expertise.

For these missional managers, the means of achieving the end—church growth—must be continually adjusted to validate their vocational existence. This helps to explain the proliferation of church growth and church planting publications, a proliferation that has warranted the codification of church planting as a distinct literary genre.[51] Each successive book provides tips and strategies to better unlock the secrets of church growth. Of course, if such numerical success were highly replicable, there would be no need for such a litany of publications.

Hirsch exemplifies this adjustment of means to ends in the second edition of his book *The Forgotten Ways*. The first edition promises a simple and replicable method for recovering the missional DNA of the early church through the replication of the six key components of "Apostolic Genius." The codification of this system as missional DNA is intended to show how a "simple, intrinsic, reproducible, central guiding mechanism is necessary for the reproduction and sustainability of genuine missional movements."[52] The use of the DNA metaphor is also meant to evoke the notion that such a system of mission is engrained in the lifeblood of all Christians, so much so that the great explosions of church growth throughout human history involve an intuitive grasp of these six components.[53] Hirsch's two examples are the growth of early Christianity and the recent growth of underground churches in China.

Yet, despite the alleged simplicity of this system, Hirsch admits in the second edition that few have been able to successfully replicate it. The lack of success in implementing this simple sixfold model, however, does not deter from the fact that those who have adopted one or two of these six critical aspects can still see great benefit.

---

51. On amazon.com, for instance, church growth is a searchable literature category, containing two thousand books.

52. Hirsch, *Forgotten Ways: Missional*, 76.

53. Hirsch, *Forgotten Ways: Missional*, 77.

But if we look for full and mature expressions of the Apostolic Genius system—where all six elements of mDNA are cooking in the one total system—there are still very few exemplary models in the West. But I am extremely hopeful: the good news is that some are now established; they are maturing and are gaining momentum, influence, and strength as viable expressions of apostolic movements. And it takes only a few of these to validate the model for others to follow. For instance, only two churches (Willow Creek and Saddleback) in effect validated the seeker-sensitive model that subsequently became the standard expression of evangelical church throughout the West! It doesn't take many to change the paradigm and demonstrate validity.[54]

There is in this instance a moving of the missional goalposts. What is promised is a simple and reproducible mission growth strategy that has proved, despite ten years and millions of books sold, not to be simple or reproducible. Hirsch is hopeful, however, that a few movements will emerge that have all six aspects of "Apostolic Genius," and that these few will validate his system.

What is obscured amidst such scheming is the simple recognition that people can, at the end of the day (not the eschaton), choose not to become Christian. The transcendent belief that every knee shall bow is confused with the immanent reality that, until that point, people may reject the gospel despite our best-laid plans. The missionary can plan and strategize the most effective APEPT leadership team, only to have members of that team unexpectedly move, fall ill, or quit. There is an over-realized eschatology undergirding the mission as growth paradigm: the belief that the kingdom of God will be made manifest through our works, and that manifestation will be the turning of souls to Jesus Christ.

THE PROBLEM OF AGENCY

THE DIMINISHED AGENCY OF THE MISSION RECIPIENT

We can codify the central issue of the mission as growth paradigm as the problem of human agency. Following the lead of the social and behavioral sciences, these missiologists attempt to elucidate law-like generalizations

---

54. Hirsch, *Forgotten Ways: Apostolic*, xxvi.

of human behavior that are predictive. As Charles Taylor puts it, such an understanding reduces personal agency to a performance criterion.[55] The behavioral sciences, taking their cue from the natural sciences, sought to provide a significance-free account of human action, that "the explanatory relationship between situation and response can be captured in an absolute description; or that ... the features picked out in the significance description are not essential to the explanation, but just concern the way things appear to us in ordinary life."[56] Taylor makes an important and nuanced distinction concerning the behavioral sciences. It is not that human beings are simplistic, or that human beings do not have complex reasons for engaging in specific behaviors. However, the assertion is that one can pick out the explanatory factors amongst these various reasons. The significance of the choice for the individual is irrelevant; what matters is the identification of the under-lying process that is ultimately determinative of the individual's choice of action. One views agency as the predictive performance of the individual with no reference to a decision's importance to that individual. Taylor gives an example of the sun rising: the individual experiences the sun going up and down each day, yet the scientist knows that this is merely the individual experience of an underlying process of the revolution of the earth around the sun.[57] The behavioral scientists apply this reasoning about the sun and the earth to human beings.

The example of church growth becomes illustrative of this point. If forty new people arrive at a church service or at an outreach event, what is import-ant is describing the factors that predicated the performative action of atten-dance. The missionary thus attempts to describe the tactics and strategies that brought about the actions of these forty people. What is irrelevant to the description are the various individual reasons that are only significant to that individual and not to their action of attendance. Some of these indi-viduals may have arrived at church because they felt a sense of obligation to the friends who had invited them, some may have attended because they had felt shame for not having engaged in the religion of their parents, some did not attend because they were sick or because the advertisements struck

---

55. Charles Taylor, *Human Agency and Language*, vol. 1: *Philosophical Papers* (Cambridge: Cambridge University Press, 1985), 106.

56. Taylor, *Human Agency*, 108.

57. Taylor, *Human Agency*, 107.

them as kitschy. However, all of these individual reasons are irrelevant. What Taylor calls the representation account seeks to redescribe these actions as naturalistic ends that are thus "discoverable by objective scrutiny."[58] The individual's reasons for showing up to church are only significant to themselves; the only descriptions that matter to the missionary are those that relate to the objective act itself and can thus be scrutinized and manipulated.

To use our example above, what matters to the church planter is not the pluriform of reasons why each of the forty people show up at a church who successfully implements its program. What matters is that the program implemented produced its desired effect, and what matters is whatever explanation best describes how these forty people showed up. The personal desires and emotions of each individual *do not matter* in regard to the missionary's primary task of numerical growth.

The consequence of the adoption of the mission as growth paradigm is thus to severely limit human agency. The primary task of the missionary is to discover the underlying processes that lead to the expansion of the church and to replicate these processes in order to bring about such growth. The enactment of this program necessarily relegates all other individual cares and desires to secondary matters. It is important to note that, under this system, there is still room to acknowledge the importance of individual's desires, emotions, and needs; however, such acknowledgment is only for the individual's benefit and must be subordinated to the overarching project of discerning and implementing the process of church growth.

---

58. Taylor, *Human Agency*, 113. One might also construe the representation account as an attempt to reduce the choice of whether to accept the gospel or to attend a church gathering to one of simple mental causation. Here I'm referring to G. E. M. Anscombe's distinction between mental causes, on the one hand, and "reasons" (motives and intentions), on the other: "the more the action is described as a mere response, the more inclined one would be to the word 'cause'; while the more it is described as a response to something as having a significance that is dwelt on by the agent, or as a response surrounded with thoughts and questions, the more inclined one would be to use the word 'reason' " (331). The attempt in the mission as growth paradigm is to reduce the receptivity of an invitation to a church gathering or an invitation to become a Christian into one of mere response, since such responses can thus be more easily predicted and thus manipulative by missional contrivance. See G. E. M. Anscombe, "Intention," *Proceedings of the Aristotelian Society* 57 (1956).

THE DIMINISHED AGENCY OF THE MISSIONARY

While it seems as though the agency of the missionary target is diminished at the expense of an enlargement of the agency of the missionary, the implementation of the growth paradigm ironically leads to a similar diminishment of agency for the missionary. The task of the missionary in this regard is stripped down to one of process and implementation, and their effectiveness becomes determinate purely on outcomes.

The role of the missionary is no longer creative, flexible, or even spiritual. The program is implemented, and the missionary is judged on the benchmarks reached or unreached. The joy that is possible in mission is determined solely on outcomes—more growth is equivalent to more joy.

This diminishment in agency on the part of the missionary is in part due to a failure to understand the task of mission as that which is ultimately the work of the Holy Spirit. The Holy Spirit is God working in and through us to accomplish his will, and John 14:6 highlights the reception of the Holy Spirit as empowering and inaugurating the era of Christian mission. Furthermore, the Holy Spirit renews moral agency: the disciple's missional actions, done in accordance with and empowered by the Spirit, become part of God's actions. "Whatever you loose on earth will be loosed in heaven" (Matt 16:19).

The Holy Spirit is the presence of God at work renewing and restoring his creation; thus, the recipients of the Trinitarian mission of the Holy Spirit find their mission in cooperating in the creative activity of the renewal of God's creation. Oliver O'Donovan remarks upon the weakened agency of sinful humanity apart from the working of the Holy Spirit. Agency is impaired because we don't know exactly what lies ahead of us: "Striving to produce something but unable to tell what it would produce, it is wholly bent upon painful effort, a world with a historical destiny but no vision of fulfilment."[59] The gift of the Holy Spirit does not give us divine foreknowledge, but rather takes our desires and aspirations and weaves them up into the purposes of God.[60]

The promise of the Holy Spirit gives the missionary not a divine foreknowledge of the end results of their efforts, but rather an assurance that

---

59. Oliver O'Donovan, *Finding and Seeking: Ethics as Theology*, vol. 2 (Grand Rapids: Eerdmans, 2014), 1.

60. O'Donovan, *Finding*, 2.

the work they do in the power of the Holy Spirit will be taken up into the divine purposes of God. This frees the missionary to be joyful and creative in their charge. The missionary is free to serve God at the behest of the movement of the Spirit, which "blows where it chooses" (John 3:8). Here lies the source of so much creativity throughout the centuries of Christian mission.

What the mission as growth paradigm offers, at its worse, is an assurance to the missionary that their efforts *will* produce the desired results. This futile attempt strips the missionary of their creative freedom, since "factual narrative of future events would entirely undercut the indeterminacy that freedom requires."[61] If the immediate future can be controlled by the implementation of a specific missional program, then the indeterminacy from which springs creative freedom is stripped.[62] The missionary is left only to implement programs and judge (and be judged) by their effectiveness in implementation.

There is in the end a sinful dramatic irony fit for a Dante poem: in their attempts to control human behavior to conjure numerical increases, the missionary becomes controlled by the ups and downs of weekly Sunday attendance figures. They are happy and content when the numbers match their projections, even if these numbers may be the result of manipulation or sheer luck. They will be sad when the numbers miss the mark, believing that they have missed a key aspect of some system.

What is offered by the mission as growth model is a false assurance that the implementation of a specific system can predict with accuracy a future that is only known by God. There is an overconfidence in the ability to predict with certainty events in the near future. In the process, what is lost is the assurance and comfort of the Holy Spirit, which gives the missionary the delight in knowing that their labors are not done in vain.

CONCLUSION

These criticisms notwithstanding, there remains much to be commended about McGavran's growth-centered approach to mission. An emphasis on mission as growth addresses some of the perpetual missiological challenges

---

61. O'Donovan, *Finding*, 156.

62. O'Donovan goes on to suggest that this desire for certainty about the near future may spring from a fear of freedom. In the present case, the missionary is attracted to the certainty of growth strategies out of a fear of failure or the possibility that the secrets to mass conversion may lie outside of their ken. O'Donovan, *Finding*, 158.

evident in an approach to mission centered on participation in the *missio Dei*. It emphasizes active participation in mission work: the missionary can get better at their job, and such improvement can yield tangible results. It also provides greater clarity in defining the work of the missionary: mission work is the focused activity of evangelism with the expressed goal of increasing the number of Christians throughout the world. Other Christian activities may be related to this task, but mission at its core is defined by such activity. These distinctive aspects of the mission as growth paradigm do have a place within mission, but the practical skills that they offer must be placed in a context free from the burdens of numerical growth and earthly success. As will be demonstrated, the development of practical skills on the part of the missionary is better conceived of as the honing of a craft whose benefits are ultimately not the numerical success of the mission, but the glory of God. This conception will be addressed in the ensuing chapter on mission and virtue. But before this discussion, it is imperative to address another major conception of mission, a conception that consciously attempts to redress the manipulative aspects of the growth paradigm by instead highlighting the dialogical aspects of mission.

3

—

MISSION AS DIALOGUE

The previous chapter examined many of the difficulties inherent in an approach to mission as church growth, particularly surrounding the idea of agency. Developed over a similar period of time, the conception of mission as dialogue directly addresses the criticisms of the mission as growth paradigm, particularly in regard to its charges of manipulation. However, its emergence was not in reaction to the work of McGavran and others, but rather in response to the perceived excesses of the missionary enterprise throughout Christian history, particularly in the occasions of missionary collusion with European colonization. Coupled with this anxiety over the history of Christian mission was an awareness of the decline of Christianity in Europe and the emergence of a de facto religious pluralism of many Western countries in the twentieth century.[1] The theological superiority of the West was challenged by the erosion of Christianity from within its European strongholds, and thus "the Eurocentric view of the world and of the Church lost its persuasiveness, undermining the territorial concept of mission at its root."[2]

The concept of interreligious dialogue emerged out of these critiques, both by those who wished to qualify the concept of mission and those who wished to abolish it. It emphasizes the intrinsic value of other persons and

---

1. Jacques Dupuis clarifies the difference between de facto pluralism and de jure pluralism. De facto religious pluralism simply acknowledges the fact of the "plurality of religions, characteristic of the landscape of today's world." Dupuis does not mean that religious diversity has not existed as a reality for millennia but rather acknowledges that what is new for many in the West is the *persistent encounter* with those of different religions. One is confronted with a plurality of religions and religious beliefs, rather than existing in relative isolation from those of differing religions. One can choose to accept this reality simply as a fact or accept it as de jure: something to be welcomed as a good development, and one that is "positively willed by God." Jacques Dupuis, *Toward a Christian Theology of Religious Pluralism* (Maryknoll, NY: Orbis Books, 1997), 386.

2. Cesare Baldi, "The Mission of the Church," in *Catholic Engagement with World Religions: A Comprehensive Study*, ed. Karl Josef Becker et al. (Maryknoll, NY: Orbis Books, 2010), 289.

their religious beliefs and the value in interpersonal encounters with others in their difference.[3] Interreligious dialogue stresses encounter rather than confrontation, the conversion to the other rather than the conversion of the other. Such an emphasis addressed both the theological anxieties of a post-Enlightenment West and the religious pluralism that emerged out of globalization, but it also created problems for traditional concepts of mission, as dialogue seemed to be at odds with the long-held Christian belief in gospel proclamation. Some sought to submerge mission into the concept of dialogue, eliminating the need for proclamation altogether.[4] Following the postmodern rejection of any universal and univocal beliefs, theologians began stressing the inherent salvific character of other religions and the rejection of certain forms of evangelization as intrinsically coercive. Here, dialogue is preeminent, and absolutist claims to truth only erect barriers to such dialogue. The affirmation of the truth claims of all religions, coupled with the intrinsic truth and goodness of other religions, demands an interreligious dialogue purged of the absolutist claims of proclamation.

It is perhaps not surprising that a conception of mission born out of both a critical reflection of missionary endeavors and a growing awareness of global religions emerged through the writings of theologians working within global ecclesial institutions.[5] The development of the mission as dialogue paradigm can be traced along two often interloping trajectories: that of the Roman Catholic Church and the World Council of Churches.

This chapter will begin by tracing the history of the mission as dialogue paradigm and offering a summation of its key tenets, followed by an extensive critique. This critique will pave the way for an in-depth analysis of the problem of persuasion in mission.

---

3. Jacques Dupuis, *Christianity and the Religions: From Confrontation to Dialogue* (Maryknoll, NY: Orbis Books, 2002), 7.

4. John Hick, for instance, rejects proclamation altogether. Dialogue should be the preeminent posture of all religious adherents, including Christians, with the goal of such dialogue being the eradication of any claims to religious superiority. John Hick, "The Next Step beyond Dialogue," in *The Myth of Religious Superiority: Multifaith Explorations of Religious Pluralism*, ed. Paul F. Knitter (Maryknoll, NY: Orbis Books, 2005), 12.

5. This is contrasted with the mission as growth paradigm, which emerges primarily through the writings of mission practitioners. Thus, the mission as growth paradigm has as many of its most important texts ones written for practical instruction and published through popular presses. In contrast, the mission as dialogue paradigm has as its most important texts official Roman Catholic and World Council of Churches documents, as well as theological texts from academic presses.

HISTORICAL BACKGROUND:
KEY THEOLOGIANS AND TEXTS

The mission as dialogue paradigm emerged in the twentieth century out of
two historical trajectories, one Protestant, the other Roman Catholic. Before
assessing the central characteristics of the mission as dialogue model, it
is important to first give an overview of its key proponents and texts, as
both theologians and conciliar gatherings (Vatican II and World Council of
Churches meetings) feature prominently in both trajectories. This overview
is not meant to be comprehensive but is intended to help provide a context
for the mission as dialogue model and help situate some of the prominent
adherents within it.

The historical development of the Roman Catholic perspective on mission
as dialogue can be charted alongside a series of official church documents
beginning with Vatican II. The most important text of Vatican II related to
dialogue is *Nostra aetate*, which articulated a positive valuation of world religions and an exhortation to engage in mutual respectful dialogue between
Christians and adherents of other religions:

> The Church, therefore, exhorts her sons, that through dialogue and
> collaboration with the followers of other religions, carried out with
> prudence and love and in witness to the Christian faith and life, they
> recognize, preserve and promote the good things, spiritual and moral,
> as well as the socio-cultural values found among these men.[6]

This exhortation to engage in interreligious dialogue inaugurated a debate
amongst Roman Catholic theologians (and reflected in official documents)
regarding this exhortation to dialogue and to the calling of Christians to proclaim the salvific work of Christ. While some interpreted *Nostra aetate* as an
affirmation of interreligious dialogue as the preeminent activity of mission
(as will be discussed below), future papal encyclicals reiterated the necessity of the proclamation of Christ. This is seen most vividly in John Paul II's
encyclical *Redemptoris missio*, which states:

> Proclamation is the permanent priority of mission. The Church
> cannot elude Christ's explicit mandate, nor deprive men and women

---

6. Paul VI, *Nostra aetate*, Vatican website, October 28, 1965, http://www.vatican.va/archive/
hist_councils/ii_vatican_council/documents/vat-ii_decl_19651028_nostra-aetate_en.html.

of the "Good News" about their being loved and saved by God. ... All forms of missionary activity are directed to this proclamation, which reveals and gives access to the mystery hidden for ages and made known in Christ (cf. Eph 3:3–9; Col 1:25–29), the mystery which lies at the heart of the Church's mission and life, as the hinge on which all evangelization turns.[7]

Much of twentieth-century Roman Catholic thought concerning the church's relationship to peoples of other religions can be characterized as a tension between dialogue and proclamation, with *Nostra aetate* and *Redemptoris missio* functioning as the boundary markers.[8] Those who promote mission as dialogue thus tend to emphasize *Nostra aetate* and deemphasize *Redemptoris missio*. At its best, this tension has helped to fuel substantial work in the fields of mission, world religions, and interreligious dialogue, with major works such as Paul Knitter's *No Other Name* and Jacques Dupuis's *Toward a Christian Theology of Religious Pluralism* interacting substantially with papal documents. At its worst, it has led to incessant internecine conflict over the interpretation of these documents. My construal of mission as dialogue will highlight the works of Knitter and Dupuis, both of whom highlight the dialogical emphases of these documents and deemphasize the aspects which promote the priority of proclamation.[9]

The roots of a Protestant approach to mission as dialogue lie in the World Missionary Conferences of the first part of the twentieth century and continue through the formation of the World Council of Churches in 1948.[10] John Cobb charts the development of dialogue through the first three

---

7. John Paul II, *Redemptoris missio*, Vatican website, December 7, 1990, http://w2.vatican.va/content/john-paul-ii/en/encyclicals/documents/hf_jp-ii_enc_07121990_redemptoris-missio.html.

8. For a detailed account of modern Roman Catholic history in regard to dialogue and proclamation, see Marcello Abp Zago, "The New Millennium and the Emerging Religious Encounters," *Missiology* 28, no. 1 (2000).

9. See Dupuis, *Toward*, 360–70; Paul F. Knitter, *Jesus and the Other Names: Christian Mission and Global Responsibility* (Maryknoll, NY: Orbis Books, 1996), 125–35.

10. The first World Missionary Conference in Edinburgh in 1910 is considered to be the beginning both of modern Christian missions and the ecumenical movement. While the gathering was exclusively Protestant and advocated for what would now be considered a conservative, exclusivist approach to mission, future conferences organized through the International Missionary Council allowed for both an expanded engagement with non-Protestant churches (Orthodox and Roman Catholic) and an expanded engagement with non-exclusivist approaches to mission centering on interreligious dialogue. The merging of the International Missionary

World Missionary Conferences, with the first clearly taking an adversarial approach to other religions, the second more accommodating, and the third a reaction against this accommodation.[11] Here there is a tension similar to the one between dialogue and proclamation in Roman Catholic circles, a tension that remained through the various consultations and statements from the World Council of Churches (WCC). Cobb's assessment of the various documents is that they both establish the necessity of dialogue while not further developing the theological grounding for such dialogue. The prevention of this grounding is due to tensions within the WCC between those who are willing to embrace full mutuality between Christianity and other religions and those who are not:

> Despite the acceptance of dialogue as a major program emphasis of the World Council of Churches, the theological grounds for dialogue are still undeveloped. This is because of a tension between two basic Christian positions. One group, and this includes many of those who participate most actively in dialogue with persons of other faiths, takes the religious conviction of these persons with great seriousness and wants to understand them better. For these Christians, dialogue is a profound spiritual sharing on the basis of full mutuality between religions movements. ... For (the other) group, there cannot be full mutuality between, for example, Christians as Christians and Muslims as Muslims.[12]

John Cobb is representative of those Protestant theologians who prioritize the mutuality of religions and the preeminence of dialogue in Christian mission.[13] Protestant views on the relationship between dialogue and mission

---

Council with the World Council of Churches in 1961, and the rejection of this merger by some conservative evangelical churches, can be seen as the culmination of this expansion. For a detailed history, see "History," The World Council of Churches, https://www.oikoumene.org/en/what-we-do/cwme/history.

11. John B. Cobb, *Beyond Dialogue: Toward a Mutual Transformation of Christianity and Buddhism* (Philadelphia, PA: Fortress Press, 1982), 15–18.

12. Cobb, *Beyond*, 18.

13. Cobb is representative of what he calls "progressive Christianity," which includes members of his own network, Protestant Christians Uniting. Other Protestant theologians who hold similar positions include Ward McAfee and the contributors to John B. Cobb and Ward McAfee, *The Dialogue Comes of Age: Christian Encounters with Other Traditions* (Minneapolis, MN: Fortress Press, 2010).

vary widely when compared to Roman Catholic positions, in part due to the potential institutional constraints of the magisterium on Catholic teaching.[14]

My assessment of the mission as dialogue paradigm will focus on the work of John Cobb for several reasons. First, his work has been highly influential within the fields of interreligious dialogue and religious pluralism, with numerous works authored and edited. Second, unlike the most prominent proponent of religious pluralism and dialogue, John Hick, Cobb does not accept the view of a universal equality of religions. The acknowledgment of robust differences between religions enables Cobb to still maintain a concept of Christian mission, albeit one that is greatly modified from traditional understandings. Hick's assertion of the universal equality of religions points instead to a wholesale dismissal of mission.[15] In the interest of providing a more complete picture of the mission as dialogue paradigm, one that accounts for the work of Roman Catholic theologians, I will also highlight the contributions of Jacques Dupuis and Paul Knitter.

FOUR KEY ASPECTS OF THE MISSION AS DIALOGUE MODEL

What follows is an assessment of the key aspects of the construal of mission as dialogue. The focus will be particularly on the communicative directives and goals that undergird this approach, which includes its understanding of persuasion and conversion, but it will also include the pertinent theological and anthropological underpinnings of this approach. The choice to emphasize communication is based on this model's emphasis on communicative acts as central to Christian mission: "To view and practice mission as dialogue is to see the church's mission essentially as one of communication."[16] The focus on

---

14. This constraint was highly visible in the trial of Jacques Dupuis by the Congregation of the Doctrine of the Faith in 2001, in which Dupuis's work *Toward a Christian Theology of Religious Pluralism* was investigated. Though Dupuis was not censured, the book was reissued with a pontifical notification clarifying official Catholic teaching: "It is therefore legitimate to maintain that the Holy Spirit accomplishes salvation in non-Christians also through those elements of truth and goodness present in the various religions; however, to hold that these religions, considered as such, are ways of salvation, has no foundation in Catholic theology, also because they contain omissions, insufficiencies and error." "Notification on the Book *Toward a Christian Theology of Religious Pluralism*," Vatican website, January 24, 2001, http://www.vatican.va/roman_curia/congregations/cfaith/documents/rc_con_cfaith_doc_20010124_dupuis_en.html.

15. See John B. Cobb, "Beyond 'Pluralism,' " in *Christian Uniqueness Reconsidered: The Myth of a Pluralistic Theology of Religions*, ed. Gavin D'Costa (Maryknoll, NY: Orbis Books, 1990).

16. Knitter, *Jesus*, 144.

mission as the engagement in communicative acts also means that a concomitant issue, religious pluralism, will only be addressed tertiarily. Concerns surrounding a theology of religions and the relationship of Christianity to those religions are intertwined with the mission as dialogue paradigm—to assert the preeminence of interreligious dialogue begs the question of what one believes about the religious views of their interlocutors.[17] Regarding the relationship between Christianity and other religions, much has been written.[18] However, few works have taken seriously the conception of dialogue as the preeminent act of mission and subsequently addressed the ethical and philosophical underpinnings of dialogue as a communicative act in which missionaries participate. It is this that a work devoted to ethics and missiology will thus address.

COMMON HUMANITY AND THE KINGDOM OF GOD

The mission as dialogue paradigm is rooted in an anthropology that rejects ethnocentrism and emphasizes the common humanity existent among all cultures. Kathryn Tanner argues that such an anthropology developed in reaction to an evolutionary anthropology of the eighteenth and nineteenth century which discerned a hierarchy amongst various cultures based upon scientific, technological, and (perceived) cultural advancement. Such evolutionary anthropology was perceived as inherently ethnocentric and in part the cause of Western colonialism. The response was to emphasize the common humanity of all and to see cultural differences as a good within this

---

17. Catherine Cornille's development of the term "soteriological agnosticism" highlights the ways in which conceptions of dialogue are intertwined with a theology of religions. Cornille advocates for a bracketing of issues of salvation—neither the exclusivist nor the pluralist can claim salvific knowledge of non-Christian religions. Yet she admits that, even with such bracketing, one's theology of religions will necessarily impact the way dialogue is conducted: "The very openness to engaging another religion in a constructive way indeed implies certain views or presumptions about the intelligibility of the teaching of the other, their compatibility with and relevance for one's own, and about the possibility of actually discerning teaching that might deepen, broaden, or generally enhance one's own religious understanding" (210). Catherine Cornille, "Soteriological Agnosticism and the Future of Catholic Theology of Interreligious Dialogue," in *The Past, Present, and Future of Theologies of Interreligious Dialogue*, ed. Terrence Merrigan and John R. Friday (Oxford, UK: Oxford University Press, 2017).

18. It should also be noted that issues surrounding Christianity and religious pluralism have been superbly addressed in two edited volumes: John Hick and Paul F. Knitter, eds., *The Myth of Christian Uniqueness: Toward a Pluralistic Theology of Religions* (Maryknoll, NY: Orbis Books, 1987); and Gavin D'Costa, ed. *Christian Uniqueness Reconsidered: The Myth of a Pluralistic Theology of Religions* (Maryknoll, NY: Orbis Books, 2004).

common humanity.[19] This is one of the preeminent markers of the modern, anthropological idea of culture.[20]

Cobb, Knitter, and Dupuis's theologies reflect this modern idea of culture in their emphasis on a universal common humanity which eschews claims of superiority and stresses the intrinsic goodness of religious diversity. The use of Scripture by the adherents to the conception of mission as dialogue reflects this emphasis on a common humanity as the grounds through which dialogue proceeds, and thus passages of Scripture that reflect the universal love of humanity and respectful dialogue become hermeneutical keys. We see this in the emphasis on the biblical concept of the kingdom of God by Paul Knitter and Jacques Dupuis: the kingdom of God is that in which all religious traditions of the world share, and the church, rather than being the kingdom of God, is in service to this kingdom. Dupuis takes the large number of Jesus's teachings on the kingdom of God and the paucity of his direct references to the church as indicative of the term's expansiveness.[21] For Dupuis, Jesus inaugurates in history the kingdom of God, to which Christians and non-Christians *already* belong.[22] This renders both Christians and adherents to other religions "co-members and co-builders with God of God's Reign on earth," and it forms the foundation for interfaith dialogue.[23] For Knitter, the distinction between the church and the kingdom, and the church's subservience to the kingdom, is foundational for a conception of mission as dialogue:

> Integral to the new paradigm for understanding the mission of the church as service to the Kingdom is the necessity of integrating dialogue into that mission-as-service. If, in this new regnocentric paradigm, the religious traditions of humankind are looked up as potential "agents of the Kingdom," then clearly, cooperation and dialogue with them are essential elements in a missioner's job description.[24]

---

19. Kathryn Tanner, *Theories of Culture: A New Agenda for Theology* (Minneapolis, MN: Fortress Press, 1997), 37.

20. Tanner sees this particular understanding of culture emerging in the United States in the 1920s, peaking in the 1960s, and coming into criticism by postmodern theorists starting in the 1980s. Tanner, *Theories*, 25.

21. Dupuis, *Toward*, 342–43.

22. Dupuis, *Toward*, 346.

23. Dupuis, *Toward*, 358.

24. Knitter, *Jesus*, 136.

Though not as central to his theology,[25] John Cobb nevertheless concurs with Knitter and Dupuis in their assessment of the kingdom of God as something shared by all, something which Christians as well as peoples of other faiths might work toward. For Cobb, the kingdom of God is

> the longed-for situation in which God's will is done on earth as it is in heaven. In the community surrounding Jesus there is already a foretaste of that situation. … But in most of the pronouncements, there is no suggestion that those who fail to believe in Jesus Christ are to be excluded or that God cannot work through those who are not believers in bring the situation to pass.[26]

For Cobb, Knitter, and Dupuis, Christians and non-Christians alike are building a common project together, the kingdom of God. They are *already* co-laborers, and, as such, competition through evangelization is rejected in favor of cooperation through dialogue.

INTENTIONAL BRACKETING OF EVALUATIVE JUDGMENTS

The modern anthropological idea of culture developed in response to previously ethnocentric understandings of culture, and its turn to an emphasis on a shared common humanity concurrently promoted a non-evaluative understanding of various cultures.[27] Similarly, the theologies of Cobb, Knitter, and Dupuis emphasize a shared common humanity and the intrinsic goodness of other religions, which leads to a rejection of any claims of religious superiority. Thus, their approaches to mission involve dialogue which is to be conducted with the *intentional bracketing of evaluative judgments*. At the heart of the conception of the mission as dialogue paradigm is the belief that unethical and immoral missionary practices are rooted in a false superiority on the part of Christian missionaries, a superiority that is part and parcel

---

25. Cobb also uses his interpretation of the Logos in John 1 as a way to conceive of a common humanity. For Cobb, the Logos is first the power of transformation in all living things, and it "is incarnate in all human beings and indeed in all creation" (138). While Christ is the fullest incarnation of the Logos, any individual can grow in their fullness of the Logos, including through the practice of other religions. John B. Cobb, *Christ in a Pluralistic Age* (Philadelphia, PA: Westminster Press, 1975), 137–46.

26. John B. Cobb, "Introduction," in *The Dialogue Comes of Age: Christian Encounters with Other Traditions*, ed. John B. Cobb and Ward McAfee (Minneapolis: Fortress Press, 2010), 16.

27. Tanner, *Theories*, 36.

of Western colonialism: "Christians have often made claims of superiority and even of exclusive possession of the way to salvation that have done great harm. We have blinded ourselves to the wisdom of other communities and have often used political, economic, and military power over them abusively. We have much of which to repent."[28] It is the presumption of superiority that compels missionaries to engage in a "monologue" with opposing worldviews, demanding assent and blinding the missionary to the ways in which they are imposing their will through economic and political power. To conceive of mission as dialogue necessarily means bracketing claims to superiority and judgments as to the truth, goodness, and beauty of other religious adherents. Before engaging in dialogue, the missionary must first reflect and assess their Christian beliefs and develop approaches that seek to minimize the ways in which they might be conceived by their interlocutors as offensive. As Cobb puts it, "We will undertake to formulate our own teachings in ways that discourage any sense of our own superiority or negative attitudes towards others."[29] Knitter similarly states that Christians cannot enter into dialogue with any "prepackaged final word."[30]

For these scholars, the desire to win adherence from an interlocutor is necessarily an imposition of power and a barrier to relational understanding. The possession of strongly held beliefs—even claims to truth—is not in and of itself problematic, but rather it is *the seeking of adherence* that is relationally damaging. Thus, those engaging in dialogue must assess the ways in which their exclusivist beliefs may erect barriers to understanding and "seek to minimize or neutralize them so they do not remain impediments."[31]

The missionary thus brackets judgments regarding the religious other under the auspices that, in so doing, one is rejecting competition for religious superiority in favor of cooperation within the common human project of building the kingdom of God.

---

28. John B. Cobb, "Rethinking Christian Faith in the Context of Religious Diversity," in *The Dialogue Comes of Age: Christian Encounters with Other Traditions*, edited by John B. Cobb and Ward McAfee (Minneapolis, MN: Fortress Press, 2010), 37.

29. Cobb, "Introduction," 21.

30. Gavin D'Costa, "Pluralist Arguments: Prominent Tendencies and Methods," in *Catholic Engagement with World Religions: A Comprehensive Study*, ed. Karl Josef Becker et al. (Maryknoll, NY: Orbis Books, 2010), 336.

31. Sonja K. Foss and Cindy L. Griffin, "Beyond Persuasion: A Proposal for an Invitational Rhetoric," *Communication Monographs* 62, no. 1 (1995): 6.

CONVERSION AS MANIPULATION

The bracketing of evaluative judgments before engaging in dialogue and the belief that all religions have the ability to cooperate (rather than compete) in the common human project of building and witnessing to the kingdom of God leads to a correlative aspect of the mission as dialogue paradigm: *the explicit rejection of conversion as inherently manipulative.*

The rejection of conversion is key to understanding the mission as dialogue paradigm, as it is often difficult to see in Knitter, Cobb, and Dupuis the relationship between dialogue and other common missional terms such as "evangelism" and "proclamation." Dupuis prefers to see dialogue as a key part of mission, but one that does not necessarily reject evangelism, although Dupuis characterizes evangelism in such a way as to make it almost entirely passive, emphasizing the change that occurs in the missionary.[32] The relationships between evangelism, mission, and dialogue are murky in Cobb's writings,[33] but one area in which there is agreement is in the rejection of the intentional desire on the part of the missionary to convert the religious other.

If the term "conversion" is to remain in the mission as dialogue paradigm, it must be radically reinterpreted to mean the growth of the individual through dialogue, and not as a change of religious affiliation. Knitter's radical reinterpretation of conversion within his understanding of the priority of the kingdom of God is demonstrative: conversion means the conversion of someone to a greater awareness of the kingdom, not to the church. Conversion is simply the change that results from dialogue—a Hindu who is changed by a dialogical encounter is "converted" while remaining Hindu.[34] Conversion as understood as the change from another religion into the Christian church, though sometimes a byproduct of mission, can never be the goal of mission. Change may occur as a result of dialogue, and such change may even be construed as a kind of conversion, but such a change cannot be the desire of the missionary as they engage in dialogue. Dialogue "does *not* ... aim at 'conversion' of others to Christianity, while, of course, it necessarily implies, on the part of the evangelizer, the witness of life."[35] One may witness to their

---

32. Dupuis, *Toward*, 382–84.

33. Donald Wiebe, "Before and after Dialogue: Is There a Significant Difference? A Response to John Cobb's 'Beyond Dialogue,'" *Buddhist-Christian Studies* 6 (1986): 147.

34. Knitter, *Jesus*, 122.

35. Dupuis, *Toward*, 360.

life and their Christianity, even to those portions of Christianity that make truth claims; however, the goal of such dialogue must never be the conversion of the other to Christianity.

Underlying this assumption is the belief that persuasion is inherently manipulative. The engagement in persuasive dialogue with the expressed goal of changing another is the attempt to exert one's superiority over another. Such an assumption is not limited to the mission as dialogue paradigm but is shared by some within the field of rhetoric and communication. For example, Sonja Foss and Cindy Griffin see the entire history of Western rhetoric as predicated upon the "conscious intent to change others,"[36] with the implicit desire to exercise domination over others. The desire to persuade is the desire to change another and thus exert control over another.[37] Foss and Griffin's rejection of intentional persuasion leads them to propose a radical reinterpretation of rhetoric predicated upon feminist principles of "equity, immanent value, and self-determination,"[38] which they dub "invitational rhetoric." Here, the goal of dialogue is to simply bring one's personal narrative to the conversation table. Intentional persuasion is rejected in favor of a witnessing of one's own life. The interactions that occur as a result of such testimonies may or may not lead to changes of opinions, but such changes cannot be the goal.

SELF-CONVERSION AS THE GOAL OF MISSION

The rejection of the intentional desire to see others convert to Christianity is rejected as the goal of mission work, which leads to the fourth feature of the mission as dialogue paradigm: *self-conversion is the goal of mission*. Rather than the goal of mission being the conversion of another to Christianity, the goal is rather the expansion and refinement of one's own Christian beliefs

---

36. Foss and Griffin, "Beyond," 2. Foss and Griffin's conception of invitational rhetoric remains both influential and controversial within the discipline of rhetorical studies. For an overview of its impact and responses to its major critiques, see Jennifer Emerling Bone, Cindy L. Griffin, and T. M. Linda Scholz, "Beyond Traditional Conceptualizations of Rhetoric: Invitational Rhetoric and a Move toward Civility," *Western Journal of Communication* 72, no. 4 (2008).

37. Foss and Griffin, "Beyond," 3.

38. Foss and Griffin, "Beyond," 4. For a more detailed comparison between interreligious dialogue and the specific concept of invitational rhetoric, see Michael Niebauer, "Dialogue or Proclamation? Communication Ethics and the Problem of Persuasion in Mission," *Missiology* 45, no. 3 (2017).

as the result of an interreligious encounter. Dupuis describes the goals of this approach to mission:

> Christians have something to gain from the dialogue. ... On the one hand, they will win an enrichment of their own faith. Through the experience and testimony of the other, they will be able to discover at greater depth certain aspects, certain dimensions, of the Divine Mystery that they had perceived less clearly. ... At the same time they will gain a purification of their faith. The shock of the encounter will often raise questions, force Christians to revise gratuitous assumptions, and destroy deep rooted prejudices.[39]

For Dupuis, genuine dialogue cannot be a means to further some predetermined ends. It is not prolegomena to evangelization. The ends are simply the enrichment and refinement of the missionary's Christian faith.

For John Cobb, the goals of enrichment and transformation are grounded in his process theology.[40] The progress of history affords the ability for personal and religious advancement. Dialogue affords the Christian the opportunity for further advancement in their faith; thus, to reject dialogue is to falsely presume that religious progress has come to an end. If the interlocutor proceeds with the utmost respect for the religious other, they will receive not the conversion of the other, nor the syncretistic blending of the two religions, but rather the further beneficial transformation of themselves:

> As dialogue proceeds, glimpses of aspects of reality heretofore unnoticed are vouchsafed the participants. This is not felt as a threat to the religious traditions from which the participants come but as an opportunity for enrichment and even positive transformation.[41]

The end of dialogue as personal transformation is in many ways the logical conclusion of a modern concept of anthropology as articulated by Kathryn Tanner. As noted above, Tanner asserts that modern anthropologies reject

---

39. Dupuis, *Toward*, 382.

40. Cobb acknowledges his indebtedness to Alfred North Whitehead throughout his writings. His view that human beings are constantly in flux and that each opportunity, including each dialogical encounter, is an opportunity for growth are predicated upon the work of Whitehead, of which he sees parallels in Buddhist thought. See John B. Cobb, *Transforming Christianity and the World: A Way beyond Absolutism and Relativism* (Maryknoll, NY: Orbis Books, 2004), 156–57.

41. Cobb, "Beyond 'Pluralism,'" 86.

anthropocentric views of culture and instead emphasize a shared common humanity amongst all peoples and cultures. Cross-cultural engagement thus becomes not the grounds to exert cultural superiority, but rather an opportunity to "further the humanistic project of social criticism."[42] The confrontation of cross-cultural differences affords the opportunity for reassessment and critique of one's own cultural assumptions.

The communicative process of dialogue is thus tailored in such a way as to further cross-cultural interaction and afford greater opportunities for mutual flourishing and enrichment. Here Foss and Griffin's characterization of "invitational rhetoric" fits well with the conception of mission as dialogue. Foss and Griffin posit invitational rhetoric as a rhetorical form, a way of intentionally engaging in dialogue that is stripped of intentional persuasion and focused instead on the dissemination of viewpoints through personal narrative. This form can be appropriated to various settings, including small group discussions and formal speeches that include audience interaction:

> In invitational rhetoric, change occurs in the audience or rhetor or both as a result of new understanding and insights gained in the exchange of ideas. As rhetors and audience members offer their ideas on an issue, they allow diverse positions to be compared in a process of discovery and questions that may lead to transformation for themselves and others ... rhetors recognize the valuable contributions audience members can make to the rhetors' own thinking and understanding, and they do not engage in strategies that may damage or sever the connection between them and their audiences.[43]

With the goal of mutual flourishing and enrichment, communication must proceed with the continual desire for respect of the other and hence the rejec tion of any claims to superiority which may sever the relationship between interlocutors, jeopardizing opportunities for further enrichment.

---

42. Tanner, *Theories*, 37.
43. Foss and Griffin, "Beyond," 6.

It is helpful in summarizing the mission as dialogue model to compare it to the previous chapter's description of the mission as growth model. In essence, the conception of mission as dialogue fundamentally inverts the mission as growth paradigm. As described in the last chapter, Donald McGavran developed his model of mission with the base assumption that the various adherents to non-Christian religions around the world are lacking and in need of the gospel message. Implicit in this assumption is a claim to the religious superiority of Christianity over the world religions. From here, the purpose of cross-cultural engagement and dialogue is conversion. The understanding of a particular culture is not meant for self-enrichment, but rather to discover the best available ways of maximizing conversion. In contradistinction to this, the conception of mission as dialogue fundamentally rejects implicit or explicit claims to religious superiority and the concomitant ends of the missionary endeavor being the conversion of others. For the growth paradigm, the goal is the expansion of Christianity to the ends of the earth; for the dialogue paradigm, the goal is the expansion of one's own Christianity through engagement with the various religions of the earth. For the growth paradigm, the differences of other religions become differences that must either be rejected or refined by the incorporation of Christianity. For the dialogue paradigm, the differences of other religions provide fodder for religious self-criticism.

Positive evaluations of the mission as dialogue paradigm stem from the ways in which it addresses some of the problems with the conception of mission as growth, particularly its lack of moral self-awareness. As stated above, a chief problem with the mission as growth model is that it views the appropriation of the social and behavioral sciences as intrinsically amoral, in the process becoming unaware of the potential ways in which their engagement with the religious other might be manipulative. Although, as we will see below, the mission as dialogue paradigm may not completely solve the problem of manipulation, it does provide a framework for approaching mission that takes seriously the ethical implications of the *ways* in which mission is conducted. For McGavran and Hirsch, missionary practices are deemed better or worse based upon efficiency—those practices that produce more churches and more converts are preferable to those that produce less.

The agency of the missionary's interlocutors is not considered, and the only responses on behalf of the missionary's audience that matter are those pertinent to their decision to convert.

The dialogist sees moral reflection on the ways in which mission is conducted as necessary prolegomena. The missionary must reflect on their biased negative evaluations of other religions and allow for the possibility that their own Christianity may be in need of correction. This should be done before, during, and after interreligious dialogue.

A CRITICAL EVALUATION OF
MISSION AS DIALOGUE

What follows is a critical evaluation of the mission as dialogue paradigm using the same communicative, anthropological, and theological tools as in the aforementioned assessment. These critiques will demonstrate how this paradigm fails to adequately address the very issues it has set out to remedy: first, that instead of eliminating evaluative judgments, it simply shifts the target of those judgments; second, that its denial of conversion strips the agency of those who wish to convert; and, third, that it denies the clear instances of intentional persuasive arguments present in Scripture. What these critiques hope to show is that the answers to the issues the mission as dialogue model hopes to address cannot be found through non-evaluative conversation. Instead, answers will come through a reevaluation of the problem of persuasion and a renewed understanding of conversion. Thus, following these critiques will be an extended section on persuasion, with conversion being taken up again in chapter five.

DISPLACED EVALUATIVE JUDGMENTS

The conception of mission as dialogue calls for an intentional bracketing of evaluative judgments on the part of those missionaries engaging in interreligious dialogue. The posture is one of self-effacement, with a rejection of one's own claims to religious superiority in the acknowledgment of a shared humanity and the intrinsic goodness of the religious other. However, the problem with this approach is that it fails to bracket all types of evaluative judgments, instead simply replacing one set of judgments for another. To enter into this type of dialogue requires refraining from absolutist claims in such a way that one does not attempt to convince others of the necessity of adopting them. However, this position itself is a type of persuasion disguised under the auspices of openness. One must accept *a priori* the belief that one should not strongly try to intentionally persuade others of their absolutist beliefs before coming to the dialogue table. One must either change, or soften their beliefs, or enter into a less fruitful form of dialogue.

By insisting on the bracketing of evaluative judgments of other religions, the mission as dialogue paradigm sets up its own set of evaluative judgments on the relative openness of others. While rejecting an evaluative judgment that another religion is lacking or deficient, the dialogist establishes new criteria for discerning the level to which another religion is open and tolerant. These criteria coincide with values prioritized by Western liberal democracies. For Cobb, those who engage in interfaith dialogue should be committed to peace, justice, the integrity of creation, community building, and social justice.[44] Knitter's approach to dialogue is "based on the common ground of global responsibility for eco-human well-being."[45]

Such evaluative judgments clearly give preference to a specific type of interlocutor. First, it prioritizes those who are committed to a non-exclusivist position regarding their own religion. As Gavin D'Costa states of Knitter's position:

> While the intention of Knitter and others is no doubt honourable in promoting peace and harmony, this would be a spurious harmony, for it … takes no one seriously by discounting their absolute claims from the outset. This would mean that only liberals within each tradition, like Knitter and Hick, could take part in dialogue.[46]

Essentially, fruitful dialogue can only take place within (to use Cobb's phrase) those "sub-traditions" that favor pluralistic understandings of their faith. There is still a judgment that occurs on the part of the dialogist: it is not a judgment as to the superiority of a particular religious standpoint, but a judgment on the degree of openness to which one approaches dialogue. For Cobb, this means, perhaps ironically, that superiority reemerges in the form of one's claims to openness: "What happens in dialogue, then, is that

---

44. Cobb, "Rethinking," 37–38.

45. Knitter, *Jesus*, 18–19.

46. D'Costa, "Pluralist," 336.

one norm that can be applied with relative objectivity to the great religious traditions has to do with their ability ... to expand their understanding of reality and its normative implications."[47] The best religious traditions and sub-traditions are those that are open and thus capable of growth and expansion. Those religions and sub-traditions (he has in mind religious fundamentalism) that claim a possession of the truth are closed and hence incapable of growth and expansion.

Not only is an evaluative judgment cast on others based upon their degree of openness, but there is also a judgment based upon the willingness to embrace an agenda for dialogue that includes criteria largely defined by the West. Terms such as "social justice," "global responsibility," and "eco-well being" are defined largely by Western scholars. In essence, Cobb and Knitter define the agenda through which fruitful dialogue can take place. John Milbank critiques this dialogical agenda:

> The terms of discourse which provide both the favored categories for encounter with other religions—dialogue, pluralism, and the like— together with the criteria for the acceptable limits of the pluralist embrace—social justice, liberation, and so forth—are themselves embedded in a wider Western discourse become dominant.[48]

From the perspective of communication ethics, the insistence on openness is a persuasive argument which attempts to limit persuasion.[49] Richard Fulkerson calls invitational rhetoric an equity critique of traditional forms of rhetoric and persuasion, criticizing it for being

---

47. Cobb, "Beyond 'Pluralism,' " 87.

48. John Milbank, "The End of Dialogue," in *Christian Uniqueness Reconsidered: The Myth of a Pluralistic Theology of Religions*, ed. G. D'Costa (New York: Orbis Books, 1990), 175.

49. While Richard Fulkerson presents critiques from the vantage point of traditional rhetoric, an interesting critique of invitational rhetoric is also levied by feminist rhetoricians. Dana Cloud and Nina Lozano-Reich argue that the requirement for a disciplined openness when engaging in dialogue often ignores the inequality of power that often exists between interlocutors: "to refuse persuasion is to refuse participation in real-world encounters marked by material and antagonistic interests" (221). When antagonistic differences exist, non-confrontational dialogue favors those in positions of power. It provides the appearance of cooperation while enabling differences to remain unchallenged, thus favoring the status quo. See Nina M. Lozano-Reich and Dana L. Cloud, "The Uncivil Tongue: Invitational Rhetoric and the Problem of Inequality," *Western Journal of Communication* 73, no. 2 (2009).

awkwardly compromised by being self-contradictory. On the broad-
est level, writers who develop it almost invariably are clearly interested in moving readers to agree that argumentation should be seen as
inherently patriarchal, oppressive, a violation of the sovereign rights
of the audience. In other words, they seek to persuade their readers of
the good sense of their views. And thus, perforce, most writers who
articulate the equity critique simultaneously violate it, by attempting
to argue readers into sharing their views.[50]

Fulkerson's critique is just as apt when applied to the mission as dialogue
paradigm. The major works of their proponents—Knitter's *No Other Name*
and Cobb's *Transforming Christianity and the World*, for instance—are written
in the interest of presenting persuasive arguments in order to convince their
audience to refrain from Christian persuasion. The persuasive elements of
this paradigm are masked by the surface appeals to openness and dialogue.
The danger in such an approach is that it is unaware of its own persuasive
underpinnings. While the mission as dialogue approach creates a welcome
awareness of the ways in which missionaries have exerted cultural dominance through the claims of religious superiority, there is the danger that it
has replaced this model for a method that is equally unaware of its cultural
embeddedness. This issue will be taken up more fully in the section on persuasion below, where I will argue for the inevitability of persuasion.

AGENCY STILL LIMITED

The mission as dialogue approach is a persuasive calling to limit persuasion,
and it is a judgment on certain types of evaluative judgments. It is also, ironically, an approach that may limit human agency even as it tries to safeguard
it. A fundamental tenet of the dialogist is their commitment not to engage
in intentional acts of conversion: "Given our history, dialogue requires that
we create a climate in which there is no manipulation, no effort on anyone's part to convert the others."[51] Intentional attempts at conversion are
equated with manipulation, and, hence, efforts to convert must be policed.
While such policing may simply mask subtler forms of persuasion, it also

---

50. Richard Fulkerson, "Transcending Our Conception of Argument in Light of Feminist
Critiques," *Argumentation & Advocacy* 32, no. 4 (1996).

51. Cobb, "Rethinking," 38.

attempts to *deny the capacity of interlocutors to be persuaded.* If the mission as growth paradigm attempts to limit human agency by contriving the means through which conversion is inevitable, the dialogist attempts to contrive a climate in which conversion is impossible. The former denies the right to reject Christianity, the latter the right to accept Christianity.

Cobb, Knitter, and Dupuis assume that interlocutors are unable to exercise personal judgment in response to intentional acts of persuasion. The mission as dialogue approach suggests that *those who are converted have been manipulated,* which denies the ability of individuals to process such calls to conversion and exercise their ability to accept, reject, or qualify such messages. An assessment of the history of missionary work shows how recipients of Christian proclamation accept, adapt, and reject the message they receive. There have been numerous missiological studies describing and analyzing the multitude of ways in which direct proclamation of the Christian message is received both by individuals and by groups. Alan Tippett categorized four ways in which indigenous populations responded to Christian missionary advocacy: rejection, total acceptance, modification, or group fission (the splitting of indigenous groups).[52] Such a process is negotiated by groups of people under the auspices of what is perceived as best for the group as a whole. According to Richard Hibbert, Tippett's framework of decision-making asserts that local people are "active agents rather than passive recipients in the process of conversion."[53] An interesting example of the plurality of ways in which such conversion does and does not take place lies in Hibbert's description of Hindus and Muslims that adopt hybrid identities, identifying as culturally Hindu or Muslim, but Christian in religion. Such individuals often vacillate between religious communities.[54]

The assertion that recipients of intentional Christian persuasion are active agents in the process of their own conversion poses difficulties for those, such as Cobb and Knitter, who see conversion as inherently manipulative. While Cobb allows for the possibility of persuasion to occur within

---

52. Alan Richard Tippett, "Conversion as a Dynamic Process in Christian Mission," *Missiology* 5, no. 2 (1977): 209–10.

53. Richard Yates Hibbert, "Negotiating Identity: Extending and Applying Alan Tippett's Model of Conversion to Believers from Muslim and Hindu Backgrounds," *Missiology* 43, no. 1 (2015): 62.

54. Hibbert, "Negotiating," 67–68.

dialogue, *intentional* attempts to convert are wrong because they invite one to abandon their traditions and communities.[55] This assumes that the abandonment of part or all of a tradition or community is de facto the product of coercion. Essentially, the recipient of Christian proclamation must either exert their freedom by rejecting this proclamation or accept this proclamation and thus accede to coercion. Tippett's research suggests that a high degree of agency is exerted by recipients of intentional Christian proclamation, and that such agency is evidenced by the multiform ways in which recipients accept, reject, or modify all or part of the Christian message that they have received. Cobb must view the assertion of this agency legitimate only if it is exercised in rejection of the Christian message. The free decision to convert is not free, despite the convert's own self-understanding. The danger in Cobb's underlying assumption of evangelization as manipulative is a type of paternalism: it *informs* those who have converted (and who believe such conversion has enhanced their lives) that they have actually been manipulated.

As stated earlier, the conception of mission as dialogue is grounded in a modernist anthropology that views cultures as distinct wholes which can be compared and contrasted.[56] While rejecting an evolutionary view of the superiority of Western culture, it embraces the view that assessments of other cultures be from the outset non-evaluative. The interaction with distinct cultures becomes instead the grounds for self-correction. Thus, attempts at conversion are damaging because they threaten the stability of a native culture, destroying difference under the auspices of a false superiority and Western dominance.

The desire in dialogue is not therefore conversion, but for each interlocutor to remain within their cultural and religious silos, somehow better

55. John B. Cobb, "Introduction," in *Death or Dialogue: From the Age of Monologue to the Age of Dialogue*, ed. Leonard J. Swidler et al. (London: SCM Press, 1990), 9.

56. Sherry Ortner traces the development of this holistic view of culture and its critique within the discipline of anthropology. However, even within the 1950s such an approach was critiqued as unduly homogenous by Oscar Lewis. Ortner believes that contemporary anthropology, what Kathryn Tanner dubs "postmodern anthropology," follows the critiques levied by Lewis. Ortner advocates for a study of community that emphasizes people as "contextualized social beings." Here, anthropology becomes the study of networks of social practices and their understandings. See Sherry B. Ortner, "Fieldwork in the Postcommunity," *Anthropology and Humanism* 22, no. 1 (1997): 63–64.

and purified as a result of an interreligious encounter.[57] The desire is for the Muslim to remain a Muslim, or a Hindu to remain a Hindu, as a result of the church's mission.

The problem with such an assumption is that, although one can identify discreet religious beliefs and practices, such beliefs and practices do not neatly map onto distinct cultural wholes. The convert is free to judge which specific practices are and are not in accordance with their changing religious beliefs. In short, a conversion to Christianity need not be a whole-scale conversion to Western culture, however it is construed. To make such an assertion is to assume a rather low opinion of the agency of the new convert.

Tippet's assessment of the actual practice of Christian missionaries suggests that the cross-cultural interactions between Christians and (in this example) Muslims are far from monolithic. Cultural adaptation of the Christian message occurs in a piecemeal fashion, both on the part of the missionary and the missionary's interlocutors. The missionary makes decisions as to which social practices can be kept, adapted, and rejected in light of the Christian message, and the interlocutor decides whether to accept, reject, or modify the message being proclaimed.[58] In such a process, the missionary targets are able to exert a large degree of agency—the ability to choose to convert and also (often to the chagrin of missionaries) synchronize their religious views.

JUDGMENT AND CONVERSION IN SCRIPTURE

Lastly, in its attempts at bracketing evaluative judgments and rejection of intentional conversion, the mission as dialogue paradigm abandons the clear exercise of evaluative judgments and intentional persuasive acts in Scripture.

---

57. For Cobb, Knitter, and Dupuis, conversion from one religious worldview to another is at best a rarity and may not come about through direct persuasion, but rather through a vague and lengthy historical process that ensures that such change is sufficiently scrubbed clean of Western imperialism.

58. This is echoed in Tanner's account of the history of Christian missionary practice: "Western Christianity's historical relations with other cultures have not always involved judgments typifying the practices of those cultures as wholes; those cultures were not viewed as having a single uniform character worthy, for example, of either simple condemnation or respect. Although often all that seemed relevant about another way of life was that it was not Christian—the basic categories to understand other cultures involved a simple distinction between Christian and heathen—the missionary impulse in Christianity tended to work against a dichotomous typification, against a 'they are all one way and we are all another' mentality." Tanner, Theories, 118.

In the book of Acts, for instance, there are clear instances of negative judgments upon false gods and, correlatively, intentional discourse which invites the rejection of false belief and the acceptance of Christianity. In approaching Scripture, the dialogist uses an inclusivist view of the biblical concept of the kingdom of God as a hermeneutical lens through which Scripture is interpreted. This enables the dialogist to continually emphasize the common humanity shared between all religions and the possibility for cooperation as they work together to further the advancement of the kingdom.

This poses enormous difficulties when approaching passages that clearly emphasize the particularity of Christ, the need to change one's worldview, and the persuasive attempts to convince others of the necessity of conversion. A kingdom of God hermeneutic renders the book of Acts especially problematic.

Of the three authors representative of the mission as dialogue perspective, Paul Knitter is most willing to accept the challenge posed by the exclusivity that seemingly backs the actions of the apostles in the book of Acts. Knitter sees this challenge codified in Peter's declaration that "There is salvation in no one else, for there is no other name under heaven given among mortals by which we must be saved" (Acts 4:12). Such an emphasis would seem to assert the exclusive soteriological claims about Jesus Christ and thus stress the priority of proclamation and conversion in mission activities.[59] The New Testament church existed in an atmosphere of religious pluralism similar to that of today, and yet it emphasized the exclusivity of Jesus and a rejection of other gods. Following the kingdom of God hermeneutic, however, Knitter views Peter's statement not as a rejection of other religions per se, but of a Roman syncretism that demanded the absorption of Christianity into the pantheon of gods, stripping it of its ethical and social attributes:

> The early Christians rejected the religious pluralism of their age not because it offended against their belief in the uniqueness of Jesus, but because it could not be reconciled with the right action or with the

---

59. As Luke Timothy Johnson comments on Acts 4:12: "The Greek sentence is awkward and somewhat tautologous; the second clause, however, does make clear that the 'no other' means 'no other name given to humans' (or: 'among humans'), and that 'salvation' means 'by which we must be saved.' The theme of salvation in the name of Jesus is announced explicitly, and involves, as we have seen, physical, spiritual, and social dimensions." Luke Timothy Johnson, *The Acts of the Apostles* (Collegeville, MN: Liturgical Press, 1992), 78.

ethical-social vision contained in Jesus' message about the Kingdom of God. Soteriocentric or Kingdom-centered motivations, rather than Christocentric or monotheistic convictions, brought about this rejection of pluralism. ... They rejected pluralism then, not because it offended against the role or nature of Jesus Christ but because it offended against the kind of God and the kind of society that were integral to Jesus' vision of God's reign.[60]

According to Knitter, the apostles' rebukes were not part and parcel of a call to convert others, but rather a rejection of the attempts of others to *be converted*. Their rejection of false idols was not a condemnation of other religions, but a condemnation of attempts to assimilate Jesus Christ into other religions, stripping Christianity of its ethical uniqueness and its calling to build a community that furthered the kingdom of God.

Situating Peter's assertion as to the uniqueness of Jesus Christ ("no other name") within the framework of his actual speech in Acts 4 clearly counters Knitter's characterization of the New Testament witness. First, Peter's audience in his speech is Jewish, not pagan: "Let it be known to all of you, and to all the people of Israel" (Acts 4:10). The assertion regarding the uniqueness of Jesus Christ is not predicated upon a fear that this uniqueness would be absorbed under a pagan pantheon—it is addressed to fellow monotheists. Furthermore, such an audience would share the same ethical framework as the apostles, as Peter's speeches affirm continuity with the Old Testament and a vision of Torah as fulfilled rather than supplanted by Jesus. One may argue that what is happening in this passage is the exact *opposite* of Knitter's construal: the rejection of an alleged syncretism is made by the Jewish leaders, who see the proclamation of Jesus as Lord and God as an attempt to destroy a monotheistic account of God.

Within the work of Cobb, Knitter, and Dupuis there is an emphasis on the distinction between the church and the kingdom of God—the church is in service to the kingdom. Such distinctions are used to assert both the distinctiveness of Christianity and the universal good of all religions that share in the kingdom. Scripture is parsed to fit this claim, with mentions of exclusivity referring only to the assertion that the church can be distinct,

---

60. Knitter, *Jesus*, 71.

and calls for repentance referring only to the calling to share in the universal kingdom.[61] Mission is then construed along the lines of this hermeneutic as the participation in the building of the universal kingdom in cooperation with those of other religions: "A lead is found in the sacred books for a positive approach to religions, firstly and principally in the biblical faith in God's universal involvement with humankind in a dialogue of salvation."[62]

The passage that most strongly counters this approach to Scripture, and the mission as dialogue paradigm, is Acts 14. Paul and Barnabas flee from persecution in Iconium and travel to Lystra, "proclaiming the good news" (Acts 14:7). During one such proclamation of the good news a man crippled from birth is healed on account of his faith. The response from the pagan crowd, however, is to confuse Paul and Barnabas for Zeus and Hermes. Paul's response is to exhort the crowd to turn from worthless idols and embrace the living God. Such idols were permitted when God "allowed all the nations to follow their own ways" (Acts 14:16), but such time has passed. Paul's words fall on deaf ears, and the crowd offers him sacrifices. Furthermore, a group of Jews come and win over the crowds, leading to Paul's stoning and near death (Acts 14:19-20).

We see in this passage several elements that challenge a conception of mission as dialogue. The free assent of the pagans in Lystra is demonstrated in their ability to hear the gospel proclamation and modify its message despite the pleadings of the missionaries. We see also the persistence of Paul and Barnabas in condemning their religion and a statement concerning the religions of the "nations": that the time of God permitting alternative worship has come to an end. As Kavin Rowe states, what is advocated by Paul and Barnabas is "not simply an admonition to tweak a rite or halt a ceremony. It contains, rather, the summons that simultaneously involved the destruction

---

61. Gerald O'Collins's *Salvation for All* is another example of an approach to Scripture that emphasizes the kingdom of God as referring to the entirety of humanity: "For all Christians the reign of God should be a decisive point of reference. The Church exists for this wider, universal reality and at its service" (250). According to O'Collins, since Jesus's teaching was about the kingdom of God and his death was for human beings in the coming kingdom of God, and since this kingdom of God refers to the entirety of humanity, then, ipso facto Jesus's death brought about salvation for all of humanity. Gerald O'Collins, *Salvation for All: God's Other Peoples* (Oxford: Oxford University Press, 2008), 192-94.

62. Dupuis, *Toward*, 51-52.

of an entire mode of being religious."[63] Furthermore, the dialogue of Paul and Barnabas is caustic, as evidenced by Paul's ensuing stoning. Here is a passage, much like the stoning of St. Stephen, that confounds conceptions of mission as dialogue and growth alike: the proclamation is judgmental yet non-coercive, well-articulated yet ultimately ineffective.

The mission as dialogue paradigm sets out to achieve a form of mission that is respectful of the religious other, rejects intentional conversion as manipulation, and focuses on the refinement of the missionary. It falls short of these goals. Its respect for the religious other is limited by the degree to which the adherents of other religions accept the dialogist's commitment to intentional openness. While it does not call for a conversion to Christianity, it does call for a conversion to an ethical and social framework that is as much, if not more, imbedded in Western values. Its focus on the refinement of the missionary misses the explicit scriptural references to acts of intentional conversion.

THE PROBLEM OF PERSUASION

Despite its flaws, the mission as dialogue paradigm offers an important contribution to the study of Christian mission, as it raises the question of manipulation and coercion in regard to evangelism, and it advocates for the need to critically reflect on the ways in which the Christian message is communicated. It stands as a necessary critique of the mission as growth paradigm as well as all attempts to engage in Christian mission in ways that do not

---

63. Christopher Kavin Rowe, *World Upside Down: Reading Acts in the Graeco-Roman Age* (Oxford: Oxford University Press, 2009), 21. Rowe will later qualify the extent of this destruction of a mode of religiosity by asserting as well Luke's portrayal of the gospel message in Acts as being "non-seditious." Christianity is about resurrection, not insurrection. While the Christian message is culturally destabilizing, such upheaval is an invitation to "an alternative and salvific way of life," a way of life that can involve both the rejection of certain aspects of pagan culture and an appropriation of other aspects. Rowe, *World*, 136. This accords with the discussion concerning the ways in which individuals and groups of individuals accept, reject, or modify the Christian message. Conversion does not entail the wholescale rejection of one culture in favor of another, but rather a conversion to a new way of life that can involve both the rejection and modification of previous social practices.

Luke Timothy Johnson's interpretation of Acts 14:1–18 is similar to Rowe's, albeit more measured: Paul and Barnabas are portrayed as "Jewish evangelists who correct misguided idolatrous impulses by means of an abbreviated but effective exhortation to conversion from such 'foolishness' to belief in the one 'living God.' " At the same time, the passage also shows the openness of the gentiles to "God's providential 'witness to himself' among these nations who until now had been allowed to 'follow their own paths.' " Johnson, *Acts*, 251.

seriously grapple with the manner in which such actions are conducted. As mentioned above, however, the issues that Cobb, Knitter, and Dupuis raise are not adequately addressed by their conceptions of Christian mission, and at the root of much of these issues lies an inadequate understanding of persuasion. In order to address the problem of persuasion in mission head on, it is thus imperative to develop a fuller understanding of persuasion using the fields of communication ethics and rhetoric.

"Persuasion," and its related term "rhetoric,"[64] connote in popular parlance the underhanded subterfuge imbedded in the tactics of a used car salesman. They are crafts devoted to winning over another for self-gain. There are no moral limits on the means employed to win assent, and whether such assent is in the best interest of the other is immaterial: the rhetor persuades for personal gain. This view of persuasion is summed up in Foss and Griffin's definition of traditional rhetoric: "Embedded in efforts to change others is a desire for control and domination, for the act of changing another establishes the power of the change agent over that other."[65]

Such a critique can just as easily be levied at the missionary enterprise. For many, anxiety over Christian mission is centered upon the problem of persuasion. If embedded in efforts to change others is the desire for control and domination, a profession devoted to efforts to change the religious affiliation of others must be a profession devoted to control and domination. Lamin Sanneh elucidates this anxiety:

> The forces pitted against a fair understanding of mission in the late twentieth century are formidable. To start with, many people are committed to the ideological position that mission is oppressive, and

---

64. The relationship between rhetoric and persuasion exists as far back as Aristotle, who defines it as the art of the discovery of the available means of persuasion in particular cases. Aristotle, *On Rhetoric: A Theory of Civic Discourse*, trans. George A. Kennedy (New York, NY: Oxford University Press, 1991), I.1.14. Contemporary definitions of rhetoric within the discipline give a much broader scope to the term, but persuasion still weighs heavily on such differences. As Bizzell and Herzberg define it: "Rhetoric has a number of overlapping meanings: the practice of oratory; the study of the strategies of effective oratory; the use of language, written or spoken, to inform or persuade; the study of the persuasive effects of language; the study of the relation between language and knowledge; the classification and use of tropes and figures; and, of course, the use of empty promises and half-truths as a form of propaganda." Patricia Bizzell and Bruce Herzberg, *Introduction to The Rhetorical Tradition: Readings from Classical Times to the Present* (Boston, MA: Bedford Books, 1990), 1.

65. Foss and Griffin, "Beyond," 3.

anachronistic to boot, and Christians have been afflicted by the con-sequences. ... Most mainline Western Christian bodies have, as a con-sequence, retreated from the subject, afflicted by a heavy sense of guilt. It is not, therefore, easy to inveigh against such strong and deep obstruction.[66]

If one starts with the presupposition that persuasion is manipulative, then mission is indeed in a precarious position, and attempts at a fair under-standing of its operations are formidable. But persuasion need not be con-sidered intrinsically manipulative. As will be shown, such an understanding of persuasion is an inheritance of Enlightenment rationality—a false split between dialectics and analytics as problematic as the split between fact and value and ought and is. Furthermore, the anxiety over the missionary enterprise described by Sanneh can be alleviated by an understanding of how acts of intentional persuasion can have the effect of changing both rhetor and their audience. Sanneh's work *Translating the Message* documents how such changes have occurred throughout the history of Christian missions. The remainder of this chapter will further a critique of persuasion within the various construals of mission and point to the possibility of a rehabili-tation of persuasion in Christian mission, which will then be explored fur-ther in chapter five.

RHETORIC AND REASON, DIALECTICS AND ANALYTICS: A BRIEF HISTORY OF THE BREAK

Rhetoric and persuasion did not always have negative connotations. While the relationship between rhetoric, persuasion, and reasoning is fuzzy in the works of Plato,[67] Aristotle forged a consensus on the relationship between rhetoric, persuasion, and reasoning that would last through the Middle Ages.

---

66. Sanneh, *Translating*, 88.

67. For an extended background on the history of rhetoric, see David S. Cunningham, *Faithful Persuasion: In Aid of a Rhetoric of Christian Theology* (Notre Dame, IN: University of Notre Dame Press, 1990), 8–27. The tension in Plato is between his negative characterization of rhetoric in "Gorgias" and his beneficial view of rhetoric, provided its use in persuading toward transcen-dental truth, in "Phaedrus": "But this ability [the art of speech] he will not gain without much diligent toil, which a wise man ought not to undergo for the sake of speaking and acting before men, but that they may be able to speak and to do everything, so far as possible, in a manner pleasing to the gods." Plato, "Phaedrus," in *The Rhetorical Tradition: Readings from Classical Times to the Present*, ed. Patricia Bizzell and Bruce Herzberg (Boston: Bedford Books, 1990), 139. It is perhaps best to say that for Plato, rhetoric is an instrument that can be used for both harm

Aristotle separates the process of reasoning into two methods: analytical and dialectical. Analytical reasoning is reasoning that occurs within agreed upon shared first principles. It takes place within a relatively closed system of agreed upon terms, and, as such, its conclusions are tautological and do not purport to discover new knowledge.[68] The most obvious example of analytical argumentation is the mathematical proof, which takes place within a set of principles and procedures agreed upon within the discipline. Modern notions of logic typically involve reasoning along analytical lines. Analytical argumentation purports a kind of absolute certainty but, because of its closed nature, does not produce new knowledge.

Analytic argumentation is contrasted with dialectics. Dialectical reasoning (which includes dialogue, rhetoric, and argumentation) is reasoning that occurs within fields of knowledge that are inherently ambiguous and contingent, of which there are not shared first principles. It is a method of arguing on practical matters that are necessarily contingent, and, as such, arguments advance not from false to true, but probable to more probable. The contingency of such arguments means that any conclusions reached cannot be universalized. However, according to Cunningham, "Its ambiguity makes it able to achieve genuinely new (nontautological) insights."[69] For instance, the assent of the validity of an analytic argument, say a simple mathematical equation, brings a definitive end to discussions. But the assent to certain dialectic arguments, say that democracy is preferred to autocracy, could be said to be merely the beginning of a long series of further discussions and insights.

What is crucial to this assessment of dialectics and analytics is the breadth of topics that fall under dialectics. For Aristotle, politics and ethics both fall under the category of dialectics.[70] Because issues in these fields are highly particular, the result of such dialectic will not be universal truths that are axiomatic. After all, if it were held to be true definitively, there would be no need of arguing. Few argue that 2+2=4; many argue over whether socialism or democracy are better for a society. However, for many, it is precisely these contingent matters—matters that are in the realm of probability and not

---

and good. For Aristotle, the connection is transparent: "Let rhetoric be [defined as] an ability, in each [particular] case, to see the available means of persuasion." Aristotle, On *Rhetoric*, I.2.

68. Cunningham, *Faithful*, 15.

69. Cunningham, *Faithful*, 15.

70. Aristotle, On *Rhetoric*, I.4–5.

certainty—that matter the most.[71] Furthermore, these are issues through which engagement with others is crucial. We argue, debate, persuade, and discuss with others in our community about what is good, what is beautiful, how we should act, and what is best for a country.

Aristotle's distinction between discussions within communities about matters of probability and formal analytic reasoning begins to break down in the Enlightenment. Here, reasoning becomes synonymous with analytic reasoning—to reason is to demonstrate syllogistically through intuitive first principles.[72] Scientific reason, so important for the advancement of the hard sciences, is extended to philosophy and the emerging social sciences. Furthermore, such reasoning can take place solely within the individual mind and is not dependent on outside forces.[73]

Since reason becomes synonymous with analytical reasoning, all reasoning that is not related to self-evidence is cast aside as irrational. In their landmark text *The New Rhetoric*, Perelman and Olbrechts-Tyteca claim this development emanates from Descartes:

---

71. According to Aristotle, "Most of the matters with which judgment and examination are concerned can be other than they are; for people deliberate and examine what they are doing, and [human] actions are all of this kind, and none of them [are], so to speak, necessary." Aristotle, On *Rhetoric*, I.2.14.

72. Stephen Toulmin traces the development of formal logic and its tendency to neglect five essential distinctions—for instance, the distinction between necessary and probable arguments and between arguments that are formally valid and those that cannot be formally valid. Logicians conflated these distinctions into "one single distinction, which they made the absolute and essential condition of logical salvation ... the analytic syllogism thereby became a paradigm to which all self-respecting arguments must conform." Stephen Edelston Toulmin, *The Uses of Argument*, updated edition (Cambridge, UK: Cambridge University Press, 2003), 138.

73. MacIntyre's summary of Kant's philosophy aptly describes this shift: "Central to Kant's moral philosophy are two deceptively simple theses: if the rules of morality are rational, they must be the same for all rational beings, in just the way that the rules of arithmetic are, and if the rules of morality are binding on all rational beings then the contingent ability of such beings to carry them out must be unimportant—what is important is their will to carry them out." MacIntyre, *After Virtue*, 43-44. Moral reasoning is of the same type as arithmetic reasoning, and reasoning becomes detached from social environment. Similarly, Descartes demonstrated an affinity toward arithmetic reasoning, questioning why it had not been applied to philosophical reasoning in the past: "I was most keen on mathematics, because of its certainty and the incontrovertibility of its proofs; but I did not yet see its true use. Believing as I did that its only application was to the mechanical arts, I was astonished that nothing more exalted had been built on such sure and solid foundations; whereas, on the other hand, I compared the moral works of ancient pagan writers to splendid and magnificent palaces built on nothing more than sand and mud." René Descartes, *A Discourse on the Method of Correctly Conducting One's Reason and Seeking Truth in the Sciences*, trans. Ian Maclean (Oxford, UK: Oxford University Press, 2006), 9.

The domain of argumentation is that of the credible, the plausible, the probable, to the degree that the latter eludes the certainty of calculations. Now Descartes' concept, clearly expressed in the first part of *The Discourse on the Method*, was to "take well nigh for false everything which was only plausible." It was this philosopher who made the self-evident the mark of reason, and considered rational only those demonstrations which, starting from clear and distinct ideas, extended, by means of apodictic proofs, the self-evidence of the axioms to the derived theorems.[74]

For Descartes, there is only the rational, which is the realm of self-evident axioms, and the irrational, which is all that is outside of the axiomatic, including that which is probable.[75] Thus, dialectic reasoning is eliminated as a form of reason—matters of uncertainty are left to the subjective whims of the individual. Rhetoric is equated not with reason but with eloquence and presentation. We see in the Enlightenment an enlargement of the number of topics that can be claimed as "facts" with a kind of mathematical certainty,[76] coupled with a rendering of topics deemed probable to the realm of "values" and individual taste.

Furthermore, in the realm of values, the individual is free to believe what they wish, so attempts to persuade are an assault on individual freedom. The demise of persuasion is articulated most vividly in Immanuel Kant's *Critique of Pure Reason*:

Persuasion is a mere semblance, since the ground of the judgment, which lies solely in the subject, is held to be objective. Hence such a judgment also has only private validity, and this taking something to be true cannot be communicated. Truth, however, rests upon agreement with the object, with regard to which, consequently, the judgments of every understanding must agree. The touchstone of whether

74. Chaïm Perelman and Lucie Olbrechts-Tyteca, *The New Rhetoric: A Treatise on Argumentation*, trans. John Wilkinson and Purcell Weaver (Notre Dame, IN: University of Notre Dame Press, 1969), 1.

75. "I deemed anything that was no more than *plausible* to be tantamount to false." Descartes, *A Discourse*, 10.

76. MacIntyre traces the expansion of mechanical causality from Newtonian physics to a wider scope of human behavior throughout the seventeenth and eighteenth century. See MacIntyre, *After Virtue*, 82–84.

taking something to be true is conviction or mere persuasion is therefore, externally, the possibility of communicating it and finding it to
be valid for the reason of every human being to take it to be true. ... I
cannot assert anything, i.e., pronounce it to be a judgment necessarily valid for everyone, except that which produces conviction. I can
preserve persuasion for myself if I please to do so, but cannot and
should not want to make it valid beyond myself.[77]

For Kant, persuasion is a "mere semblance" that cannot be communicated. There is according to Kant a universalizable morality that is objectively
binding on the human will, yet such morality is accessible through the subjective reason of the individual. The grounds for judgment of moral claims
exist solely in the individual, yet these judgments can be claimed to have
universal validity and so are objective. So, for something to be true, it must
be capable of being communicated in a way that garners assent from every
human being. One cannot assert anything that cannot be judged valid for
everyone. What is probable can only be stated as a mere opinion. Persuasion
is thus privatized: we should not attempt to communicate persuasively, since
that which is in the realm of persuasion cannot be proved valid for everyone.

Rhetoric, stripped of its persuasive connotations, must now be rendered
inert. For nineteenth-century rhetorician and Church of Ireland bishop
Richard Whatley, rhetoric becomes subservient to logic, becoming not the
discovery of the available means of persuasion but the available means of
argument, defined as logical proof. Rhetoric becomes the art of effectively
arranging and communicating logical arguments,[78] its role reduced to the eloquent presentation of these logical arguments. Whatley's definition of rhetoric is of particular importance due to the popularity of his work *Elements*

---

77. Immanuel Kant, *Critique of Pure Reason*, trans. Paul Guyer and Allen W. Wood (New York:
Cambridge University Press, 1998), 685.

78. Richard Whatley, *Elements of Rhetoric: Comprising an Analysis of the Laws of Moral Evidence
and of Persuasion, with Rules for Argumentative Composition and Elocution* (Carbondale, IL: Southern
Illinois University Press, 2010), 6. According to Douglas Ehninger, "Whatley is successful in
carrying out his design of treating rhetoric as an 'off-shoot from Logic.' Conceiving of logic as
methodology of proof, he consistently treats rhetoric as the application of that methodology in
actual attempts to influence, so that while logic is the process of establishing truth by reasoning,
rhetoric becomes the process of conveying truth to others by reasoning." Douglas Ehninger,
"Introduction," in *Elements of Rhetoric: Comprising an Analysis of the Laws of Moral Evidence and
of Persuasion, with Rules for Argumentative Composition and Elocution* (Carbondale, IL: Southern
Illinois University Press, 2010), xiv.

of Rhetoric, which became the standard English textbook on rhetoric in the nineteenth century.[79] There are those, however, who are not content even with this reduced role of rhetoric as eloquence. For John Locke, rhetoric can only be the clear, orderly, and efficient transmission of knowledge through language, and "all the artificial and figurative application of words eloquence hath invented, are for nothing else but to insinuate wrong ideas, move the passions, and thereby mislead the judgment."[80]

Despite the widespread critique of Enlightenment rationality,[81] its impact on an understanding of persuasion still remains. For MacIntyre, an acceptance of the Enlightenment's failures means either to accept a "genealogical" (Nietzschean) morality, which asserts that moral claims are simply impositions of the will on others, or to return to some form of Aristotelianism. For rhetoric, a similar choice is posed: one must either accept that all attempts at persuasion, including those that are moral and religious, are the imposition of the will on others, or return to a form of reasoning as argumentation and persuasion regarding that which is probable. Foss and Griffin's conception of invitational rhetoric is an example of the former, as are the communicative presumptions of the construal of mission as dialogue.

For Foss and Griffin, since persuasion is intrinsically coercive, and since rhetoric occurs outside of the realm of the hard sciences (i.e., it is not subject to formal logic and inference), any attempt at communication must be scrubbed clean of persuasion. Any change that occurs from an encounter must not be due to the intentional persuasive force of the interlocutor but must emanate from the individual. Here one sees echoes of Kant in Foss and Griffin's model: persuasion may still occur, provided that it exists firmly and completely within the subjective will of the individual.

This is precisely what is happening in the conception of mission as dialogue. The attempt of the missionary to convert another is intrinsically coercive; therefore, persuasion must be eliminated in the communication of the

---

79. Cunningham, *Faithful*, 24.

80. John Locke, "An Essay Concerning Human Understanding," in *The Rhetorical Tradition: Readings from Classical Times to the Present*, ed. Patricia Bizzell and Bruce Herzberg (Boston, MA: Bedford Books, 1990), 710.

81. As has already been mentioned in the work of Alasdair MacIntyre, the Enlightenment's attempt at grounding morality in universal principles that are self-evident failed. Morality must be rendered, in the Enlightenment framework, also to the arena of private validity (what MacIntyre calls "emotivism").

Christian message. Note, however, that conversion can still occur, but it must solely be the product of the internal movements of the individual. It cannot come as a result of the intentional actions of the missionary.

PERSUASION IS UNAVOIDABLE, SO ATTEMPTS TO
LIMIT IT MAY THEMSELVES BE MANIPULATIVE

What follows is a critique of the mission as dialogue paradigm based upon its limited notion of persuasion. I echo the assertion of Perelman and Olbrechts-Tyteca in *The New Rhetoric* that the Cartesian rejection of argumentation is a "perfectly unjustified and unwarranted limitation of the domain of action of our faculty of reasoning and proving."[82] The following critiques stem from the false attempts at limiting persuasion, as well as the ways in which persuasion does not have to limit the personal faculties of reasoning and proving. Both critiques take as their starting point the assertion of the inevitability and unavoidability of persuasion.

We exert influence on others in a variety of ways, both intentionally and unintentionally. To encounter another is to be changed in some way, whether we desire that change or not. This point is brought out famously in Martin Buber's *I and Thou*: we know ourselves as "I" only through our relationship to the "You."[83] In the exchanging of ideas, the selection of what topics to discuss and what to omit will affect the impact of our ideas. Speech is not value neutral and cannot be scrubbed clean of its judgments. As the prominent twentieth-century rhetorician Kenneth Burke states, "Speech in its essence is not neutral. Far from aiming at suspended judgment, the spontaneous speech of a people is loaded with judgments. It is intensely moral—its names for objects contain the emotional overtones which give us the cues as to how we should act towards these objects."[84] For Burke, the simple expression of an opinion or belief changes the ways another thinks, as does the wording we use to formulate a belief. Even the selection of the word we use to name something—for instance, whether someone is "pro-life" or

---

82. Perelman and Olbrechts-Tyteca, *The New Rhetoric*, 3.

83. Martin Buber, *I and Thou*, trans. Walter Arnold Kaufmann (New York: Charles Scribner's Sons, 1970), 62.

84. Kenneth Burke, *Permanence and Change: An Anatomy of Purpose* (Berkeley, CA: University of California Press, 1984), 176–77.

"anti-choice"—can speak volumes about both what we believe and what we hope others will believe.

It is therefore extraordinarily difficult to define what intentional persuasion is and what it isn't. Gass and Seiter state that a definition of persuasion should "take into account the rich complex of verbal, nonverbal, and contextual cues found in interpersonal encounters ... these elements do not function separately, but rather, they operate in an interrelated manner."[85] Once one factors in nonverbal communication, as well as contextual and implicit cues, it becomes clear that persuasion can take place without intent being obviously stated. The danger in a communication ethic that attempts to purge intentional persuasion is that it could potentially enable subtler and more deceptive forms of persuasion to occur, a form of argumentative seduction. Using the metaphor of arguers as lovers, Wayne Brockriede says that "such devices as ignoring the questions, begging the question, the red herring, appeals to ignorance or to prejudice all aim at securing assent through seductive discourse that only appears to establish warrantable claims."[86]

The attempts to construe mission as dialogue that intentionally bracket calls to conversion do not safeguard against the possibility that such encounters will exert influence on another, whether such influence is welcome or not. In limiting the possibility of manipulation to the act of intentional conversion, they miss the other ways in which one may be persuaded. Aristotle's critique of the sophists is pertinent: He does not condemn their love and use of rhetoric, since persuasion is necessary in things that cannot be proved certain. Instead, his critique is that they are people of bad character. Rhetoric is a tool which can be wielded to enact great good or great harm depending on who is using it and how they wield it: by using the power of words "justly, one would do the greatest good and unjustly, the greatest harm."[87] Whether one is attempting to persuade another to convert to Christianity, or persuade another to reject conversion and embrace dialogue, ethical issues may emerge because the one persuading is of a bad moral character. There is no communicative context that safeguards the power of words from their unjust use.

---

85. Robert H. Gass and John S. Seiter, *Persuasion, Social Influence, and Compliance Gaining* (Boston: Allyn and Bacon, 1999), 20.

86. Wayne Brockriede, "Arguers as Lovers," *Philosophy & Rhetoric* 5, no. 1 (1972): 4.

87. Aristotle, *On Rhetoric*, I.1.13.

PERSUASION IS UNAVOIDABLE, SO PROCLAMATION
ENTAILS RISKS ON THE PART OF THE MISSIONARY

The belief that persuasion is to an extent inevitable entails a correlate: that the ones engaged in intentional persuasion open themselves up to *being* persuaded. The mission as dialogue paradigm is right in asserting that a conversion may occur in the self after engaging in interreligious dialogue. What it fails to acknowledge is that a conversion of the self may also occur through intentional acts of persuasion. Just because someone intends to convince another of a belief does not mean that they themselves are closed off from change. Cobb makes this false assumption: the more "conservative" Christians will be less open to change than the more "progressive" Christians.[88]

Sanneh's monograph *Translating the Message* gives a historical account and assessment of Christian mission that highlights the complex ways in which the missionary enterprise shaped both the missionary and the mission. While not denying the cases in which missionaries colluded with oppressive imperialist regimes, Sanneh emphasizes the ways in which missionaries, through introducing the gospel message, helped foster significant benefits for local cultures. At the same time, he also showcases the ways in which many missionaries became more critical of their home churches as a result of spreading the gospel: "Missionaries accepted the indigenous culture as the final destination of the message, and they were prepared to go to similar lengths in renouncing Western culture as the normative pattern for all peoples."[89] Such a critique of Western culture was done in part in order to advance the success of the missionary venture. For instance, Sanneh cites the missionary work of Alexandro Vilignano in sixteenth-century Japan, tracing the changes in his views of Japanese culture as a result of his work. Vilignano arrives convinced of European superiority. "However, as field experience mellowed him, Vilignano adopted a different course, still critical, but this time toward the Western cultural assumptions of Christian mission."[90] *Hence missionaries, in their attempts to intentionally convert others, experienced a conversion themselves.* Significantly for reflecting on Cobb's critique of conversion is that this change did not take place through a radical

---

88. Cobb, "Beyond 'Pluralism,' " 87–88.
89. Sanneh, *Translating*, 93.
90. Sanneh, *Translating*, 96.

open dialogue but through the intentional proclamation of the gospel. The type of mutual conversion so desired by the dialogist was achieved through a method of intentional proclamation that they reject. Chapter five will take up this issue more fully in showing how the work of the Holy Spirit in prayer and the desire to discover the available means of persuasion in the acts of proclamation effect a change in the life of the missionary.

CONCLUSION

The conception of mission as dialogue sets out to address the seemingly ethnocentric and coercive aspects of Christian mission by conceiving of it as the process of engaging in interreligious dialogue that is non-persuasive, the goal of which is the conversion of the self rather than the other. While it may have failed in many of its objectives, it does provide for a missiology that is morally reflective, as well as press the point regarding the alleged coerciveness lurking behind the missionary enterprise as a whole. It has brought the problem of persuasion to the forefront of discussions concerning mission, yet it has failed to adequately address these issues. The ensuing chapter on proclamation will address the issue of persuasion head on, but first we must establish a way of speaking about mission that takes seriously the moral actions of the missionary.

Part II

—

THE CONSTRUCTIVE TASK: MISSION, VIRTUE, *and* THE PRACTICES *of* PROCLAMATION *and* GATHERING

4

—

MISSION AS VIRTUOUS PRACTICE

In part I of this book, I used theological ethics to critically assess three rival versions of mission in order to better understand their philosophical and theological underpinnings, as well as their strengths and weaknesses. What emerged from these discussions were three perpetual challenges, what I have called the problems of distinction, agency, and persuasion. While each of the three previous chapters has included an extended analysis of one of these problems, it has been shown that such challenges are not limited to that specific model. Indeed, each of these models bears traces of all three of these perpetual issues.

In highlighting the ways in which the problems of distinction, agency, and persuasion perpetually recur throughout these various models of mission, I am suggesting that the potential solutions to these issues lay outside of dogmatic and anthropological approaches to mission, and that the field of missiology lacks the resources to adequately solve them. While the discipline of theological ethics has provided the primary critical tools for identifying the perpetual problems of mission, it also provides the resources for solutions. In the next section of this book, historical and recent scholarship in ethics—drawn both from virtue ethics and communication ethics—will help forge a model of mission that better addresses these challenges. As Aquinas and MacIntyre have been aids in the critical task, so they will also aid the constructive task.

This chapter begins by setting forth the goals of this constructive part of the book, which centers on the ways in which my casting of mission through the lens of virtue ethics better addresses the problems generated in the critical section of the book. Following this will be the articulation of my conception of mission, beginning with this thesis: *Christian mission is best construed as specific activities (proclamation and gathering) that develop virtue in its practitioners, moving them toward their ultimate goal of partaking in the glory of*

God. The remainder of the chapter will then be spent tracing the key lines of thought inherent in this statement.

WHY VIRTUE? THE GOALS OF THIS
CONCEPTION OF MISSION

Before expanding on my conception of mission as virtuous practice, it is imperative to understand the purposes of such a construal: Why virtue? What do I hope to accomplish? What are the goals to which this conception of mission aspires?

ADDRESSING THE PROBLEMS OF DISTINCTION,
AGENCY, AND PERSUASION

The assertion that mission is best construed as virtuous practices comes with three primary goals. First, such a theory aims to address the three perpetual issues involved in the study of mission—what I have codified as the problems of distinction, agency, and persuasion. But the goal is not simply to address these problems adequately, but to do so in such a way that the answers to these problems are intelligible within the logic of the aforementioned models. Here I am appropriating Alasdair MacIntyre's understanding of competing moral traditions and how the conflicts between such traditions might be resolved, and I am showing how a similar adjudication might take place amidst rival conceptions of mission. In his book *Three Rival Versions of Moral Inquiry,* MacIntyre elucidates how particular moral traditions can supersede their rivals through integration rather than domination. This happens when a particular tradition can be shown to better address the problems of their rivals, yet in a way that is intelligible from within their rival's tradition.[1] For instance, in his analysis of Thomas Aquinas, Alasdair MacIntyre describes how Thomas was able to integrate Aristotelian and Augustinian epistemologies into a coherent whole. The importance of Aquinas's system was not that it fit perfectly together, as if Thomas split the difference between the two systems, but rather that Thomas's system of thought was able to answer the concerns of each system better than that system could on its own terms: "Aquinas integrated both rival schemes of concepts and beliefs in such a way

---

1. Alasdair C. MacIntyre, *Three Rival Versions of Moral Enquiry: Encyclopaedia, Genealogy, and Tradition* (Notre Dame, IN: University of Notre Dame Press, 1990), 119–24.

as both to correct in each that which he took by its own standards could be shown to be defective or unsound and to remove from each, in a way justified by that correction, that which barred them from reconciliation."[2]

My portrayal of mission as virtuous practice attempts to address the problematic areas of the *missio Dei* consensus and models of mission based on growth or based upon dialogue, with the hope that such attempts may be intelligible to the adherents of each. It should be noted that what is attempted is not a type of Hegelian synthesis of opposing missiologies. It is tempting to simply categorize mission as growth and mission as dialogue as conservative and liberal binaries, with a third way magically striking a golden mean. To do so would ignore deficiencies, particularly in the realm of human agency, that belie both. This is the second key assertion that MacIntyre makes regarding the development of Thomas's moral system. While Aquinas attempted to answer the concerns internal to each rival view, he was not beholden to either view: "If one is compelled to enquire where the truth lies between alternative, rival, and incommensurable overall points of view, one cannot but entertain the possibility that either or both of these points of view is systematically false, false as a whole in its overall claims."[3] While one can attempt to address internal concerns to systems of belief, the judgments made on the truth or falsity of these systems are judgments that are made outside of these systems: "Hence in judging of truth and falsity there is always some ineliminable reference beyond the scheme within which those judgements are made and beyond the criteria which provide the warrants for assertablity within that scheme."[4] The goal of my model of mission is thus to better address the aforementioned problems of distinction, agency, and persuasion in the field of Christian mission, drawing upon conceptual resources within the fields of missiology, moral theology, philosophy, and rhetorical studies,

2. MacIntyre, *Three Rival Versions*, 123.

3. MacIntyre, *Three Rival Versions*, 121.

4. MacIntyre, *Three Rival Versions*, 122. It should be noted here that MacIntyre embraces a Thomistic notion of the natural law, which he sees as providing the framework through which individuals are able to properly pursue the good in community. Natural law in this rendering is, first, principles that provide the norms for shared rational enquiry and an objective standard through which such inquiry can take place. Alasdair C. MacIntyre, "Intractable Moral Disagreements," in *Intractable Disputes about the Natural Law: Alasdair MacIntyre and Critics*, ed. Lawrence S. Cunningham (Notre Dame, IN: University of Notre Dame Press, 2009), 24–25.

while reserving the right to pronounce judgment on parts of each system that are not in harmony with what God has revealed in Scripture.[5]

FITTINGNESS WITH THE NEW TESTAMENT DEPICTION OF MISSION

This leads to the second goal: to present a way of construing mission that fits the New Testament witness. I am committed to the historical affirmation in Anglicanism that Scripture is God's written word and contains all things necessary for salvation, articulated clearly in Article Six of the Thirty-Nine Articles:

> Holy Scripture containeth all things necessary to salvation: so that whatsoever is not read therein, nor may be proved thereby, is not to be required of any man, that it should be believed as an article of the Faith, or be thought requisite or necessary to salvation.

Such a statement asserts both the necessity and sufficiency of the Bible for salvation. Oliver Crisp codifies this belief in Scripture as "the *norma normans non normata*—that is, the norming norm that is not normed by anything

---

5. This assertion that the judgments of models of mission are predicated on Scripture departs from MacIntyre's notion of the natural law as the objective standard of moral enquiry. In this regard, my approach is more akin to Oliver O'Donovan. For O'Donovan, there is a rationality inherent in the created order that can be discerned by human beings, yet sin has the effect not only of making such rationality difficult for human beings to discern, but it also involves a rupture in the rationality of the created order itself. The resurrection of Jesus Christ thus becomes the way through which created order is restored, and it provides Christians the opportunity to become moral agents "involved in deciding what a situation is and demands in the light of the moral order," provided they do so through the revelation of Jesus Christ as attested to in the entirety of the biblical canon. Oliver O'Donovan, *Resurrection and Moral Order: An Outline for Evangelical Ethics* (Grand Rapids: Eerdmans, 1994), 24.

While such an approach is perhaps distinctly Protestant, it does have similarities with some Catholic theologians. Gerald McKenney argues that Josef Ratzinger grounds moral truth in the Christian historical tradition. While such a tradition is only accessible by faith, its embodiment in the church provides evidence for its truth claims that can be acknowledged even by nonbelievers. See Gerald P. McKenny, "Moral Disagreements and the Limits of Reason: Reflections on MacIntyre and Ratzinger," in *Intractable Disputes about the Natural Law: Alasdair MacIntyre and Critics*, ed. Lawrence S. Cunningham (Notre Dame, IN: University of Notre Dame Press, 2009), 219.

My own approach is particularly suitable for rendering judgments on models of Christian mission. MacIntyre's depiction of rival traditions is concerned primarily with models of moral enquiry, not rival theologies or rival Christianities. Appeals to Scripture are thus not authoritative. An assessment of Christian mission, however, is distinctly Christian, and the practice of mission is largely defined by the initial missional activity of the apostles as depicted in the book of Acts. Thus, in this case, the use of Scripture as a criterion for judgment is highly warranted. This will be addressed in the ensuing paragraphs.

else."[6] Because of this belief, it is imperative that an account of mission remain faithful to Scripture as God's written word.

An affirmation of Scripture as God's word written only begs the question of how it should be interpreted, an issue whose importance and contentiousness is evidenced by the fact of entire academic journals devoted to it. As far as my own commitments, the aforementioned statement regarding Scripture as the norming norm, as well as my particular ecclesial commitments as an ordained clergyman, provide boundaries for my interpretations. Novel scriptural proposals that violate the doctrine and discipline of the church are out of bounds. However, I do not believe such boundaries are meant to stymie creativity—G. K. Chesterton's statement on the boundaries of the church being less like the walls of a prison and more like the fencing of a playground is adroit.[7] Just as a creative child can venture throughout a playground seeing such fencing but having no desire to breach it, so too can creative scriptural interpretation reside joyfully within the boundaries of doctrine.

Chapter two raised the issue of interpretation, and there I mentioned the work of David Kelsey and his evaluation of the ways in which theologians construe the texts of Scripture. Richard Hays's *The Moral Vision of the New Testament* contains a detailed explanation of the ways in which this might be done particularly when using the New Testament to make ethical claims. Hays lists four types of appeals that theologians make when using Scripture as a source of ethical reflection: rules, principles, paradigms, and the symbolic world.[8] For Hays, "each of these modes of discourse may be found *within* Scripture as well as in secondary theological reflection about Scripture's ethical import."[9] Since all of these types of appeals are present in Scripture, they are all legitimate for making ethical claims. The task of

---

6. Oliver Crisp, *Deviant Calvinism: Broadening Reformed Theology* (Minneapolis, MN: Fortress Press, 2014), 17. This term is used summarily to denote the relationship between the authority of Scripture, of confessions and creeds, and the church, particularly as it developed in the Lutheran tradition and Matthias Flacius Illyricus's 1567 work *Clavis scripturae sacrae*. See Richard A. Muller, *Post-Reformation Reformed Dogmatics*, vol. 2 (Grand Rapids: Baker Academic, 2006).

7. G. K. Chesterton, *Orthodoxy* (New York: Barnes and Noble, 2007), 137.

8. Richard B. Hays, *The Moral Vision of the New Testament: Community, Cross, New Creation; A Contemporary Introduction to New Testament Ethics* (London: T&T Clark, 2003), 209.

9. Hays, *The Moral Vision*, 209.

theologians is the "task of rightly correlating our ethical norms with the modes of Scripture's speech."[10]

Following this framework, my own approach to Scripture will seek an imaginative construal of the pertinent texts related to mission, particularly in the New Testament, being sensitive to Scripture's own appeals to rules, principles, paradigms, and the symbolic world. An area of emphasis will be on paradigms, which Hays states are "stories or summary accounts of characters who model exemplary conduct."[11] While I will at points appeal to various parts of Scripture, the interpretative focus will be this: *the words and actions of the apostles, as well as the depiction of their character, demonstrated principally in the book of Acts, are meant to model exemplary conduct for missionaries today.*

Part of the critiques in the aforementioned chapters centered upon the ways in which conceptions of mission both misconstrue Scripture and fail to sufficiently account for the wide range of missional activity of the apostles as depicted in the book of Acts. For instance, Alan Hirsch's construal of Scripture as possessing the keys to unlocking replicable church growth conflicts with the clear depictions of the rejection of the gospel message in the book of Acts. Furthermore, Paul Knitter's conception of mission as dialogue ignores passages in the New Testament that depict intentional persuasion meant to encourage conversion. Neither of these approaches adequately attends to the complex ways in which the disciples engage in persuasive activity while at the same time remaining relatively unconcerned when such persuasion is met with failure and hostility.

What is needed is a *fitting* account of mission, one which accounts for the complex ways in which the proclamation of Jesus as Lord and the expansion of the Christian church is displayed in the biblical text. The term "fittingness" has its roots in theological aesthetics, as it refers to the "due proportion or consonance" that a person or object has to itself.[12] For Aquinas, this is one aspect of beauty—that something is perfectly in harmony with what it ought to be. Hence, the Son is beautiful because he is the perfect image of the Father. Kevin Vanhoozer appropriates this conception of fittingness to express the

---

10. Hays, *The Moral Vision*, 209.

11. Hays, *The Moral Vision*, 209.

12. Aquinas, *Summa Theologiae*, I, q. 39, art. 8.

relationship between theological concepts and Scripture.[13] A theological concept "depends for theology not only on whether it seems to fit experience, but on whether it illuminates, and is illuminated by, the scriptural text."[14] Fitness is not, however, a mere static equivalence between dogma and Scripture, but rather the beautiful and harmonious ways in which such concepts cohere with the drama of Scripture, with Jesus Christ as the center.[15] Furthermore, a concept is fitting not just because it is in accordance with a large collection of biblical texts, but also because it better aids those who see themselves as continuing the biblical story. The goal of formulating doctrine is to aid in the dramatic performance of the biblical canon by the church today.[16]

Vanhoozer's concept of fittingness bears resemblance to what Frances Young describes as the exercise of "mimetic exegesis" in the ancient church. Young describes how early Christian theologians appropriated the ancient practice of dramatically performing texts for the purpose of pedagogy. Exegesis here "assumes the replay of a drama—an act or plot—and so had a place in forming ethics, lifestyle, and liturgy."[17] One of the focuses of such mimetic exegesis was on the way specific characters in the Bible assumed the role of literary heroes: paragons of virtue who model how Christians ought to live their lives. Thus, "a character like Job came to embody patience, and Christ's life and death were set forth as a way to be imitated."[18]

What is aimed at in this study is a conception of mission that both draws from the biblical witness and helps better shed light on the biblical witness. The point of developing concepts of mission that fit with the biblical

---

13. While Vanhoozer's appropriation of the term "fittingness" has not been specifically appropriated by other contemporary theologians, the concept resonates with the work of other modern theologians, most notably Hans Urs von Balthasar, whose casting of Christian action through the lens of dramatic performance was an important influence on Vanhoozer's work.

14. Oliver O'Donovan, Self, World, and Time: Ethics of Theology, vol. 3 (Grand Rapids: Eerdmans, 2013), 7.

15. Kevin J. Vanhoozer, The Drama of Doctrine: A Canonical-Linguistic Approach to Christian Theology (Louisville, KY: Westminster John Knox Press, 2005), 258.

16. "Fittingness involves more than conceptual consistency. The criterion for correct doctrine is not simply logical but dramatic consistency: performing the same kind of communicative action—a matter of being constant in word, thought, and deed. ... Doctrines help us discern what, in light of the drama of redemption, is fitting language and action for Christian disciples." Vanhoozer, The Drama, 109.

17. Frances Margaret Young, Biblical Exegesis and the Formation of Christian Culture (Cambridge: Cambridge University Press, 2007), 209.

18. Young, Biblical Exegesis, 209.

narrative is not just to provide terms that are logically coherent with the complex ways in the which mission is displayed in the Bible; it is also to provide better opportunities for the church to carry on the task of mission today in a way that is pleasing to God. In this sense, fittingness is as much an aesthetic term as it is a scientific one. To say that a concept of mission aids in a fitting performance of the biblical narrative is to say that such performances are beautiful, as one might call a contemporary performance of Beethoven's Ninth Symphony by the Chicago Symphony Orchestra a fitting performance of the composer's score.[19] This touches upon what St. Paul describes as the sacrifices of the people—"Holy and Pleasing to God—this is your spiritual act of worship" (Rom 12:1 NIV84). The offering of our bodies as spiritual sacrifices to God—to perform the biblical narrative—is an act that calls forth holiness and is in turn pleasing to God.

To this end, the book will draw largely upon biblical accounts of mission, focusing primarily on the preeminent missiological text in Scripture: the book of Acts.[20] One particular area of emphasis will be on a kind of mimetic exegesis of the book of Acts, where the characters of the biblical drama—specifically Peter, Paul, and Stephen—are paragons of virtue who teach missionaries how to perform their task in a way that is holy and pleasing to God. The hope is that my account of mission will be illuminated by the witness of holy Scripture, and that my account will better enable readers to glean new insights from Scripture as a result.

MORAL REFLECTION ON THE PERFORMANCE OF MISSION

Furthermore, the hope is that this characterization of mission will aid in the practical performance of mission. This leads to the third goal of the mission as virtuous practice model: that those engaged in mission will be better equipped to morally reflect on their actions. Moral reflection is the

---

19. Ellen Davis and Robert Hays make a similar point in regard to the collective activity of the church: "Scripture is like a musical score that must be played or sung in order to be understood; therefore, the church interprets Scripture by forming communities of prayer, service, and faithful witness. The Psalms, for example, are 'scores' awaiting performance by the community of faith." Ellen F. Davis and Richard B. Hays, "Nine Theses on the Interpretation of Scripture," in The Art of Reading Scripture, ed. Ellen F. Davis and Richard B. Hays (Grand Rapids: Eerdmans, 2003), 3–4.

20. According to Stephen Bevans and Roger Schroeder, for instance, "Acts, it is generally acknowledged, constitutes our principal source of information on the origins of Christian mission." Bevans and Schroeder, Constants, 11.

process of thinking about our doing, both our past actions and our immediate future actions. It is "how we think what we are to do, which is to say, how we act."[21] This is an important assertion, since a common misperception of ethics and moral theology is that it is simply the listing of dos and don'ts, with the presentation of increasingly complex (and obscure) scenarios in which the ethicist renders definitive judgment. Instead, the task of moral reflection is the discernment of what is good and right in accordance with God's goodness. Although such moral reflection may not be immediately practical, it does have practical import, since by such reflection persons will become a people through which the goodness of God flows. We don't love God because of God's effects, but loving God necessarily affects us. Moral reflection thus "generates and supports useful goods of deliberative thought toward action."[22]

This book carries with it the very basic desire to help those engaged in Christian mission to be better missionaries. By reflecting on the missionary task, one can better discern what is good and right about it, and such reflection will support good and right deliberative thought toward further action.

The remainder of this book will develop my conception of mission, with this chapter unpacking my thesis statement, the following chapters developing my concept of proclamation and gathering as virtuous practices, and the concluding chapter discussing briefly how such practices are involved in a life lived well. In so doing I will demonstrate how this conception of mission meets the aforementioned goals.

Each of these chapters emphasizes specific portions of these goals: The reframing of mission in relation to Aquinas's moral theology and the use of Alasdair MacIntyre's concept of a virtuous practice are meant to specifically address the problems of distinction and agency in mission. The following chapter on proclamation is meant to address the problem of persuasion and highlight how a conception of proclamation as a virtuous practice fits with the portrayals of mission in Scripture. The examination of the virtuous practice of gathering in chapter six takes up the question of agency again and shows how the acts of mission may reach their completion. That chapter and

---

21. O'Donovan, *Self*, 3.

22. Oliver O'Donovan, *Common Objects of Love: Moral Reflection and the Shaping of Community; The 2001 Stob Lectures* (Grand Rapids: Eerdmans, 2002), 19.

the conclusion together highlight how this approach to mission encourages moral reflection both on the performance of mission and its place in a life lived for the glory of God.

THESIS STATEMENT: KEY LINES OF THOUGHT

Now that the critiques of mission have been articulated and the goals of my conception of mission established, I will elucidate my construal of mission as virtuous practice, demonstrating how this approach offers a better way for addressing the challenges within mission and meets the stated goals. The proposal is this: *Christian mission is best construed as specific activities (proclamation and gathering) that develop virtue in its practitioners, moving them toward their ultimate goal of partaking in the glory of God.*

The remainder of this chapter traces the key lines of thought related to my thesis, the discussion of which will aid in further defining and clarifying its key terms and assertions. It begins first by using Thomas Aquinas's moral theology to build a foundation which will provide a way of speaking of mission that best meets the aforementioned goals. This foundation involves first a discussion of the relationship between God, creation, and agency, followed by an examination of how a theory of action and virtue fits into this relationship. Then, I will demonstrate how this foundation provides an appropriate grammar for speaking of mission.

The chapter then moves from doctrinal and theoretical considerations to more practical ones, beginning with an examination of Alasdair MacIntyre's notion of a virtuous practice, how mission can be construed as the virtuous practices of proclamation and gathering, and finally how the engagement in these activities promotes specific virtues.

The structure of this chapter runs roughly along the same progression as the *Summa Theologiae*. It starts first by discussing the relationships within the Triune God and between God and creation, followed by an account of human agency. This follows the progression of the *Prima Paris* of the *Summa*. From here, I progress to discuss humankind's ultimate end, the vision of God, how human beings move toward this end through deliberate action, and how human beings cultivate virtue toward this end. This corresponds with the *Pars Prima-Secundae* of the *Summa*. Following this section, I will proceed to discuss Alasdair MacIntyre's conception of virtuous practices, which is akin to what Aquinas calls habits, also covered in the *Pars Prima-Secundae*.

Following this section, I will discuss how mission fosters specific virtues, drawing from the *Pars Secunda-Secundae* of the *Summa*.

The reason for such structuring is partly due to my reliance on Aquinas for many of the theological foundations for my concept of mission, though my use of Aquinas is by no means exclusive. The section on virtuous practices, for instance, is highly indebted to Alasdair MacIntyre. The ensuing chapters will expand on various aspects of my model of mission with the aid of Augustine, Gregory of Nyssa, and John Henry Newman. Other theologians such as Oliver O'Donovan also provide insight. Another reason for structuring the chapter in this way is for heuristic purposes. The first two parts of the *Summa* take the reader from lofty considerations of God and creation, to an understanding of human action within this relationship with God, to the particular details of how human beings cultivate virtue. The hope is that tracing my concept of mission along these same lines will enable a more comprehensive view of what mission is and what role human beings might play in it.

MORAL THEOLOGY AND MISSION: BUILDING A FOUNDATION

Chapter one traced the breakdown of ruled language concerning God's transcendence and immanence and between human and divine agency, showing how the loss of these careful distinctions has muddled the distinctive aspects of Christian mission and created confusion as to the workings of human agency within the activities of mission. In order to redress these issues, it is imperative to set mission on a more solid foundation. This section turns to Thomas Aquinas's moral theology to build such a foundation.[23]

---

23. My use of the phrase "Aquinas's moral theology" is meant to be broad, as it includes aspects, such as the relationships within the Trinity, that are typically considered part of dogmatics. However, the distinctions between dogmatics and moral theology are not clear cut, and my examination of Aquinas's understanding of the relationships between God, creation, and agency are crucial for understanding how Aquinas believes human beings can grow in virtue. Furthermore, my reading of Aquinas on these issues is as one who is largely consistent with the Christian tradition. To appropriate Tanner's words, Aquinas stands within a broad category of orthodox, pre-modern theologians whose language of God affirms both God's radical transcendence and radical immanence. See Tanner, *God and Creation*, 56–80. It is my own assertion that Aquinas provides the most astute articulation of these relationships, and that Aquinas stands largely, though not completely, in harmony with the tradition, most notably Augustine. As such, I will at times refer also to Augustine, as well as the contemporary Trinitarian scholar Giles Emery's assessment of the traditional articulation of the Trinity.

God, Creation, and Agency

Conceptualizing mission in relation to Aquinas's moral theology begins by first affirming key distinctions between God and creation within classical Trinitarian theology as articulated by Thomas Aquinas, with the hope that such affirmations can help alleviate the problems of distinction and agency that have plagued the study of mission.

Aquinas's conception of moral agency is grounded in his broader articulation of the Trinity and the relationship between God and creation. For Aquinas, the relations within God's very self—the relations among Father, Son, and Holy Spirit—are different from God's relations to his creation. Within God's self there are "real relations," relationships that involve procession within persons of the same nature.[24] The relationships within the Trinity "imply ontological similarity and dependence."[25] This ontological similarity and dependence aids in a Trinitarian grammar that enables human beings to speak of one God, Father, Son, and Holy Spirit. The difference in the persons are differences of relation and not substance. The relationship between God and creation, however, cannot be spoken of in such terms. To make the relationship between God and creation interdependent and ontologically similar would be to make God dependent upon creation, which would either "divinize creation or mythologize God by turning God into a creature."[26] God's relationship to creation is instead referred to as "logical," meaning that the relationship does not imply dependence or change.[27] Aquinas sees the relationship between God and creation as asymmetrical:

---

24. "When something proceeds from a principle of the same nature as itself, then both of them—viz., what proceeds and what it proceeds from—must belong to the same ordering, and so they must have real relations with respect to one another. Therefore, since, as has been shown [q. 27, art. 3], the processions in God involve an identity of nature, the relations associated with the divine processions must be real relations." Aquinas, *Summa Theologiae*, I, q. 28, art. 1.

25. Long, *Triune God*, 57.

26. Long, *Triune God*, 57.

27. An assertion that God is not in real relation to creation does not necessitate a belief in a God that is distant or uncaring. Robert Sokolowski describes how Aquinas's formulation of the traditional understanding that God is not dependent upon the world means that creation is the result of the sheer goodness and generosity of God: "And the world is not diminished in its own excellence, it is not somehow slighted because God is not related by a real relation to it; rather the world is now understood as not having had to be. If it did not have to be, it is there out of a choice. And if the choice was not motivated by any need of completion in the one who let it be, and not even motivated by the need for 'there' to be more perfection and greatness, then the world is there through an incomparable generosity. The world exists simply for the

God is outside the order of all creatures and does not by His nature have a relation to creatures. ... He produces creatures not by a necessity of nature, but through His intellect and will. And this is why in God there are no real relations to creatures. However, in the creatures there is a real relation to God, since creatures are contained under God's ordering and by their nature depend on God.[28]

Human beings have a real relation to God since they exist under God and are dependent on God as the source of their existence. Yet God relates to creation in a way that does not change God.[29] To speak of the relationships within God's self is to speak analogously, since human beings are not God.

This principle of analogy when speaking of the relationships within God's self and the relationship between God and humanity is particularly important in regard to the language of agency. God exercises divine agency in a way that is different from and only analogous to human agency. For Aquinas, God exists in all things: "God exists within all things and intimately so."[30] God acts as the "donating source" of all that exists, operating in a way that neither changes God nor displaces human agency. D. Stephen Long sees Aquinas's notion of infinity as key to understanding how divine agency differs from human agency:

God is the donating source of everything in creation such that it is both like and unlike God, which is how a term like *infinity* functions. It allows for God to be "in all things" without displacing them or being composite with them. ... Infinity is God's lack of limitation so that

---

glory of God." Robert Sokolowski, *The God of Faith and Reason: Foundations of Christian Theology* (Notre Dame, IN: University of Notre Dame Press, 1982), 34.

28. Aquinas, *Summa Theologiae*, I, q. 28, art. 1.

29. Aquinas parses this distinction even further, stating that, although God does not have a real relationship to creation, creation does have a real relationship to God: "And this is why in God there are no real relations to creatures. However, in the creatures there is a real relation to God, since creatures are contained under God's ordering and by their nature depend on God" (*Summa Theologiae*, I, q. 28, art. 1). Creatures depend on God, but God does not depend on creatures. Aquinas posits a third type of relationship, one that is mixed, which is evidenced in the incarnation, which "effects a real change in humanity without changing God." Long, *Triune God*, 57.

30. Aquinas, *Summa Theologiae*, I, q. 8, art. 1.

God and creatures can inhabit the same space and time because God's essence is not *in* space or time.[31]

God is not in space or time and, as such, can act in created things without displacing created things. God's agency is thus not competitive with human agency: "Because of God's infinity, the two agencies are not competitive, as if God acts 75 percent and the creature 25 percent."[32] The activity of God is differentiated from the activity of human beings: God is able to send himself in ways that human beings cannot.[33] God's agency functions in a way that human agency cannot. God can go to where he already exists; humans go to where they do not exist. God can act without displacement; human beings act through displacement.

The Vision of God, Action, and Virtue

The *Prima Pars* of the *Summa* is focused on God and God's relation to creation. In the second part (which encompasses both the *Prima Secundae Partis* and the *Secunda Secundae Partis*), Aquinas shifts his focus from God to humankind. Roughly speaking, the first part is about God and how God relates to creation; the second part involves how creation relates to God. This section will thus focus specifically on how human beings relate to God, first by defining the ultimate goal of human life, then proceeding to how human beings might act so as to move toward this goal, and finally addressing how they might develop virtues through such actions.

One of the potentially problematic aspects of the asymmetrical relationship between God and creation, at least on the surface, resides in the description of the relationship between God and creation as logical, since this would seem to imply remoteness and distance. However, the fact that God does not

---

31. Long, *Triune God*, 25.

32. Long, *Triune God*, 26.

33. Sokolowski shows how this understanding of divine agency is critical for understanding the Chalcedonian assertion of the full humanity and full divinity of Christ. Since God is not dependent upon creation, he is capable of involvement with creation without abolishing or displacing it: "God does not destroy the natural necessities of things he becomes involved with, even in the intimate union of the incarnation. What is according to nature, and what reason can disclose in nature, retains its integrity before the Christian God. ... If the incarnation could not take place without a truncation of human nature, it would mean that God was one of the natures in the world that somehow was defined by not being the other natures; it would mean that his presence in one of these other natures, human nature, would involve a conflict and a need to exclude some part of what he is united with." Sokolowski, *The God of Faith*, 35–36.

exist in a dependent relationship with creation entails that God does not create out of necessity, but out of love: "God produced creatures not because of any need on His part or because of any other extrinsic cause, but because of the love of His own goodness."[34] Because God creates out of the love of his own goodness, human beings have as their end goal entering into this love in the beatific vision: "Our end is not found in ourselves, but God alone."[35] It is toward this end, entering fully into God's glory and his love, that human beings are given the possibility of moving.

A key assertion by Aquinas is that the ultimate goal, or telos, of the human being is the vision of God. God is the greatest good, and since the good is that which is desirable and the terminus of desire, God is what human beings are created to desire, as well as where their desires terminate: "Final and perfect happiness (in Latin *beatitudo*) can consist in nothing else than the vision of the Divine Essence."[36] Aquinas here quotes St. John: "When He shall appear, we shall be like to Him; and we shall see Him as He is" (1 John 3:2). The term "vision of God" can be difficult to understand in modern parlance. By "vision of God," Aquinas means "knowing and loving God."[37] Sight in this case can be thought of both as a "seeing" of the mind's eye in the act of knowing, as well as the actual visual perception of Jesus that Scripture states will occur in the eschaton (Rev 22:4-6).

Paired with the vision of Jesus in Revelation is the partaking of the glory of God—the glory of God in the heavenly temple so radiant as to not require any other source of light. Hence, the goal of human beings is conterminously that of seeing God and partaking in his glory. Aquinas likewise speaks of the glory of God as humanity's created end in his explanation of the transfiguration:

> Now in order that anyone go straight along a road, he must have some knowledge of the end: thus an archer will not shoot the arrow straight unless he first see the target. ... Therefore it was fitting that He should show His disciples the glory of His clarity (which is to be transfigured), to which He will configure those who are His.[38]

---

34. Aquinas, *Summa Theologiae*, I, q. 32, art. 1.
35. Long, *Triune God*, 60.
36. Aquinas, *Summa Theologiae*, I-II, q. 3, art. 8.
37. Aquinas, *Summa Theologiae*, I-II, q. 1, art. 8.
38. Aquinas, *Summa Theologiae*, III, q. 45, art. 1. This material can be accessed online at "Summa Theologiae," New Advent, https://www.newadvent.org/summa/.

Another way that this ultimate end is described is as friendship with God, since friendship is a kind of shared knowledge and loving. Expanding on John 15:15 (where Jesus says "I no longer call you servants, but my friends"), Aquinas states that "since man shares something in common with God insofar as God communicates His own beatitude to us, it must be the case that some sort of friendship is founded upon this sharing. ... But the sort of love built on this sharing is charity. Hence, it is clear that charity is a certain sort of friendship of man with God."[39] Gregory of Nyssa states similarly that the goal of the virtuous life is "to be known by God and to become his friend."[40] As Aquinas uses at various points "vision," "glory," and "friendship" to describe the one and same end of humankind, so will my conception of mission, with a particular emphasis on glory in the ensuing chapter.

Aquinas's account of humanity's ultimate end as the vision of God is grounded in the work of God himself in divine revelation. Not only is the ultimate goal the vision of God, but such a goal is not the product of human reason but is revealed by God in Holy Scripture:

---

39. Aquinas, *Summa Theologiae*, II–II, q. 23, art. 1. Aquinas's codification of happiness, defined as the beatific vision of God, as the ultimate telos of humankind provides a corrective to some of the deficiencies in other ancient accounts of virtue. Julia Annas sees in ancient accounts a definition of happiness (*eudaimonia*) that is to some extent platitudinal, a kind of placeholder for stating the final good of a person: "Happiness is stable, active and objective just because the final good is. In saying that the final good is happiness we are thus adding very little. But that is just what Aristotle says: what we have really done is give the final end a handy name." Julia Annas, *The Morality of Happiness* (New York: Oxford University Press, 2009), 46.

Added to this rather thin account of happiness is its contingency, at least according to Aristotle, on friendship for its fulfillment: "a happy man needs friends." Aristotle, *Nicomachean Ethics*, trans. Martin Ostwald (Upper Saddle River, NJ: Prentice Hall, 1999), 264. Stanley Hauerwas and Charles Pinches see in Aristotle a tragic flaw: happiness is contingent on the ability to have close, intimate friendships, yet, because of the contingencies of life—most notably, death—lasting friendships are often elusive: "Aristotle suggests we can be happy only if we achieve a self-sufficiency that guards us against outrageous fortune. Christians claim, on the other hand, that we are happy only to the extent that our lives are formed in reference to Jesus of Nazareth." Stanley Hauerwas and Charles Robert Pinches, *Christians among the Virtues: Theological Conversations with Ancient and Modern Ethics* (Notre Dame, IN: University of Notre Dame Press, 1997), 16.

What Aquinas's account of happiness as the beatific vision provides is a "thick" account of the end of life. The end is not a vague placeholder that must only be filled in with a lifetime of virtuous activity, but a person: God the Father, Son, and Holy Spirit, revealed to humankind. Furthermore, this end consists in friendship with God, who is eternal and everlasting; therefore, happiness is not limited to the lucky few who maintain lifelong human friendships.

40. Gregory of Nyssa, *The Life of Moses*, trans. Abraham Malherbe and Everett Ferguson (New York: Paulist Press, 1978), 137.

It was necessary for human salvation that, over and beyond the philosophical disciplines devised by human reason, there should be a doctrine conformable with divine revelation. For, first of all, according
to Isaiah 64:4 ("The eye has not seen, O God, apart from You, what
things You have prepared for them that wait for You"), man is ordered
toward God as an end who exceeds the comprehension of reason. But
the end must first be known to men, since they have to order their
intentions and actions toward the end. Hence, it was necessary for
man's salvation that certain things exceeding human reason should
be made known to him through divine revelation.[41]

This is the opening salvo of the *Summa Theologiae*, and the biblical underpinnings of the work are not to be taken lightly. God's revelation of himself to
humanity is necessary for their salvation. Human beings are ordered toward
God as their end, and since this end is supernatural, it can only be obtained
through the work of God.[42] However, the gift of God's revelation to humanity
is not to be simply passively received; instead, Aquinas asserts, it has been
given so that human beings might order their actions toward that end.

And so, Aquinas's discussion of the ultimate goal of human life in *Prima
Secundae Partis*, question 1, is coterminous with an elucidation of how human
beings might progress toward this goal through actions. In order to understand how this is possible, one first has to understand what Aquinas means
by "good," and goodness in general.

For Aquinas, goodness and being are integrally related; they are "the same
in reality and differ only conceptually."[43] Goodness is perfection of being,
so to say that something exists is to say that we can know it and describe
what it would be like to be perfected. To call something good means that it

---

41. Aquinas, *Summa Theologiae*, I, q. 1, art. 1.

42. Thomas O'Meara points out that Aquinas's prioritization of divine revelation and the
necessity of divine grace are often missed in contemporary revivals of virtue. According to
O'Meara, "Aquinas's theology is not an Aristotelian psychology grafted onto some phrases about
Christ. Aquinas employs an Aristotelian philosophy of nature to explain aspects of Christian
revelation, a revelation that is, as he sees it, of realities believed and not just of beliefs." Thomas
F. O'Meara, "Virtues in the Theology of Thomas Aquinas," *Theological Studies* 58, no. 2 (1997): 258.
Aquinas's theory of virtue is not a kind of natural/supernatural, Aristotle/Scripture layer cake.
Aristotelianism is instead used as a kind of explanatory tool to help unpack and elucidate the
revelation of God through Jesus Christ.

43. Aquinas, *Summa Theologiae*, I, q. 5, art. 1.

is desirable—it draws someone toward their perfection: "For something is good insofar as it is desirable and is the terminus of a movement of desire."[44] This eradicates the chasm between "ought" and "is" that plagues much moral theology and philosophy, as has been addressed in chapter two. For Aquinas, Jean Porter explains, to know what something is, is to know what it ought to be.[45] This connection between goodness and desire is meant as well to show that the point of moving toward the end is not simply one of rote accomplishment.[46] One apprehends the good, sees that it is beautiful and desirable, and thus moves toward it: the end is "not first set before us as an object to attain, but as a model to admire."[47]

To the extent to which human beings comprehend the good and act rightly, they are able to progress toward their final end. Aquinas states that those actions that are distinctively human are those which are done deliberately: "Therefore, the actions that are properly called human actions are those that proceed from a deliberate act of willing."[48] Human actions in this case are distinguished from acts of man, which are actions without deliberation. Such actions of this type are those that human beings share with non-rational animals, such as scratching one's face. Furthermore, for Aquinas, those actions that are distinctly human are also called "moral actions." All activity that is deliberate bears a moral character, providing the opportunity for human beings to act according to their good and move toward their final end. Charles Pinches summarizes this relationship between action, morality, and ultimate ends in Aquinas:

> The description of all human acts is essentially related to the fact that they proceed from a human being who is, distinctively, capable

---

44. Aquinas, *Summa Theologiae*, I, q. 5, art. 6.

45. Jean Porter, *The Recovery of Virtue: The Relevance of Aquinas for Christian Ethics* (Louisville, KY: Westminster John Knox Press, 1990), 44.

46. Gregory of Nyssa makes this point clearly: "This is true perfection: not to avoid a wicked life because like slaves we servilely fear punishment, nor to do good because we hope for rewards, as if cashing in on the virtuous life by some business-like and contractual arrangement. On the contrary, disregarding all those things for which we hope and which have been reserved by promise, we regard falling from God's friendship as the only thing dreadful and we consider becoming God's friend the only thing worthy of honor and desire." Gregory of Nyssa, *Life of Moses*, 137.

47. O'Donovan, *Finding*, 89.

48. Aquinas, *Summa Theologiae*, I–II, q. 1, art. 1.

of deliberation and choice. This makes all human acts moral … choice, deliberation and action all have their place in relation to the final end of human beings, happiness, and so ultimately to God. Human acts, then, have their meaning in terms of this final end to which all other ends are subordinate. "Morality" or the "moral life" is a way of speaking about our journey to this end.[49]

The assertion that all deliberate activity is moral will be important in the next section, as it will be my claim that mission involves deliberate activity, and thus such actions should be considered moral.

It is within this broader framework of goodness, happiness, and action that one can begin to unpack Aquinas's theory of virtue. Through the engagement in deliberative activity, human beings have the ability to develop habits that incline them to either move closer toward or further away from their ultimate end. Those habits that incline one to their ultimate end are called "virtues." When human beings develop virtue through the cultivation of good habits, they are to an extent actualizing their natural potential. The development of these habits both strengthens our ability to do good and causes good in their performance. Herbert McCabe puts it best: "Virtues are dispositions to make choices which will make you better able to make choices."[50] The cultivation of these habits has a real effect on the character of the individual, yet it is important to note even here that such activities are not done completely apart from God. God still remains the first cause of all human

---

49. Charles Robert Pinches, "Human Action and the Meaning of Morality: A Critique of Jean Porter on Action and Aquinas," *Pro Ecclesia* 12, no. 2 (2003): 143. Pinches's description of moral action is meant to challenge a portion of Jean Porter's work, which Pinches sees as attempting to block off certain deliberate actions as moral from those that are morally neutral. This leads to an incessant debate over what constitutes moral action and interminable attempts to break down actions into constituent parts in order to demarcate the moral from the amoral. What Aquinas offers is instead a simplified account of moral action, since it is all action that is deliberate. This places the emphasis then on describing individual actions (rather than action in general) and attempting to understand how such actions accord with the good. I think Pinches is right in his assessment of Aquinas here, and his argument is strengthened when one takes into account Aquinas's assertion of the necessity of the exercise of prudence for the development of all of the virtues. Prudence seems to have a near ubiquitous role in Aquinas's moral theology, which indicates the need for its exercise in all human activity in order for such activity to be properly moral.

50. Herbert McCabe, *The Good Life: Ethics and the Pursuit of Happiness* (London: Bloomsbury, 2005), 29.

activity, since God is the source of both the existence of humanity and the one who creates the ability to choose in the first place.[51]

In Aquinas there is a hierarchy of the virtues, beginning with the individual virtues that control and direct the passions (temperance and fortitude), followed by the way in which one acts toward the benefit of others (justice). Prudence is the pinnacle of the cardinal virtues: it involves the integration of these lower virtues into an act of discernment regarding proper action.[52] These cardinal virtues, however, are not enough for lasting peace, which ultimately comes through the principle theological virtue of charity. Charity is the greatest virtue, as it unites us to God and aligns and encompasses (but does not abrogate) the other virtues.[53] Jean Porter sees this system as addressing both the complexities of the individual and the relationship between the individual and the community since, for Aquinas, both the common good and the individual good are mutually interdependent.[54]

The necessity of divine grace for the perfection of *all* of the virtues is key to understanding how Aquinas can speak of the development of habits by human beings that promote virtue while also insisting that their final end cannot be obtained by such efforts. On the one hand, human beings have in their nature the aptitude of certain virtues: "Accordingly, one man has a natural aptitude for scientific knowledge, another for fortitude, another for temperance. And it is in these ways that both the intellectual virtues and the moral virtues exist in us by nature because of a certain initial aptitude."[55] While human beings can work to cultivate virtues, none can be perfected without the infusion of grace that is a supernatural gift of God. The cardinal virtues of temperance, fortitude, justice, and prudence can only be perfected

---

51. This is made explicit in Aquinas's account of free choice in *Summa Theologiae*, I, q. 83, art. 1: "Free choice is a cause of its own movement in the sense that through free choice a man moves himself to act. However, freedom does not require that what is free should be the first cause of itself—just as, in order for something to be a cause of another, it is not required that it be the first cause of that thing. Therefore, God is the first cause and moves both natural causes and voluntary causes. And just as, in the case of natural causes, He does not, by moving them, deprive their acts of being natural, so too He does not, by moving voluntary causes, deprive their actions of being voluntary, but instead He brings this very thing about in them."

52. Porter, *The Recovery*, 155.

53. Porter, *The Recovery*, 170–71.

54. Porter, *The Recovery*, 124–25.

55. Aquinas, *Summa Theologiae*, I, q. 2, art. 63.

by those who receive the Holy Spirit. The cardinal virtues are thus, for the justified, infused virtues.[56]

To further understand this relationship, it is helpful to understand the relationship between nature and grace in Aquinas's thought. For Aquinas, nature and grace are not opposites to be held in dialectical tension. Instead, human beings are ordered by their very nature toward a supernatural end, the beatific vision, that can only be obtained through God's grace. According to Hans Urs von Balthasar, Aquinas's views on nature and grace are in accordance with that of the church fathers in the insistence that there is "one, indivisible world order, which nature and grace together form a unity: nature exists for the sake of grace and is ordered to it, having its ultimate finality in it ... the nature of created spirit is directed beyond itself."[57] This relationship between nature and grace is vital for understanding how human beings can both grow and develop their created potential while maintaining their reliance on God's grace as the source of their existence and the necessity of God's grace to bring individuals to the supernatural end for which they were created. As this applies to the infused virtues, those who are filled with the Holy Spirit do not possess separate natural and supernatural virtues, but rather one virtue that is a unity of nature and grace. Josef Pieper enunciates Aquinas's notion of prudence in this way: infused prudence does not mean

---

56. Jean Porter, "The Subversion of Virtue: Acquired and Infused Virtues in the *Summa Theologiae*," *The Annual of the Society of Christian Ethics* (1992): 41. This is another example of how Aristotle's theory of virtue remains helpful for providing "categories of thought derived from human reason" to aid in the reception and appropriation of divine revelation.

57. Balthasar, *Theology of Barth*, 268. Balthasar here quotes Aquinas: "The beatific vision and knowledge are to some extent above the nature of the rational soul, inasmuch as it cannot reach it of its own strength; but in another way it is in accordance with its nature, inasmuch as it is capable of it by nature, having been made to the likeness of God, as stated above. But the uncreated knowledge is in every way above the nature of the human soul." Aquinas, *Summa Theologiae*, III, q. 9, art. 2 (see "Question 9. Christ's knowledge in general," New Advent, https://www.newadvent.org/summa/4009.htm#article2). A recovery of Aquinas here remedies the unhelpful split between nature and grace that characterizes a certain strain of Barth's thought, as well as the thought of those adherents of mission as the *missio Dei*. For Aquinas, nature is not static, but dynamic—all creatures are created with the ability to grow and move toward their created ends, but such ends necessarily require things outside of themselves. A sparrow, for instance, is created to fly, but this natural goal requires air and gravity to accomplish. Human beings are unique in that their created, natural ends are in fact supernatural: human beings have as their created goal the vision and worship of God. Because this end is supernatural, human beings require the grace of the Holy Spirit to obtain it, in the same way that a sparrow needs air and gravity in order to fly. This allows a way of speaking of salvation in terms that affirm the inherit natural goodness of creation while acknowledging the inability for human beings to obtain salvation apart from an outpouring of God's grace.

"a pre-eminence of natural and 'acquired' prudence over supernatural and 'infused' prudence; rather, he means the pre-eminence of that 'fuller' prudence in which the natural and the supernatural, the acquired and the given, are combined in a felicitous, in a literally 'graced' unity."[58]

The notion that virtue may be acquired through natural habituation yet perfected only through supernatural infusion is vitally important for affirming the real exercise of agency by individuals while maintaining their reliance and dependence on God.[59] This safeguards against any notion that human achievement can be grounds for salvation and perfection: "God's saving agency directly issues in a new created habitus: an infused created habit sufficient for further increases in the gifts of God's grace heads off the idea that God's power becomes the creature's own, and makes clear that human free will unrevised by grace is not a principle factor in God's salvation of us."[60] Aquinas asserts a supernatural telos while affirming that such a supernatural end is at least partially advanced through participation in the material world. The insistence on the cultivation of virtue to further one toward their goal of the divine vision prevents Christians from falling into a kind of overly contemplative retreat from the material world.[61] His insistence on the need for God's grace to infuse such labors prevents the church from falling into Pelagianism.

---

58. Josef Pieper, *Prudence* (London: Faber and Faber, 1960), 31.

59. Jennifer Herdt draws the connection between Aquinas's conception of virtue and the assertion of the non-competitive workings of divine agency. She concludes her assessment of Aquinas's theory of virtue by stating that "there is no competition between divine and human agency here, such that if human beings are moved by God they must themselves be passive. At the same time, human agency is fulfilled not through independence or self-sufficiency but instead by being willingly dependent, fully open to God's gift, thus perfecting the charity that unites human beings with God." Jennifer A. Herdt, *Putting on Virtue: The Legacy of the Splendid Vices* (Chicago: The University of Chicago Press, 2012), 91.

60. Tanner, *God and Creation*, 118.

61. We see this in Aquinas's distinction between virtues and gifts of the Spirit. Both move the person toward their end and spur movement and participation in the material world, yet only through the exterior gift of the Spirit can one achieve their supernatural end: "Now inspiration denotes motion from without. For it must be noted that in man there is a twofold principle of movement, one within him, viz. the reason; the other extrinsic to him, viz. God." Aquinas, *Summa Theologiae*, I–II, q. 68, art. 1.

Mission and Virtue

The previous sections laid a theological foundation on which to build an account of mission. Now it is imperative to begin to situate mission within this foundation, as well as to show why doing so best addresses the stated goals of this project.

First, Aquinas's moral theology provides a grammar to speak of the exercise of human agency in a way that gives it real value while also delineating it from the exercise of divine agency. Chapter one highlighted the problems in missiology resulting from a collapse of the distinctions between human and divine agency. This loss of distinct language rendered the relationship between human beings and God as competitive and contrastive, with human beings either competing with God or ceding their agency to God. The result is a kind of missional occasionalism, where the activities of the missionary are simply the occasion for God to show up in history.

Casting mission in the key of Aquinas's moral theory restores a proper distinction between God and creation, one that affirms real relationships within the Triune God and an asymmetrical and loving relationship between God and creation. To speak of the relationships within God's self is thus, for human beings, to speak analogously. To speak then of the mission of God and the missionary activities of human beings is to speak of actions that are similar yet different.

We see this at work in Aquinas's definition of mission itself, where he describes how the term "mission" can denote two different types of sending:

> The concept mission implies that the one who is sent either (a) begins to exist where he previously did not exist, as happens with created things, or (b) begins to exist, but in a new mode, where he previously existed—and it is in this latter sense that missions are attributed to the divine persons.[62]

Mission, for Aquinas, relates to sending, and the preeminent act of sending is that which occurs within the Trinity. The Father sends the Son, and the Father and Son send the Holy Spirit. To be sent is to bear the authority of the one who sends and entails "exclusive origin and close intimacy."[63] This

---

62. Aquinas, *Summa Theologiae*, I, q. 43, art. 6.
63. Emery, *The Trinity*, 25.

sending which occurs within the Trinity is unique in that it involves a sending of God to where God already exists.[64] Aquinas draws here on Augustine's explanation of Old Testament missions—the Son and the Spirit are sent to the Old Testament patriarchs, and yet, with the sending of the Son in the incarnation, God exists in a new way where he previous has existed.[65] This distinction is crucial for understanding how God works in new ways while still being the same God; to mistake God's missions as the sending of God to places where God did not previously exist is to fall into Arianism.

For human beings, the sending of the Son and the Holy Spirit reveals the identity of God as Father, Son, and Holy Spirit, and it provides the way through which they may enter into the divine life of God through the life, death, and resurrection of Jesus Christ. We may call this, at least from a human perspective, the purpose of the Trinitarian missions: the revelation of God as Triune and the salvation of humankind.

The mission of the church is an extension of the Trinitarian missions,[66] and it is Aquinas's detailed account of the relationships between God, creation, and agency that helps parse the similarities and differences between the church's mission and Trinitarian missions. First, *as the Father sends the Son and the Holy Spirit, the Son sends the church*. The church is sent by God the Son on mission, and thus it is given the authority of Jesus as the one who sends it. As the sending of the Son and the Holy Spirit both reveal God as Trinitarian and enable salvation, the church likewise is sent to testify to this revelation and gather those who receive this salvific message. We see this displayed most vividly in the last Farewell Discourse in John 17. Here, Jesus reveals himself as the one sent by the Father and as being one with the Father ("All mine are yours, and yours are mine," John 17:10), and he in turn sends the disciples to reveal this truth to the world: "Sanctify them in the truth; your word is truth. As you have sent me into the world, so I have sent them

---

64. Augustine highlights the ability of the Father to send the Son in a way that nevertheless maintains their unity and equality: "If however the reason why the Son is said to have been sent by the Father is simply that the one is the Father and the other the Son, then there is nothing at all to stop us believing that the Son is equal to the Father and consubstantial and co-eternal, and yet the that Son is sent by the Father. Not because one is greater and the other less, but because one is the Father and the other the Son." Augustine, *The Trinity*, trans. Edmund Hill (Hyde Park, NY: New City Press, 1991), 179.

65. Augustine, *The Trinity*, 182–83.

66. Emery, *The Trinity*, 26.

into the world. And for their sakes I sanctify myself, so that they also may be sanctified in truth" (John 17:17–19).

Second, *as the Father, Son, and Holy Spirit are one, the church is called to reflect this unity.* The sending of the disciples is linked as well to their unity, just as the sending of the Son reveals the essential unity of the Father and the Son: "I ask not only on behalf of these, but also on behalf of those who will believe in me through their word, that they may all be one. As you, Father, are in me and I am in you, may they also be in us, so that the world may believe that you have sent me" (John 17:20–21). So, in addition to being sent to preach, the disciples are also commissioned to remain as one, and such unity must be visible to the world.[67] Hence, the gathering of Christians becomes an essential task of the church's mission, as such gatherings become visible signs of the unity of the church, and, hence, the unity of the Father, Son, and Holy Spirit. According to Raymond Brown, the Farewell Discourses of John reveal an interrelationship between sending and unity: Jesus is revealing "at least one christological dogma, namely, the relationship of the Son to the Father,"[68] and belief in this unity of Son and Father is made known through those sent to proclaim the gospel.[69] As will be demonstrated, these two marks of mission (sending and unity) correspond to my conception of mission as proclamation and gathering.

While the mission of the church is integrally related to the sending of the Son and the Holy Spirit, it is not identical to it. Human beings are sent on mission in a way that is analogous to the mission of God. God moves to where God already exists; human beings can only be sent to where they have not existed. The reintegration of the distinctions between human and divine mission is vital to understanding what is being described when one is discussing mission. We can speak of the discreet actions of missionaries, of proclaiming the gospel and starting churches, while also acknowledging that God can and does work both through these actions and above and beyond these actions.

---

67. Raymond E. Brown, *The Gospel according to John*, vol. 29-29A (Garden City, NY: Doubleday, 1966), 776. Augustine makes a similar point in regard to John 17:22: "Just as Father and Son are one not only by equality of substance but also by identity of will, so these men, for whom the Son is mediator with God, might be one not only by being of the same nature, but also by being bound in the fellowship of the same love." Augustine, *The Trinity*, 166.

68. Brown, *John*, 29-29A: 774.

69. Brown, *John*, 29-29A: 774.

Human beings cooperate, rather than compete, with God in their mission activities. Since God is the donating source of all being, and because God is not in space or time, God can work through human beings without displacing or being composite with them. Human beings are free to act, knowing that their actions truly matter while also affirming that all good that is accomplished through their endeavors is at the same time attributable to God as the source of all being and all that is good. Human beings are in control of their deliberation and their actions, yet the source of their deliberation is ultimately God.[70] Aquinas gives an example of a soldier being moved to seek victory by the motions of the leader and the flag bearer. The soldier both decides to step forward in battle while also being caused to move by the actions of the leader. For those who engage in proclamation and gathering, we can say that they freely engage in these practices while acknowledging that the source of these missional movements is from God.

Situating mission within Aquinas's understanding of God, creation, and agency helps to parse the differences and relationships between the missional activity of God and missional actions of human beings. From here, we can situate mission within Aquinas's description of the ultimate end of human beings and their growth toward that end in order to better understand the purpose behind the performance of these human actions and specify the ways in which such actions should be conducted.

Aquinas states that human beings can move toward their natural and supernatural end through engaging in specific activities that promote virtues. While complete happiness can only be found in the beatific vision of God, and such a vision is ultimately possible only through an act of divine grace, human beings nevertheless can participate in God's goodness through the development of virtues toward their final end. Thus, what is required is a life that "calls for deliberate activity guided by knowledge of what is truly

---

70. "A man is the master of his own acts, of both his willing and his not willing, because of reason's deliberation, which can be turned toward one part [of a contradiction] or the other. But if he is likewise the master of whether or not he deliberates, this must be because of a previous deliberation. And since there is no infinite regress here, one must in the end arrive at the point at which the man's free choice is moved by some exterior principle that lies beyond the human mind, viz., God." Aquinas, *Summa Theologiae*, I–II, q. 109, art. 2.

good for human beings."[71] The acts of mission, the act of bearing witness to the resurrected Christ, the act of gathering Christians for worship of God the Father, Son, and Holy Spirit, are just such deliberate activities. In performing such activities well, human beings actualize their potential and move toward their goal of partaking in the glory of God.

Setting the goal of mission activity as the glory of God remedies the major issues in both the mission as growth and mission as dialogue models. One of the problems in these approaches is that their goals are partially dependent on the reaction of their audiences. Chapter three examined how the centering of mission on dialogue fails to adequately account for the multitude of persuasive speeches in the book of Acts, nor does it account for the ways in which the activities of the apostles offended the sensibilities of their interlocutors. The temptation in the mission as dialogue model is thus to modify the Christian message with the aim of being inoffensive, in the process adapting the gospel in ways that no longer accord with Scripture.

On the other hand, if the goals of mission are tethered to specific numerical outcomes, then there will always be an element of successful mission that is dependent on the decisions of others. As noted in chapter two, human beings cannot completely control their environment and cannot master other human beings. For this reason, even the best gospel proclamations and the most skilled church plants may in the end fail to achieve numerical success because individuals decide not to respond.

If the goal of mission is, however, the glory of God, it places limits on the extent to which the content of its activity can be adapted. Aquinas notes, for instance, that there are certain times and places that obligate a Christian to publicly confess their faith, in particular when "honor is due to God."[72] This would include times in which such confessions may be deemed offensive by one's audience, as well as times in which such a confession may not lead to numerical success. However, the benefit of such a goal is that its attainment is not dependent on the capricious responses of others. *One can glorify God simply in the activity of mission itself.*

Furthermore, interpreting the goal of mission as the glory of God helps to address the problematic aspect of agency in regard to the recipients of these

---

71. Porter, *The Recovery*, 72.

72. Aquinas, *Summa Theologiae*, II–II, q. 1, art. 2

missional activities. Chapter two focused on the ways in which missionaries attempt to manipulate their audiences by presuming to predict the responses of individuals with objective scrutiny. The only individual reasons that one may give for accepting or rejecting the Christian faith are those reasons that can be described in such a way so as to be controlled by the missionary in order to maximize numerical growth and efficiency. Placing the glory of God as the telos of mission places the burden of mission activity on honoring God, rendering all attempts at manipulation, no matter how successful, as off limits, thus affirming the agency of recipients to accept or reject their message. This issue will be taken up further below with MacIntyre's understanding of internal goods and virtuous practices, as well as in the ensuing chapter on proclamation.

To state that the goal of mission is the glory of God, and that mission is not dependent on the response of others for its successful performance, would seem on the surface to render the quality of such performances immaterial. However, placing mission within Aquinas's moral theology implies both that such activities can be performed well, and that such activities have the real ability to promote virtue in the individual. For Aquinas, all deliberate action is moral action. Every deliberate action taken is an opportunity to act in accordance with what is good and, hence, is an opportunity to grow toward our ultimate end. Put simply, placing mission within this context asserts that all missional activities are intrinsically moral activities. There is not a bifurcation between the moral, "spiritual" activities and the amoral, "practical" activities.

This imbues all activity with a greater importance—it is not just the big decisions that matter, and it is not just the ethical dilemmas that require moral enquiry. To adopt the glory of God, rather than growth, as the telos of mission means that one cannot be inattentive to the day-to-day details of ministry. As Jonathan Edwards puts it, to have the glory of God as one's end is not to abandon our activities, but instead to use all members of our bodies in activity that glorifies God.[73] Events still need to be planned, Bible studies scheduled, relationships developed. And for these activities, the cardinal virtues need to be honed. To be on mission means that one has to

---

73. Jonathan Edwards, *The Works of Jonathan Edwards*, vol. 8, *Ethical Writings*, ed. Paul Ramsey (New Haven: Yale University Press, 1989), 480–81.

make choices—who to speak to, how to run a Bible study, when to gather for worship—and the development of virtue aids in this basic decision-making ability. These seemingly mundane decisions that a missionary makes each day are not irrelevant or amoral, but instead afford the missionary the possibility of honoring God, developing virtue, and growing toward their final end of partaking in God's glory. The last section of this chapter will expand on this by showing how the engagement in mission can promote the specific virtues of temperance, prudence, and faith.

Aquinas asserts that all deliberate activity is moral, granting a degree of importance to the smaller day-to-day decisions of one's life. However, a potential problem exists with this affirmation, as this could seem to imply that there is no real difference between small actions and more complex ones. If this were the case, it could encourage a kind of punctilious existence—life becomes simply a string of small, unconnected events that afford opportunities for good decision-making. This is not, however, what Aquinas means by stating that all human action is moral action. He does, for instance, state that there are certain activities that require less deliberation than others, such as actions that require a relatively fixed means and end in order to be accomplished.[74] It follows from this that prudence, that virtue of good deliberation, would be more greatly developed through engagement in more complex activities. Aquinas, however, does not spend much more time developing this train of thought. This leaves my conception of mission somewhat incomplete—what is needed is a description of the complex activities involved in mission and a discussion of why it is important and helpful that such activities be performed well.

VIRTUOUS PRACTICES

The previous section sought to situate mission within the broader context of Thomas Aquinas's moral theology. However, several questions remain: What are the specific missional activities that promote virtue? How does the performance of such activities develop virtue? How does one get better

---

74. Aquinas, *Summa Theologiae*, I–II, q. 14, art. 4. Charles Pinches summarizes Aquinas's view as follows: "As his logic goes, there are some individual acts of which, while necessarily either good or bad, it makes little sense to inquire or deliberate about their goodness or badness." Pinches, "Human Action," 154.

at these missional activities? What specific virtues are developed through their performance?

It is thus imperative to flesh out my conception of mission, examining with greater specificity the types of activities that constitute mission and how the engagement in such activities holds the potential to glorify God and promote virtue. To do this, we turn to a notion of mission as virtuous practice.

Alasdair MacIntyre's Definition of a Virtuous Practice

Aquinas's moral theology does a great deal in articulating the distinctiveness of God and creation, of clarifying the supernatural end of human life, and of understanding the role of actions in developing virtue. However, there remains large terrain to still be covered. We have the ends clarified and the path to virtue for human beings spelled out, but what remains to be explored is the type of activities in which human beings engage that further this growth, as well as the ways in which individuals may draw connections between these activities to form a coherent understanding of their life as a whole. Virtue is developed through habitual actions, which prompts a desire to clarify the kinds of activities that promote flourishing and the ways in which such activities are performed well. Alasdair MacIntyre's conception of a virtuous practice, and the connection between the engagement in such practices and the life well lived, provide the tools for sufficiently addressing such concerns.

MacIntyre develops his notion of a virtuous practice first in *After Virtue* and further develops the concept through his ensuing works *Three Rival Versions* and *Ethics in the Conflict of Modernity*. In *After Virtue*, MacIntyre describes a practice as:

> Any coherent and complex form of socially established cooperative human activity through which goods internal to that form of activity are realized in the course of trying to achieve those standards of excellence which are appropriate to, and partially definite of, that form of activity.[75]

---

75. MacIntyre, *After Virtue*, 187.

For MacIntyre, a practice is a cooperative activity which contains goods that can only be realized through the performance of that activity. There are several salient features of MacIntyre's definition.

First, a practice is both *complex* and *coherent*. These two adjectives form a kind of loose boundary for what denotes a practice and what doesn't. Defining a practice as complex means that it is something that cannot be easily mastered. Landscaping could be considered a practice, but perhaps not mowing the lawn. Chess a practice, but not Candyland.[76] Coherence, on the other hand, ensures that one can define a practice as a discernable and unique activity with a beginning point and endpoint. As stated above, the aim in using the term "practice" is to help provide concrete and discernable ways of defining a particular activity so that one can in turn better define what makes a good or poor performance of such an activity.

Second, it has internally realized goods. In *After Virtue*, MacIntyre distinguishes between internal and external goods inherent in sustained activities. External goods are those that can be achieved through other activities, or goods that are attached to a practice through social circumstance. MacIntyre cites a few examples of external goods, such as prestige, status, and money, that can be acquired through numerous activities and are, in many cases, the product of external happenstance.[77] Internal goods, however, are unique to a particular practice, and they can only be "recognized by the experience of participating in the practice in question."[78] The discovery of the internal goods of such practices comes as one begins the process of learning such activities. As one learns to play chess, for instance, one also learns what is uniquely good about playing chess and how such good cannot be derived through other activities. In so doing, one learns to enjoy this practice "for its own sake."[79] As we will see, this distinction between internal and external goods will be particularly important in the development of specific missional practices since the goal is to define practices that cannot be performed through other avenues and are not determined wholly upon worldly success.

---

76. For a further examination of particular activities that constitute practices according to MacIntyre, see MacIntyre, *After Virtue*, 188.

77. MacIntyre, *After Virtue*, 188.

78. MacIntyre, *After Virtue*, 189.

79. McCabe, *The Good Life*, 54.

The development of excellences in such activities is twofold: First, one must be initiated into a process of life-long learning. One must have teachers who are able to impart the basic knowledge and skills of such practices, and the learner thus begins to discern with greater clarity how to apply such knowledge and skills in their particular circumstances.[80] This first step highlights the complexity of a practice—it is sufficiently complex as to require some kind of training. Added to this definition is that practices are non-repeatable. These activities are sufficiently complex that their ends cannot "be adequately specifiable by us in advance of and independently of our involvement in those activities through which we try to realize them."[81] What is required by the practitioner of these activities is the enactment of prudence, good judgment, to be exercised afresh in each situation in order to perform the activity well. At the heart of practices is that they are performative and, as such, are not merely a matter of copying what has been done in the past. To elaborate on MacIntyre's own example of chess, one begins the art of mastering chess by learning from other masters. While such a learning process may begin with learning to copy specific moves and countermoves, in order for the student to become a master, the student must go beyond copying to learning how to judge within specific games which moves are best. Or, for example, the process of becoming a master painter may begin with copying specific styles or works, but the goal of such learning is to enable new creative works. As we will see, such skilled performances are at the heart of mission activities: each instance of gospel dissemination is new since the recipients of the message are unique individuals.

The second major step in the development of a practice is the necessity of the learner to develop not only the skills and discernment necessary for a good performance, but also the ability to discern what is good and right in regard to their overarching telos. "The apprentice has to learn to distinguish between the kind of excellence which both others and he or she can expect of him or herself here and now and that ultimate excellence which furnishes

---

80. MacIntyre, *After Virtue*, 191.

81. Alasdair MacIntyre, *Ethics in the Conflicts of Modernity: An Essay on Desire, Practical Reasoning, and Narrative* (Cambridge: Cambridge University Press, 2016), 50. This performative aspect of practices is something that is only implicit in MacIntyre's definition in *After Virtue* but is made explicit in this most recent work.

both apprentices and master craftsmen with their telos."[82] Hence, the need to develop the virtues. The virtues both help the learner grow in their particular craft and help them discern how such crafts fit into the broader picture of the life lived well.[83] MacIntyre believes that the initiation into this process of developing a practice can lead the learner to develop virtue. This is perhaps the genius of MacIntyre's term—while practices possess unique, internal goods, the practitioner must develop and exercise the virtues (temperance, fortitude, etc.) in order to master such practices. These virtues become sedimented in the character of the individual, thus enabling them to exercise these virtues in the performance of other activities as well. Here MacIntyre is assuming, alongside Aquinas and the majority of ancient philosophers, the unity of the virtues.[84] The development of a particular virtue leads the individual to think not only of the place that virtue has in their life as a whole, but also how that virtue might be exercised in other situations.[85]

The development of virtue will thus lead to a discernment on the part of the individual as to how such practices fit within the broader context of the good life. This means also the discernment of when and where to engage in such activities as opposed to others. Competing responsibilities—to one's spouse, children, church—may require an individual to postpone the development of practices in one area of life for the sake of another area. In these cases, the life well lived is good yet tragic. The finitude of corporeal existence means that one often cannot achieve excellency in multiple areas of life. But such tragedy does not mean one has not lived a good or virtuous life. We call the devoted artist but terrible father a flawed individual—we call the talented artist who gives up his craft to care for their father a good yet tragic individual.

82. MacIntyre, *Three Rival Versions*, 62.

83. Julia Annas makes a similar point in regard to the intelligibility of actions. The mastering of particular practices in part requires the individual to articulate what they are doing and why. This articulation extends to the broader question of how such practices fit within a life lived well: "Your actions fit into structured patterns in your life; a snapshot of what you are doing at one time turns out to reveal, *when you think about these structures*, what your broader aims and goals in life are." Julia Annas, *Intelligent Virtue* (Oxford: Oxford University Press, 2013), 122.

84. For a fuller examination of ancient accounts of the unity of the virtues, see Annas, *The Morality*, 67–84.

85. Annas, *The Morality*, 75.

Missional Practices: Proclamation and Gathering

The remainder of this chapter will be devoted to developing an understanding of mission as constituted by two specific virtuous practices: proclamation and gathering. While the following chapters will further expound these terms, it is important to provide a brief definition before continuing. By "proclamation," I mean the persuasive communication of the Christian message and invitation to assent to the contents of this message. By "gathering," I mean the formation of a community of persons who have assented to this message. These two specific actions are chosen because they fit best with MacIntyre's notion of a practice and accord best with the particularities of mission as expressed in the New Testament.

How do the practices of proclamation and gathering fit with MacIntyre's notion of a practice? First, proclamation and gathering are both complex and coherent activities. Their coherence comes with their ability to be described as particular events taking place in time. A conversation in which a missionary speaks about the death and resurrection of Jesus Christ, persuading and inviting another person to receive this information and make a profession of faith, has a clear-cut beginning and endpoint. The gathering of individuals for public worship of God the Father, Son, and Holy Spirit also has a discernable beginning and end—from the opening prayer to the closing benediction. In addition, they are both complex activities. Proclamation of the gospel requires a degree of knowledge and understanding of the Christian faith, the ability to understand the particular beliefs of the interlocutor, and the ability to creatively present the faith in particular instances in a way that both remains faithful to the gospel message and accords with its intrinsic persuasiveness. The gathering of Christians into a new church congregation involves a similarly complex set of tasks—from catechizing new believers to helping them develop relationships with others in the community and enabling their gifts for the benefit of the community as a whole. Such activities require the creative application of specific skills. The complexity and coherence of such practices help to prevent mission from dissolving into ambiguity.

Proclamation and gathering contain unique internal goods that can only be obtained through their performance. These goods are the participation of the individual in the mission of God. In each faithful act of proclamation and gathering, the Holy Spirit enables the missionary to become "caught up" in the salvific mission of God. They participate in the sending action of God analogous to the sending of the Son and Spirt by the Father. Jesus's commissioning of the disciples in John 20 becomes axiomatic: "As the Father has sent me, so I send you" (John 20:21). It is through engagement in the practices of mission that one begins to understand the unique good of participation in the mission of God, learning to enjoy such activity for its own sake.

This assertion helps draw a distinction between my conception of mission as virtuous practices and a construal of mission based upon growth, since the goal of growth, numerical success, is an external good. Success can be achieved through a whole host of practices that have little or nothing to do with mission. Event planning, for instance, is another type of activity in which one may strive to obtain increase in attendance figures.[86] Furthermore, the drive for the obtainment of such external goods opens mission to the temptation of seeking methods and procedures to achieve success that compromise the activity itself. In contrast, mission as virtuous practice focuses on cultivating internal goods that enable one to grow in character and glorify God despite the fruits of their labors not yielding external numerical growth. For MacIntyre, the acquisition of internal goods requires the development of the virtues and that such virtues be "exercised without regards to consequences."[87] This is important, as the acquisition of external goods, such as worldly success, can be obtained through the subversion of virtue. The book of Acts shows how the disciples engage in proclamation as a kind of virtuous practice, obtaining the internal good of participation in God's mission through the exercise of such virtues as prudence and fortitude. These virtues are exercised even when it might entail a diminishment of external goods, for instance in persisting to proclaim the gospel even when such attempts have yielded little numerical success, or when such persistence threatens one's own life. Acts 5, for instance, depicts in an almost comical way how the apostles are arrested, told not to proclaim the gospel, and nevertheless continue to do so:

---

86. This is not to say that the obtainment of such external goods should not be welcomed. They are, in fact, *goods*. This will be noted in the next chapter as well: when large numbers of people assent to the gospel proclamation of a missionary, such conversion can certainly be celebrated. However, the setting of such external goods as the telos of mission leads to a host of issues, as has already been noted.

87. MacIntyre, *After Virtue*, 198.

And when they had called in the apostles, they had them flogged. Then they ordered them not to speak in the name of Jesus, and let them go. As they left the council, they rejoiced that they were considered worthy to suffer dishonor for the sake of the name. And every day in the temple and at home they did not cease to teach and proclaim Jesus as the Messiah. (Acts 5:40–42)

This illustration leads to a final point: that the codification of proclamation and gathering as missional practices best accords with the presentation of Christian mission in the Bible, particularly the book devoted to the mission of the disciples, the book of Acts. In his monograph *World Upside Down*, Kavin Rowe identifies three core practices performed by the disciples in the book of Acts: confession of Jesus as Lord, active mission to the end of the earth, and assembly of the "Christians."[88] These three practices correlate well to my construal of two core missional practices—mission is proclamation with the hope of confession of Jesus as Lord, and mission is the gathering of those who confess into Christian community. The mission of the church "to the ends of the earth" is done with these goals in mind. Furthermore, a key assertion from Rowe is that the other important actions performed by the church, such as economic redistribution, can be traced to these core practices.

---

88. Rowe, *World*, 6. Rowe's book remains a source of intense scholarly praise and debate. However, his characterization of the three core practices in Acts remains relatively unchallenged. A much broader critique of *World Upside Down* comes from the book's conception of Acts as a complete narrative. John Barclay claims that Rowe does not do justice to the unique situations of the various Christian communities which form the backdrop of much of Acts. John M. G. Barclay, "Pushing Back: Some Questions for Discussion," *Journal for the Study of the New Testament* 33, no. 3 (2011): 323.

Rowe states in response that Luke's omission of specific details about much of these communities in many ways proves that Luke's intention is to give a narrative account of the early church rather than a comprehensive sociological study: "On the one hand, the claim for a new culture would obviously benefit from local illustrations thereof. On the other hand, Acts itself does not seem so concerned to provide us with the information on which to speculate. At this point at least, my reading may simply reflect the narrative foreground more so than the modern concern to illumine the sociological gaps in the story's detail. But the point is nevertheless an important one." Christopher Kavin Rowe, "Reading World Upside Down: A Response to Matthew Sleeman and John Barclay," *Journal for the Study of the New Testament* 33, no. 3 (2011): 337.

These controversies aside, the list of core practices listed by Rowe are not too dissimilar from the lists of the core themes of Acts listed by other scholars, though such lists are complicated by the fact that many commentaries group the discussion of the core themes of Acts together with the Gospel of Luke. Luke Timothy Johnson lists several themes in Acts that he joins to a broader list of themes characteristic of Luke-Acts as a whole. These themes include the life of the church and universality of the apostle's mission to preach the gospel to the gentiles. Johnson, *Acts*, 15–17.

For Rowe, these practices constitute the narrative center of the book, and the removal of any of them would render it incoherent. While other activities in the life of the church are important, they can be bracketed without compromising the narrative structure of Acts as a whole: "One cannot conceive of an Acts-like narrative without mission. Nor can one conceive of Acts' narration of cultural disruption ... without the formation of concrete communities with noticeably different patterns of life."[89] Rowe's identification of core practices as essential to defining the overall narrative of Acts has parallels to MacIntyre's definition of virtuous practices as those that have internally realized goods. My assertion is that proclamation and gathering are the two essential missional practices because the removal of either renders mission (particularly as it is portrayed in Acts) incoherent.

This leads to an important, and perhaps controversial, conclusion: activities such as caring for the poor, economic redistribution, and other social works are not core missional practices. This is not to say that such activities are not essential to the life of the church, but simply that they are not *constitutive* of mission. To put it in MacIntyrean terms, such social works are externally realized goods: one can serve the poor and not be a Christian, but one cannot proclaim Christ's resurrection as good news without being a Christian. One can assemble a gathering of people—say, a nonprofit organization—with some particular social good in mind. However, the gathering of the church around the Eucharist table is a specifically Christian gathering. The missional practices of proclamation and gathering are exclusively Christian activities that cannot be performed outside of the Christian faith.

In addition, we see this distinction between core mission activities and the care for the poor played out in the book of Acts itself in the inauguration of the diaconate in Acts 6:1-6.

The establishment of the first deacons occurs because of the pressing needs of the local church, in this case for the feeding of widows, coupled with the desire for a division of labor so that the apostles might better focus on the missional task of preaching the word. There is no indication that such a division is hierarchical—it is simply part of the ordering of the church so that it may thrive both in the spreading of the gospel and in its service to

---

89. Rowe, *World*, 103.

those in need.[90] Here we see the demarcation of the specific vocations for proclaiming the gospel and serving the poor, yet this demarcation does not entail the exclusion of any Christians from engaging in either of these activities. This is one of the more intriguing parts of Acts 6: Stephen is set aside as the first deacon yet is quickly depicted proclaiming the gospel.

This matter will be addressed further in the next chapter. However, it should be stressed here that the soft division of labor in Acts 6 between those focused upon proclamation (apostles) and those focused upon the needs of widows (deacons) is done so that each of these activities could be *better* performed. The demarcating of such activities as discreet need not diminish the importance of either. The church should proclaim Christ and sacrifice as Christ did for the sake of the poor. Placing these activities under the one umbrella of mission only creates a false competition between such essential Christian practices.

As mentioned in chapter one, the subsuming of all activity under the *missio Dei* helped to create such a precarious position for the term "mission." "Mission" here becomes used as a label to stress the importance of an activity. My assertion here is that, by limiting the scope of the term "mission," "mission" does not have to be synonymous with "important." To state that proclaiming the gospel is an act of mission and feeding the hungry is an act of service need not spark an instantaneous and incessant debate over the relative importance of each to the life of the Christian and the life of the church.

My desire to limit mission to the practices of proclamation and gathering is in keeping with the desire to address the perpetual problem of definition with missiology. It is not to say that the various other practices of the church are unimportant, but rather that there is merit in examining the essential aspects of mission and how these activities can help shape a virtuous Christian existence.

---

90. Furthermore, this soft division of labor does not entail that proclamation and service to the poor are completely unrelated. Indeed, the proclamation of the gospel is good news to the poor and oppressed, and service to the poor does bear witness to Christ. Calling a practice distinct does not mean that it shares nothing in common with other practices.

MISSION AND THE DEVELOPMENT OF SPECIFIC VIRTUES

My conception of mission states that the practices of proclamation and gathering have the potential to develop virtue in missionaries, but, as of yet, the specific ways in which such missional practices might promote specific virtues has been understated. As Aquinas's moral theology in the *Summa Theologiae* moves from developing the relationship between ends, actions, and virtues in *Prima Secundae Partis* (I–II) to an examination of specific virtues in *Secunda Secundae Partis* (II–II), this chapter ends with a brief examination of how engagement in the missional practices of proclamation and gathering might promote the specific virtues of temperance, prudence, and faith. The choice of these three virtues is by no means meant to be exhaustive. Time, location, and the personal characteristics of the individual all may determine which virtues may be more or less needed in specific instances of the practice of mission. In this way, "The differentiated nature of the virtues reflects the differentiated character of the world and its events."[91]

Temperance

Temperance is the virtue by which the individual moderates their passions so as to desire what is truly best for themselves.[92] Temperance is not abstention from material things but rather the moderation of appetite whereby one orders their desires to conform with their specific good. For Aquinas, food, clothing, and sex are all goods that, when inordinately indulged, obscure one's desires for higher goods, most specifically the good of union with God. However, temperance is not simply a virtue regarding food, clothing, and sex, but is best seen as the ways in which one tames and directs all of one's passions so that their desires are properly ordered. This includes desires for leisure, travel, and hobbies.

There are a host of virtuous practices which promote temperance. The athlete must learn to check their appetite as part of their conditioning. The violinist must learn to deny their desires to watch TV and devote that time to the practicing of scales and arpeggios. The missional practices of proclamation and gathering also aim to promote the virtue of temperance through the development of similarly mundane disciplines. In order to proclaim the

91. O'Donovan, *Finding*, 95.
92. Porter, *The Recovery*, 166.

gospel well, one must engage in prayer, in the study of effective communication, in the devotion to understanding the gospel which they intend to
proclaim. Such exercises require time and energy and, hence, the need to
reign in inordinate desires for more frivolous pursuits.

While the virtue of fortitude is perhaps more needed for those missionaries who endeavor under the threat of persecution and martyrdom, the
virtue of temperance is particularly needed for those who pursue mission
in an age of comfort, security, and extravagance. The particular vice of the
modern West is that which Aquinas called curiosity (*curiositas*): the pursuit of knowledge and experience simply for their own sake, which keeps a
person from pursuing higher goods.[93] Similarly for Augustine, the pursuit
of knowledge is one that must be tempered, since the desire to know about
frivolous things can divert one from their pursuit of God. At its worst, such
pursuits can be a kind of lust of the mind's eye, "a cupidity which does not
take delight in carnal pleasure but in perceptions acquired through the flesh.
It is a vain inquisitiveness dignified with the title of knowledge and science."[94]
Gilbert Meilaender understands Augustine as indicating that such desires
are simply a "greedy longing for a new kind of experience."[95]

The danger for missionaries, as with the danger for those who wish to
excel in a host of other practices, is that of dissipation. The dissipated man
of Victorian literature, exemplified best by Jane Austen's Mr. Willoughby, is
the man who travels to London and expends copious amounts of time and
wealth on frivolous pursuits, winding up with very little. They become dis-
solved, hollow, and empty. C. S. Lewis calls this pursuit the desire for nothing:

> And Nothing is very strong: strong enough to steal away a man's best
> years not in sweet sins but in a dreary flickering of the mind over it
> knows not what and knows not why, in the gratification of curiosi-
> ties so feeble that the man is only half aware of them, in drumming

---

93. Aquinas, *Summa Theologiae*, II–II, q. 167, art. 1. Aquinas lists several ways in which the
pursuit of knowledge can be evil, including "when a man desires to know the truth about
creatures, without referring his knowledge to its due end, namely, the knowledge of God." (See
"Question 167. Curiosity," New Advent, https://www.newadvent.org/summa/3167.htm#article1.)

94. Augustine, *Confessions*, trans. Henry Chadwick (Oxford: Oxford University Press, 2008),
211.

95. Gilbert C. Meilaender, *The Theory and Practice of Virtue* (Notre Dame, IN: University of
Notre Dame Press, 1984), 139.

of fingers and kicking of heels, in whistling tunes that he does not like, or in the long, dim labyrinth of reveries that have not even lust or ambition to give them a relish, but which once chance association has started them, the creature is too weak and fuddled to shake off.[96]

The temptation to dissipation is only amplified through the internet, which creates what Bradford Littlejohn calls a "restless seeking." Such seeking is:

an increasingly pervasive feature of our increasingly digital lives. Hence the compulsive urges to open emails or web pages for no particular reason, to pursue long periods of mindless browsing, particularly of images, following link after link of "clickbait," as we now call it, even when we neither really expect nor really experience pleasure in the process are obvious enough.[97]

The danger of dissipation is no longer restricted, as it may have been in Austen's time, to wealthy nobility traveling to London, but is now open to seemingly anyone with access to the internet. Those missionaries who bemoan the difficulty of proclaiming Christ in the West are often quick to blame the so-called "secular culture" but are remiss in acknowledging the barriers which emerge not from external institutions but rather from their own internal desires. Here, the passionate flames of mission are tamed one frivolous click at a time.

Hence, those who wish to become experts at proclamation and gathering must first begin by moderating their desires. They must spend less time on lesser things—on television, video games, and social media—and devote more time to prayer and the study of Scripture. In so doing they begin to grow—from people of incontinence to continence, from continence to temperance.

---

96. C. S. Lewis, *The Screwtape Letters with Screwtape Proposes a Toast* (New York: HarperOne, 2015), 60. Quoted in W. Bradford Littlejohn, "Addicted to Novelty: The Vice of Curiosity in a Digital Age," *Journal of the Society of Christian Ethics* 37, no. 1 (2017): 180.

97. Littlejohn, "Addicted to Novelty," 190.

Prudence

Prudence is the "application of right reason to an act."[98] It is the virtue by which one decides how to act in a specific situation. For Aquinas, prudence is both an intellectual and moral virtue—intellectual in that it requires proper deliberation of the specific situation, and moral in that it ends with an action. The prudent person deliberates, makes judgments on their information, and finally commands an action that is in accordance with their ultimate good.

Prudence is the virtue required for the contingencies of life. Each life is unique and consists of various decisions that must take into account a whole host of contingent factors. The prudent person is one who has perfected the ability to make the right choices in any and all of these unique situations. This is one of the reasons why Aquinas considers prudence to be the most important of the cardinal virtues, since temperance, fortitude, and justice all require prudence for their proper exercise in new and unique situations. Prudence is thus required to instantiate the other virtues in particular situations.

For the Christian infused with the Holy Spirit, the ends to which prudence commands become the ultimate good of the glory of God. This is a crucial distinction to note, as prudence can be misconstrued as a utilitarian means to an end.[99] For the Christian, the end to which prudence commands is eschatological, and, as such, the goal of action is not simply the effects

---

98. Aquinas, *Summa Theologiae*, II–II, q. 47.

99. It is also important to note here that the exercise of prudence for the Christian does not entail an abandonment of Scripture or its sidelining in favor of consequentialist calculation. The insistence of divine revelation for Aquinas already speaks to this, as well as the fact that his discussion of the virtues includes various discussions on sins (such as theft and gossiping) in which Scripture is cited as the final authoritative word. To state that the goal of human life is the beatific vision does not mean that the laws in Scripture are abrogated by the exercise of prudence. Oliver O'Donovan makes the point that consequentialism, particularly in Christian forms that seek to subsume all ethics to a command of love, miss the essential interconnectedness of the laws in Scripture. Jesus's summation of the law as loving God and loving one's neighbor as yourself is just that: a summation. The sum "is not totaled without its constituent elements." O'Donovan, *Finding*, 200. This does not absolve the individual from discernment, since the unique situations in which they are presented require faithful deliberation as to how to love God and neighbor, given its elaboration in the various laws in Scripture, at this particular moment. This is nowhere more evident than in contemporary bioethics, where the seemingly straightforward commandment forbidding murder is complicated by various reproductive technologies. The virtue of prudence is thus necessary to make such discernments in accordance with the good of humankind. Hence O'Donovan remarks about the "interdependence of law, prudence, and the quest for wisdom" that permeates the Old Testament wisdom literature. O'Donovan, *Finding*, 197.

which it brings about in the world, but rather its effect on the character of the one who commands.[100]

Prudence is a virtue that is both required and honed through the missional practices of proclamation and gathering. As mentioned above, both of these practices are performative: each situation in which one proclaims the gospel is unique, as is each community that is gathered in response to this proclamation. Thus, what is required is first the acquisition of knowledge—the content of the gospel which is being proclaimed, the types of structures needed for a church to be gathered, etc. When presented with situations which require action, such information is then deliberated upon in prayer, a judgment is made, and an action is commanded. The contingencies of the missionary, their audience, and their specific place and time ensure that such decisions will need to be made anew in each given situation. Each moment in which the missionary is called to proclaim the Christian message thus becomes an opportunity to exercise prudence. The termination of such proclamative acts affords the opportunity for reflection upon such decisions as one discovers how they were (or were not) in accordance with the ultimate good of partaking in the glory of God.

The failure to exercise prudence in the practice of mission may manifest itself in a variety of maladies. First, there can be mission that is performed without a crucial component of prudence which Aquinas calls *docilitas*. Josef Pieper describes Aquinas's notion of *docilitas* as "a kind of open-mindedness which recognizes the true variety of things and situations to be experienced and does not cage itself in any presumption of deceptive knowledge."[101] It is the perfection of deliberation in the course of the exercise of prudence. One can characterize some of the issues with the mission as growth model as the lack of *docilitas*. Here, there is a type of direct correlation between knowledge and action that forgoes deliberation and judgment. One reads a book which gives the steps to church planting success, and one simply acts upon such prefabricated plans with the expectation of the achievement of the promised results. A lack of deliberation sets up the missionary for failure, since the contingencies of the moment necessarily require more than the simple enactment of a program, while also ensuring that the engagement

---

100. O'Donovan, *Finding*, 195.
101. Pieper, *Prudence*, 34.

in such activity will not lead to any growth in virtue on the part of the missionary. There should be no surprise then at the various recurring scandals surrounding popular North American pastors and church planters. If what it takes to build a large church is more a matter of technical efficiency than the development and exercise of prudence, then the character of the pastor is no more necessary to success than the character of a mechanic is necessary to the successful repair of a transmission. Such is the case when results are honored above rectitude.

There is another aspect of prudence that is necessary for the effective engagement in mission, and that is what Aquinas refers to as *solertia*. *Solertia*, often translated as "shrewdness," is for Aquinas the application of a quick wit to matters which require prudent action.[102] It is the ability to engage in swift decision making that is nevertheless prudent; it is the perfection of the command aspect of prudence. The virtuous practices of mission require deliberation and judgment upon specific actions, and such deliberation concludes in a command to act. Mission is not merely an intellectual or theoretical activity. Those who have *solertia* are able to quickly and appropriately make the right decisions to act in new and differing situations. Those lacking in *solertia* plunge into the vice of irresoluteness, with "deliberation and judgment tumbling uselessly into futility instead of pouring usefully into the finality of a decision."[103]

If the danger in the mission as growth model is thoughtlessness, or action without deliberation, the danger of the *missio Dei* model is irresoluteness, or deliberation without command. It is the treatment of mission as a mere theoretical activity, capable of criticizing the actions of missionaries but never itself terminating in missionary activity. The failure to see mission as a discrete activity enables and perhaps encourages endless discussion and critique but does not require action.

Faith

Averring that faith might be developed through the virtuous practices of proclamation and gathering requires first an insistence on the theological virtues of faith, hope, and charity as those which, following Aquinas, cannot

102. Aquinas, *Summa Theologiae*, II–II, q. 49, art. 4.
103. Pieper, *Prudence*, 29.

be obtained by human effort, but can only be acquired through a supernatural infusion of the Holy Spirit: "And so as regards the assent, which is the principal act of faith, faith is from God moving the man interiorly through grace."[104] For Aquinas, faith is a movement in the will of believers, but such a movement of the will is itself a movement of the Holy Spirit working within the individual: "The act of faith exists in the will of believers, but, as has been explained, a man's will has to be prepared by God through grace in order that it might be elevated to those things that lie above its nature."[105] This statement is in accord with Augustine's explanation of the movement of the will in the act of faith, whereas "the whole work belongs to God, who both makes the will of the man righteous, and thus prepares it for assistance, and assists it when it is prepared."[106]

Given that faith is a work of God in the human heart, how can it also be a virtue that can be nurtured? Aquinas makes a key distinction regarding exterior and interior causes of assent to the Christian faith. While we might be convinced in part by exterior persuasions—miracles, the arguments of others, for example—no exterior acts are *sufficient* to bring about faith. Instead, what is necessary is the interior assent to faith that can only come through the workings of God. However, these exterior acts are helpful for bringing about faith and, as Aquinas argues, sustaining and nurturing the faith of the believer. For Aquinas, confessing is the external act that is intrinsically related to the interior acts of faith:

> Now confessing what belongs to the Faith is by its species ordered, as to an end, toward what belongs to the Faith—this according to 2 Corinthians 4:13 ("Having the same spirit of faith, we have faith and, because of this, we speak"). For exterior speaking is ordered toward signifying what is conceived in the heart. Hence, just as the interior conceiving of what belongs to the Faith is properly an act of faith, so, too, the exterior confessing is likewise an act of faith.[107]

104. Aquinas, *Summa Theologiae*, II–II, q. 6, art. 1.

105. Aquinas, *Summa Theologiae*, II–II, q. 6, art. 1.

106. Augustine, *The Enchiridion on Faith, Hope and Love*, trans. J. B. Shaw (Washington, DC: Regnery Publishing, 1996), 40.

107. Aquinas, *Summa Theologiae*, II–II, q. 3, art. 1.

Confession is thus an act of faith, confirming and strengthening the work of God in the heart of the Christian. The principal act of confession is the confessing of what belongs to faith, which Christians do when they share their faith with others.[108]

The practice of proclamation is the preeminent exterior act of faith. It is at once persuasive speech meant to encourage assent to faith, as well as a confession of the very content of the faith. In confessing their faith, the missionary declares externally what they believe internally, strengthening that very belief.

The oft-used speech act example of a wedding is illustrative of this point. The married couple professes their love and commitment to each other, and the words of the ceremony bring about a change in the life of the couple. However, the ceremony itself is not the only instance in which love is professed in words. The thousands of "I love yous" exchanged over the course of the marriage are actions that do not bring about something new, but rather strengthen and nurture the initial bond forged in the marriage ceremony. The verbal confession of faith in the proclamation of the gospel is akin to these "I love yous" uttered throughout a marriage. Such confessions do not bring about new faith, but rather strengthen the initial assent of faith on the part of the missionary.

Alistair McFadyen's notion of sedimentation is helpful for understanding this process. For McFadyen, one's identity is developed in part through a history of communicative actions between others and God: "personal identity is a sedimentary history of response, that which endures through time."[109] Just as a farmer's body will adapt itself in accordance with its history of bodily movements—say, their hands will become calloused from physical labor—so the identity of individuals can be molded through a history of their communicative actions. The practice of proclamation, exercised over time, has just such an effect. In performing one's faith in a communicative action before others and God, one's identity is sedimented, molded by that very same faith.

---

108. Aquinas also lists two other exterior acts of faith: confession of thanksgiving or praise and confessing one's sins. While not the focus of this book, the practice of gathering can be said to develop the virtue of faith in that it provides the context through which both confession of the content of faith (in the creeds) and the confession of thanksgiving (in common worship) are instantiated.

109. Alistair I. McFadyen, *The Call to Personhood: A Christian Theory of the Individual in Social Relationships* (Cambridge: Cambridge University Press, 1990), 89.

GOALS (PARTIALLY) ADDRESSED

The beginning of this chapter set forth three goals regarding my conception of mission as virtuous practice: first, that it sufficiently addresses the problems of distinction, agency, and persuasion; second, that it fits with the New Testament depictions of mission; and, third, that it calls forth moral reflection on the performance of mission. At various points in the preceding sections I have indicated how my conception has met these goals. While not all of these issues are completely addressed in this chapter, this section will draw together and summarize the various ways in which these goals have been addressed so far.

First, situating mission within the broader framework of Aquinas's moral theology reestablishes traditional language concerning the transcendence and immanence of God and the distinctions between God and creation and human and divine agency. Since God is not defined within the horizon of creation, he is able to be "present and interior to things and yet beyond them,"[110] capable of working within human nature without violating human nature. This in turn enables the parsing out of the distinct ways in which human beings participate in mission and the ways in which their work is distinguished from and superseded by God.

Furthermore, the adoption of MacIntyre's concept of a virtuous practice also addresses the problems of distinction and agency. Practices involve discreet activities that can be identified and which can be performed with varying degrees of excellence. By conceiving of mission as virtuous practices, I am describing distinct activities which can be identified and which can be performed well or poorly. This coheres with the contribution of the mission as growth paradigm, which takes seriously the desire to improve upon the tasks of mission by identifying specific actions that are mission and attempting to discern the ways in which these actions might be better performed.

The second goal, the fitness of my conception of mission with the New Testament witness, is partially addressed through the demonstration of the ways in which human missions are related to, yet distinct from, the Trinitarian missions as depicted by Jesus in the Farewell Discourse of John 17. In addition, I have shown how the codification of proclamation and gathering as virtuous practices coheres with the essential activities of the apostles

---

110. Sokolowski, *The God of Faith*, 33.

in the book of Acts, and I have begun to show how the codification of these activities as virtuous practices might capture an intriguing aspect of Luke's portrayal of the apostles: that the superior performance of their mission work does not seem to be dependent upon the reactions of their audiences, but instead on their fidelity to the message which they are presenting. This will be taken up more fully in the ensuing chapter.

The last goal, moral reflection, is demonstrated through the situating of missional practices within Aquinas's moral theology and in the examination of the virtue of prudence. Mission involves deliberate activity and is thus, according to Aquinas, moral activity. All actions performed by missionaries carry the possibility of furthering them toward their goal of partaking in God's glory. Proclamation and gathering are practices which require the development of the virtues. The ultimate good of these practices are not the external ones of numerical increase, but the unique and internal good of delighting in participating in the mission of God and delighting in God's glory. This provides the opportunity for missionaries to reflect upon their actions, discerning whether virtues such as fortitude, temperance, or prudence might need to be further honed for the perfection of such actions, as well as assess whether these actions were performed for the glory of God or the glory of self.

CONCLUSION

This chapter has sought to show how a conception of mission as virtuous practice better addresses the perpetual problems in mission, encourages moral reflection, and accords with the conception of mission particularly evidenced in the book of Acts. These goals are only partially achieved, however, and a more complete picture is required. The reader will notice that the particular problem of persuasion is yet to be adequately assessed, and that more of the practical implications for this approach to mission need to be fleshed out. For this reason, it is imperative to give a more robust account of mission and virtue by examining in detail each of the specific practices of proclamation and gathering. As such, the remainder of this book will be devoted to unpacking the content and shape of these practices as well as showing how these practices fit into the broader context of the Christian life.

5

—

PROCLAMATION

The proclamation of the gospel is the preeminent missionary activity in the New Testament. Jesus's exhortation at the end of Mark, "Go into all the world and proclaim (*kērussō*) the good news to the whole creation" (Mark 16:15), echoed at the end of Matthew's Gospel, sets forth an imperative to go throughout the world and proclaim the resurrection of Christ. There is a connection between the sending of the disciples and the purpose of this sending, which is the act of proclamation. This connection is exemplified in the book of Acts with the linking of the apostles (those sent) with the vocational activity of preaching the word of God (Acts 6:2). Likewise, nearly all of Peter and Paul's activity in the book of Acts involves "proclamation" (*kērussō*) or a similar verb such as "preaching" (*euangelizō*, Acts 8:35; 11:20) or "testifying" (*martureō*, Acts 2:40).

That mission should involve some form of proclamation is relatively uncontroversial. Bevans and Schroeder's influential work *Constants in Context* asserts its preeminence in mission: "The explicit proclamation of the person and message of Jesus Christ, or at least the burning intention to do so, is what ultimately makes mission *mission*."[1] However, as seen in earlier chapters, the ways in which it should be conducted are highly contested. Rival conceptions of proclamation threaten to render the term indistinct, morally unreflective, or non-persuasive. The ensuing chapter will rehabilitate proclamation as a virtuous missional practice whose telos is the glory of God, in the process addressing many of the aforementioned critiques. In line with the previous chapter's discussion concerning virtue and mission, this conception has three key dimensions.

First, in keeping with Alasdair MacIntyre's conception of a virtuous practice, this construal of proclamation will be distinct, complex, coherent, and

---

1. Bevans and Schroeder, *Constants*, 358.

performative. It will be distinct enough that it can be defined as a discrete activity separate from other actions, coherent enough to function as a skill which one can improve upon, and complex enough to clarify that such skills cannot be easily mastered. Furthermore, it will be performative—the engagement in the activity of proclamation is non-repeatable, creatively performed anew by the missionary in each instantiation.

Second, as a virtuous practice, it will take seriously the ethical implications of such performances. Because proclamation is a distinct, complex, and coherent activity, the completion of individual performances of such activities enables the possibility for such performances to be evaluated by the missionary. Proclamation, like other practices, can be performed well or poorly, and the missionary is afforded the opportunity to reflect on previous performances in order to discern the good from the bad. In addition, the definition of proclamation as a practice that gives glory to God implies that there are moral as well as performative standards with which the missionary should evaluate their actions. The missionary reflects not just upon the ways in which their actions are in accordance with the mastery of some skill, but also whether their actions honor God and fit with the ways in which mission is performed in God's word. As Kevin Vanhoozer states, what is reflected on is whether such acts of proclamation are *faithful* performances.[2]

Relatedly, this development of proclamation will seek to fit with the ways in which such activities are carried out in Scripture, particularly in the book of Acts. As mentioned above, Luke describes in great detail the manifold ways in which the disciples proclaim the gospel in varying contexts. This chapter will attempt to construct a notion of proclamation that is in accord with such descriptions. In keeping with the previous chapter's discussion concerning Scripture, particular attention will be paid to the words and actions of the apostles as moral exemplars for missionaries. Peter, Paul, and Stephen are paragons of virtue who model the ways in which proclamation is beautifully performed and set examples for contemporary missionaries as to how they might faithfully proclaim the gospel in vastly different circumstances.

This chapter will proceed first by defining the penultimate goal of proclamation through an extended examination of Christian conversion. This section will draw heavily on John Henry Newman's conception of conversion

---

2. Vanhoozer, *Drama*, 183.

as a uniquely personal act of assent which is predicated upon an accumulation of "antecedent probabilities" and is thus essentially non-syllogistic. This
elaboration of conversion is meant to show how Christian proclamation can
be conceived of as an intentional act of persuasion that respects both the
desire of missionaries to persuade well and the ability of individuals to exert
their agency in accepting, rejecting, or modifying the missionary's message.

From there, it will proceed to examine the four interrelated activities that
together make up the discreet practice of proclamation, progressing linearly
beginning with prayer, to preparation and communication, and returning
to prayer after completion of the communicative act. The final part of this
chapter will demonstrate how this depiction of proclamation aligns with
MacInytre's notion of a virtuous practice and helps to meet the overall goals
of my conception of mission and virtue.

CONVERSION: THE PENULTIMATE
GOAL OF PROCLAMATION

Within MacIntyre's definition of a virtuous practice there is a distinction
between the activity performed and the unique goods internal to that activity: the unique, internal goods are achieved through a striving for excellence
while engaged in said activity. It is perhaps best to clarify this distinction by
speaking of penultimate and ultimate goals. The penultimate goal of a practice is what is typically achieved through the performance of such activity,
while the ultimate goal is the internal goods realized. For instance, the penultimate goal of chess is winning a single game of chess, while the ultimate
goal would be acquisition of the unique joys of being a master at chess.[3]

---

3. For MacIntyre, the success gained from winning a game of chess would be an example
of an external good, since one can experience the joys of winning through various other types
of competitions. My use of the language of penultimate and ultimate goals is meant to provide
greater clarity on the specific external goods that are aimed at in the process of engaging in a
practice. MacIntyre refers to a whole host of external goods that one could receive in various
practices, such as wealth, success, and prestige. Such a broad conception of external goods is
helpful for understanding the difference between such goods and the internal joys of activities,
but it does not further distinguish between the kind of external goods that are nevertheless
aimed at in the performance of a practice. For instance, one aims at winning when they play
a game of chess, though they may also receive other external goods such as wealth. Though
winning is an external good, it still shapes how the player goes about learning how to play chess
well. In terms of proclamation, one aims at conversion, though they may receive other external
goods in the process. This penultimate goal lends shape to how one learns how to proclaim the
gospel well, even if the ultimate goal is beyond it.

Before the missionary engages in the virtuous practice of proclamation, they must have some understanding of the penultimate goal of such activity, which is the conversion of their interlocutors to Christianity. While the ultimate goal of proclamation is partaking in the glory of God, the penultimate goal, that which is aimed at by the performance of proclamation, is the assent to Christianity from someone who was previously not a Christian. An understanding of conversion is imperative for addressing many of the issues raised in the examination of the various models of Christian mission, particularly the problem of persuasion. To understand the problem of persuasion, it is important to examine what happens when someone is persuaded.

NEWMAN: CONVERSION AS A UNIQUELY PERSONAL EVENT

We have already seen in chapter three how individuals exert agency in response to intentional acts of persuasion on the part of missionaries by either accepting, rejecting, or modifying the Christian message. The exercise of agency on the part of individuals in response to intentional acts of persuasion indicates the deeply personal nature of conversion. A key text for understanding what happens in such personal acts of conversion and the interplay between persuasion and agency in these acts is John Henry Newman's *An Essay in Aid of a Grammar of Assent*, which is both a systematic treatment of assent as well as an examination of the particular case of assent to Christian propositions in the act of conversion.[4]

In *Grammar of Assent*, Newman is trying to answer a seeming paradox: How does one come to give unconditional assent to propositions that are grounded in conditional propositions? How does one believe in something to be true even though it is based on claims that are fundamentally unprovable? Newman gives as an example the proposition "I shall die": such a proposition is intrinsically unprovable—it will only be proved true if we actually die.[5] In terms of mission, the question can be formulated thusly: How does one

---

4. For Newman, assent refers more broadly to mental acts of affirmation to propositions, and conversion refers to the particular case of assent to the propositions of revealed religion. John Henry Newman, *An Essay in Aid of a Grammar of Assent* (London: Oxford University Press, 1985), 13.

5. Newman, *Grammar*, 157. Newman's example is important for demonstrating the ubiquity with which people hold certain beliefs with certainty even though they are fundamentally unprovable.

come to confess a faith in Christ even though such beliefs cannot be proven for certain?

For Newman, one comes to assent to such propositions through an accumulation of "antecedent probabilities." We are convinced by a whole host of influences that, at some moment, bring us to a decision of belief. There are two key facets to Newman's approach. First, there are a profundity of such probabilities accumulated, and as such they are incapable of being quantifiable:

It is the cumulation of probabilities, independent of each other, arising out of the nature and circumstances of a particular case which is under review; probabilities too fine to avail separately, too subtle and circuitous to be convertible into syllogisms, too numerous and various for such conversion, even were they convertible.[6]

This is in line with the statement that persuasion is inevitable and pluriform. We are persuaded by a whole host of intentional and unintentional words and non-verbal communications, and such communicative acts are impossible to disentangle. In mission terms, the process through which one is converted is impossible to codify in simple, logical progressions or syllogisms. One may be persuaded through specific arguments, through the character of the missionary, through the actions of a Christian community, and through the beliefs of their friends and family.[7]

---

6. Newman, *Grammar*, 187.

7. The assertion that there exists a pluriform of avenues through which one may assent to belief in Christianity helps to mitigate the differences between those who construe such assent as coming either purely through rational discourse and those who see such assent as coming principally through rhetorical persuasion. The difference between these two positions is articulated most clearly by John Milbank's critique of Alasdair MacIntyre in his monograph *Theology and Social Theory*. When confronted with rival incommensurable traditions, MacIntyre sees the need for figures to emerge who will be able to successfully reason for the superiority of one tradition over the other in terms that are intelligible to adherents of that rival tradition and in ways that better address the internal issues within that rival tradition. MacIntyre's paradigmatic example is Aquinas, whose work was able to mitigate the differences between rival Augustinian and Aristotelean moral traditions yet do so in a way that better addressed the recurring issues within each of these traditions. MacIntyre thus advocates for a return of the contemporary university to a system that resembles Aquinas's University of Paris: one where rival traditions are able to both simultaneously advance their claims and continually engage in conflict with their rivals. See MacIntyre, *Three Rival Versions*, 230–32.

Milbank, on the other hand, believes that rational dialogue is ultimately insufficient in the face of rival traditions. For Milbank, "decisive shifts within traditions, or from one tradition to another, have to be interpreted as essentially 'rhetorical victories' " (347). The argument for

Related to this assertion is that the act of assent is deeply personal. The complex and intricate web of probabilities that influence a person are hyper contextual—the individual is uniquely convinced and thus exercises their agency in a unique act of assent:

> As a man's portrait differs from a sketch of him, in having, not merely a continuous outline, but all its details filled in, and shades and colours laid on and harmonized together, such is the multiform and intricate process of ratiocination, necessary for our reaching him as a concrete fact, compared with the rude operation of syllogistic treatment.[8]

That such conversions defy "syllogistic treatment" means that the process by which someone is converted cannot be broken down into replicable stages. For Newman, the actual moment of assent is unique, and although it comes through the accumulation of probabilities, that accumulation is not a linear progression: one does not advance from being 10 percent to 20

---

a particular tradition lies in the various stories, sermons, histories, saints, miracles, etc. that make up that tradition. What wins people over is the adoption of a new mythos, a new way of life that is appealing enough to evoke a rejection of their old tradition. For Milbank, this is crucially important for Christianity, which offers not a better rationality, but the adoption of a new mythos that is established through nonviolence. John Milbank, *Theology and Social Theory: Beyond Secular Reason* (Oxford: Blackwell, 2006), 376. This is also the position adopted by Stanley Hauerwas and Charles Pinches in their assessment of Milbank's critique of MacIntyre. They see MacIntyre as starting with the virtues and presenting a case for the rationality of Christianity. The flaw in such an approach is that aspects of an Aristotelian account of the virtues contradict Christianity. "We cannot ... as Christians, defend virtue first and Christianity later." Hauerwas and Pinches, *Christians*, 68.

The conception of conversion I am advocating here, one that relies heavily on Newman, would seem to give preference, to some extent, to Milbank's approach. However, Newman's assertion concerning the pluriform and complex ways in which one comes to assent does not entail that such assent cannot be brought about through rational discourse. Conversion is a unique and personal event, and the contribution of rational discourse to such conversions can range from the substantial to the insignificant.

It is also important to note, however, that MacIntyre's discussion concerning rival traditions is principally concerning rival philosophies, not rival religions. MacIntyre does not give an account of Christian conversion, so it is not entirely clear whether MacIntyre himself would disagree with my assessment of the role of rationality in conversions to Christianity. MacIntyre's assessment of the arbitration between rival traditions is helpful for understanding a way to approach rational discourse, and my use of MacIntyre in chapter four is meant to highlight how this can be helpful for critiquing various rival conceptions of mission. However, when it comes to the proclamation of the gospel, the limits of rational discourse must be acknowledged. An account of conversion in Scripture clearly indicates that rational discourse is but one of many avenues through which the gospel is persuasive. For every Areopagus speech there is a road to Damascus.

8. Newman, *Grammar*, 187.

percent converted. Instead, one is influenced in a whole host of ways up until the point in which they go from unbelief to belief.[9] One can think here of a dam bursting: while one cannot predict when and if the dam will burst, one can *post facto* examine the multitude of factors that contributed to the break. This is crucial, since if assent were a linear and hence predictable process, it could be susceptible to manipulation. This complements the afore-mentioned critiques of the mission as growth model—the means through which one assents to the Christian faith cannot be converted into a simple syllogistic process and are thus resistant to being manipulated: conversion is never as simple as the sharing of the four spiritual laws or the recitation of the sinner's prayer.

This also suggests that individual agency is exerted in the act of assent. It is not that any one argument is incontrovertibly persuasive for all people at all times in all places; it is that certain aspects are deemed persuasive for that individual. This is why, when asked to give an account of one's conversion, one gives a narrative. Such stories may involve accounts of certain arguments that they found persuasive, certain people who were influential, or certain actions on the part of Christian communities that were impactful.[10] The act of assent may acknowledge these exterior influences while affirming the personal nature of the act.

This also helps to mitigate the perpetual debate between event-oriented and process-oriented conceptions of conversion. Elizabeth Cochran describes the ways in which Luther, Calvin, and Edwards seemed to vacillate between emphasizing a radical event of conversion and a conversion that develops over time.[11] A way out of this impasse is to simply assert that the uniquely

---

9. This conception of conversion shares certain affinities with those of prominent Protestant thinkers, including Martin Luther, John Calvin, and Jonathan Edwards. Elizabeth Cochran describes how these thinkers share a conception of conversion as "an occurrence that radically transforms one's identity," and notes that such a dramatic shift, similar to Stoic accounts of virtue, defies "overly mechanistic or casual accounts of moral formation, so that one cannot strictly prescribe or predict conditions that will make someone virtuous." Elizabeth Agnew Cochran, *Protestant Virtue and Stoic Ethics* (London: Bloomsbury T&T Clark, 2018), 114–15. As will be discussed below, these Protestant thinkers differ, often within their own writings, over the extent to which such a dramatic shift can still be predicated on a host of other influences which precede such a shift.

10. It is important to note that the recitation of such conversion stories rarely involves a simple recitation of the Apostles' Creed. The creeds describe the content of the Christian faith, but the act of coming to profess this faith is not so easily codified.

11. Cochran, *Protestant Virtue*, 116–20.

personal aspect of conversion means that the trajectory of such conversions will vary based on both the person and that person's narrative rendering of their conversion. The Christian may reflect upon their conversion, discerning the point at which they went from unbelief to belief, yet the events leading up to this point may be either gradual or dramatic or both. For instance, one may grow up going to church while also having a dramatic conversion experience in their teenage years. Hindsight may demarcate a particular point in which allegiances shift while simultaneously acknowledging an indebtedness to the ways in which childhood experiences in church contributed to this shift. Cochran's description of the controversy over Luther's conversion is illustrative of this point. Luther's famous "tower experience" of conversion while reading Romans is posited by many scholars to be a retroactive condensing of various events by Luther "so that he is representing the date and precise details of this moment poetically."[12] The "tower experience" marks for Luther this decisive shift in belief, yet it may also mark the culmination of a large series of events which gradually prepared the way for such an event.

It may be added that the act of assent, being unique to the individual and typically enunciated narratively, may help to explain that phenomena that heretofore perplexes the missionary dialogist: the happy convert. The dialogist must view such cases as the products of exterior persuasion that are intrinsically coercive, and thus the convert is manipulated, or perhaps delusional. The individual convert, however, sees their conversion as an individual choice that is nevertheless influenced by a whole host of people, arguments, and observations. Here, the recipient receives the message as a gift which is received with great happiness,[13] with the convert expressing gratitude for the individuals who helped persuade them to make such a choice.[14]

---

12. Cochran, *Protestant Virtue*, 117. See also Alister E. McGrath, *Luther's Theology of the Cross: Martin Luther's Theological Breakthrough* (Oxford: Wiley-Blackwell, 2011), 98–99.

13. For Jean-Luc Marion, the reception of the gift as the free decision of the recipient is what makes the gift a gift: "The gift consists ultimately in the fact of self-decision, exactly as from the perspective of the giver." For one who proclaims the gospel, such proclamation may only be considered a gift by the one who assents. Others may ignore it or see such proclamation as offensive. The free decision to receive is what renders it a gift and not a nuisance. See Jean-Luc Marion, *The Visible and the Revealed* (New York: Fordham University Press, 2008), 92–93.

14. David Cunningham notes how the Greek term used for "faith," *pistis*, is also the word for "persuasion." The suggestion is that the confession of faith may have persuasive and rhetorical overtones: the statement "I believe" may be akin to "I have been persuaded." Cunningham, *Faithful*, 39.

CHRISTIAN CONVERSION, LOGIC AND EXCESS

In addition to being a unique personal event that is described narratively by the individual, assent specifically to the Christian faith exceeds such descriptions. This act of assent, though predicated in part on the arguments of the missionary, goes far beyond them. Such acts can be conceived of as what Jean-Luc Marion calls "saturated phenomena." They are experiences that flood the senses, making themselves so overabundantly present that they defy complete description: "To define the saturated phenomenon as incapable of being looked at amounts to envisioning the possibility of a phenomenon imposing itself with an excess of intuition that it could neither be reduced to conditions of experience, and thus to the *I* who sets them, nor thereby forego appearing."[15]

Such assents are so deeply complex and personal that to describe them through logical means is to merely scratch the surface of their meaning. The love between two people may be described logically and intelligibly, but never exhaustively. And so it is for the one who assents to Christ. As Newman puts it:

> And so of the great fundamental truths of religion, natural and revealed, and as regards the mass of religious men: these truths, doubtless, may be proved and defended by an array of invincible logical arguments, but such is not commonly the method in which those same logical arguments make their way into our minds. The grounds, on which we hold the divine origin of the Church, and the previous truths which are taught us by nature—the being of a God, and the immortality of the soul—are felt by most men to be recondite and impalpable, in proportion to their depth and reality. As we cannot see ourselves, so we cannot well see intellectual motives which are so intimately ours, and which spring up from the very constitution of our minds; and while we refuse to admit the notion that religion has not irrefragable arguments in its behalf, still the attempts to argue, on the part of an individual *hic et nunc*, will sometimes only confuse his apprehension of sacred objects, and subtracts from his devotion quite as much as it adds to his knowledge.[16]

---

15. Marion, *The Visible*, 43.
16. Newman, *Grammar*, 217.

The convert may point to the array of arguments proclaimed by the missionary as having a part to play in their conversion, but the description of the act itself far exceeds such arguments. Indeed, as Newman suggests, the convert may prefer *not* to attempt a deep analysis of their conversion, as such an act is an attempt to reduce the irreducible. What Newman is suggesting is that although Christian truth is defended with arguments that are logical, these logical arguments are rarely those that convince the unbeliever. Furthermore, Newman asserts that the pursuit of such logical arguments by believers is not necessary—some may be content with the wonder of belief.[17]

Amalgamating these strands of thought in Newman and Marion, we arrive at the conclusion that the process of conversion, though it may begin through a cumulation of probabilities, is not necessarily a logical process. Yet, the act of assent saturates our understanding. We may (if we are inclined) proceed to grasp the logical underpinnings of such belief, knowing that, while such endeavors may provide greater coherence, they will never exhaust the significance of belief.[18]

Likewise, the missionary gives arguments in favor of a relationship with God through Jesus Christ. They extol the virtues of such a life and give arguments in its favor and an invitation to encounter. If successful, the arguments may be described later by the convert as contributing to such a conversion, yet the relationship established with God will far exceed them.

THE ACT OF PROCLAMATION

With this penultimate goal of conversion in mind, the missionary partakes in the act of proclamation. This complex virtuous practice is composed of four discernible actions: it begins with prayer, proceeds through preparation

---

17. Newman's understanding of the logic of faith anticipates that of Paul Ricoeur, who remarks on the inherent incomprehensiveness of belief due to the hermeneutic circle: to express any belief requires language and, as such, is imbedded in preconceptions of thought and meaning. However, if one acknowledges these presuppositions, this may be a starting point through which belief may be explored, with the hope of both a greater depth and coherence of belief. For Ricoeur, one "wagers" a better understanding, which becomes itself "the task of verifying my wager and saturating it." Paul Ricœur, *The Symbolism of Evil*, trans. Emerson Buchanan (Boston, MA: Beacon Press, 1967), 355.

18. The Nicene Creed, for instance, can be seen as the development, post-belief, of a greater coherence of Christian thought regarding the Trinity and the nature of Christ. The creed, however, is not the starting point for Christian proclamation, nor does it exhaust its content. Indeed, it becomes the grounds for further exploration of the divine mysteries, as evidenced in so many of the Greek fathers. Perhaps not only *Lex Orandi, Lex Credendi*, but also *Lex Credendi, Lex Orandi*.

and communication, and ends with a return to prayer. Such actions are quasi-linear, highlighting a discernable progression in the process of proclaiming the gospel while acknowledging that, particularly in the case of prayer, such actions may be performed contiguously. What follows is an examination of each of these actions, highlighting particularly the ways in which these actions contribute to an understanding of proclamation as a virtuous practice, how such actions enable critical and moral reflection, and how these actions are exemplified in the book of Acts. It will conclude with a description of proclamation's ultimate goal, the partaking in the glory of God, followed by a summary of how this examination as a whole is in accord with the three key dimensions described in the beginning of this chapter.

PRAYER

Prayer is an integral part of the missionary actions of the disciples. It is in prayer that Luke portrays the reception of the Holy Spirit and the identification of the audience to which the gospel should be proclaimed. This is seen most vividly in Acts 4: "When they had prayed, the place in which they were gathered together was shaken; and they were all filled with the Holy Spirit and spoke the word of God with boldness" (Acts 4:31).[19] As such it can be seen as an integral part of the practice of proclamation—not simply a pre-evangelistic act, but something that inaugurates and undergirds the entirety of the act, perhaps akin to the way that running may be said to be a fundamental action within certain sports, such as soccer.

The emphasis on prayer as both the beginning of oration and undergirding the entire act of oration is a key distinction between classical rhetoric and Augustine's Christian rhetoric. What sets the Christian speaker apart is not that they strive to be people of good character (for that is a key component of Aristotle's rhetoric), nor even that they should be people who are humble (for Cicero acknowledges this), but instead that they should be people who pray. For it is in prayer that one receives the teaching they wish to proclaim and give their own assent to such teaching: "When he is going to preach, before he loosens his tongue to speak, he should lift up his thirsting soul to God, in order to give forth what he will drink in, and to pour out what he will

---

19. Cf. Acts 13:1–4; 16:11–34.

be filled with."[20] What follows is thus an examination of the key aspects of prayer in relation to proclamation, focusing on how it forms both the rhetor and his or her message.

Prayer as Persuasion

Prayer is dialogue with God. It is an event in which the individual acknowledges the presence of God and their dependence on him. We are born into a world of relationships and realize ourselves as individuals through our relational communications, whether those communications be material or verbal.[21] Preeminently, human beings are created in relationship to God and are given freedom to engage within this relationship in communication with God. As Alistair McFadyen states, "We live and breathe within the parameters set by the divine intention in communication of dialogue-partnership with God as a more or less distorted image of and response to God. We can refuse to enter into dialogue: we cannot, however, avoid being in relation with God."[22] This is echoed in Augustine's famous assertion that human beings cannot hide from God and, as a result, should turn to God and "make confession." In light of the ever presence of God, human beings should respond by engaging in speech before God.[23]

In prayer, one acknowledges their relation to God and accepts the invitation to dialogue with God. By accepting this invitation, they accede to the possibility of being changed by God as a result of these dialogical encounters. For the missionary, this means that, before they may begin to persuade others of the good news, they themselves must be persuaded by God: "Prayer is aligning oneself with God's purposes in the world; it is opening ourselves

---

20. Augustine, *On Christian Teaching*, trans. R. P. H. Green (New York: Oxford University Press, 2008), 105.

21. Louis-Marie Chauvet stresses this point in regard to language. Human beings are born into a symbolic world mediated by language. "Like the body, language is not an instrument but a *mediation*; it is in language that humans as subjects come to be. Humans do not preexist language; they are formed in its womb." Human beings encounter their world through communications—human beings speaking to other human beings. Louis-Marie Chauvet, *Symbol and Sacrament: A Sacramental Reinterpretation of Christian Existence* (Collegeville, MN: Liturgical Press, 1995), 87. Herbert McCabe makes a similar point by insisting that speech is not *ad extra* to human actions, but is intertwined in the meaning and significance of all human action: "Man does not just *add* speech on to such things as eating and sexual behavior; the fact that these latter occur in a linguistic context makes a difference to what they are." McCabe, *What Is Ethics?*, 68.

22. McFadyen, *The Call*, 22.

23. Augustine, *Confessions*, 73.

up so that God's will may be done in us and in God's creation."[24] The Christian rhetor must thus be a "petitioner before a speaker."[25] To be a petitioner is to acknowledge a need and to be open to change.

To enter into discourse is to open oneself up to the possibility of change. Lloyd Bitzer describes what he calls rhetorical situations, which are contexts of persons, places, and objects that invite utterance and the possibility of change from those involved in such utterances.[26] Thus, for Bitzer, "rhetoric is a mode of altering reality, not by direct application of energy to objects, but by the creation of discourse which changes reality through the mediation of thought and action."[27] The key advancement made by Augustine is to acknowledge that prayer itself is as much a rhetorical situation as the act of verbal communication intent upon convincing others of the gospel. Prayer can be considered the initiation of a rhetorical situation by the missionary, or rather it is the acknowledgment that God has *already* created this discourse situation. In prayer, one risks being changed through the mediation of thought with God.

This account of prayer as a starting point for proclamation has profound implications for the way in which the proclamation of the gospel with others will proceed. The practice of proclamation includes activity meant to acknowledge need and dependence. The missionary must begin as a learner, listening to God for the content of their proclamation and acknowledging the ways in which they are invited to assent anew to this content. Psalm 19 provides the most vivid example of how such prayers may take form: there is a declaration of the goodness of God's statutes, which give "light to the eyes" (19:8 NIV), followed by a supplication for the strength to keep such commands (19:11–12), and, last, a prayer that one's speech may be in line with what God has communicated: "Let the words of my mouth and the meditation of my heart be acceptable in your sight, O Lord, my strength and my redeemer" (19:14 NKJV).

This plea for the acceptability of one's speech shows how prayer may provide a check on the proclamations of the missionary. Before engaging in

---

24. Bevans and Schroeder, *Constants*, 367.

25. Augustine, *On Christian Teaching*, 105.

26. Lloyd F. Bitzer, "The Rhetorical Situation," *Philosophy & Rhetoric* 25 (1992): 5.

27. Bitzer, "The Rhetorical Situation," 4.

persuasion with others, one asks that the words that they are about to share are deemed acceptable to God. When one speaks to a potential convert, they are also speaking before God. While this may not guarantee that such speech avoids becoming manipulative, it does set forth a precedent that missionary speech should be morally aware—it is open to judgment by God.

Prayer and Ethos

A practice of proclamation that begins in prayer establishes itself as an act that begins with the conformity of the missionary to the message which they will communicate. An added benefit is that such conformity helps to establish character on the part of the missionary. If God's words are just and good, then the missionary who conforms to these words will, over time, conform to this goodness. This growth in character will lend a degree of gravity and authority to the words they proclaim to others.

For Aristotle, a person who seems to possess practical wisdom, virtue, and goodwill is "necessarily persuasive to the hearers."[28] Aristotle, however, believes that such character, or ethos, must be constructed by the speaker: it is the perception of character that is important, leaving open the possibility that the rhetor may not actually be of good character. There is thus the possibility for hypocrisy within Aristotle's rhetoric.[29]

A Christian view of rhetoric asserts that character is persuasive, but that such character should not be an artificial construction of the speaker, but rather constructed *by* God in prayer.[30] Gregory the Great draws this relationship between character and speech in *The Book of Pastoral Rule*: before

---

28. Aristotle, *On Rhetoric*, 121.

29. While Christian rhetoric would reject the construction of a false ethos on behalf of the promotion of Christian proclamation, this does not necessarily mean that God may not use such hypocrisy for his aims. As Paul notes, God may still use the duplicitous person to bring about his will: "Some proclaim Christ from envy and rivalry, but others from goodwill. These proclaim Christ out of love, knowing that I have been put here for the defense of the gospel; the others proclaim Christ out of selfish ambition, not sincerely but intending to increase my suffering in my imprisonment. What does it matter? Just this, that Christ is proclaimed in every way, whether out of false motives or true; and in that I rejoice" (Phil 1:15–18). Augustine reiterates this assertion by Paul, stating that the formation of genuine character is important for the Christian rhetor, while acknowledging at the same time that God can still use those of poor character. In these situations, God works through the listeners who, in their own obedience, are able to hear not the voice of the deceitful teacher, but the voice of their Lord. Augustine, *On Christian Teaching*, 142.

30. In this regard, a Christian understanding of rhetoric in relation to truth and character is more akin to that advocated by Socrates at the end of "Gorgias." Human beings should not strive to be persuasive by creating a semblance of goodness, but by striving to *actually* be good in

speaking, the preacher "strikes themselves with the wings of their thoughts," examining themselves before God to see if their deeds align with the content of their speech.[31] It is God who forms one in the image and likeness of Christ, a likeness which holds the potential to help authorize the gospel proclamation: the goodness of the missionary bolsters their claim that the information they are imparting is not from them, but from God. Paul draws out this connection between his own character and the reception of the gospel by the church in Thessalonica:

> You remember our labor and toil, brothers and sisters; we worked night and day, so that we might not burden any of you while we proclaimed to you the gospel of God. You are witnesses, and God also, how pure, upright, and blameless our conduct was toward you believers. As you know, we dealt with each one of you like a father with his children, urging and encouraging you and pleading that you lead a life worthy of God, who calls you into his own kingdom and glory. We also constantly give thanks to God for this, that when you received the word of God that you heard from us, you accepted it not as a human word but as what it really is, God's word, which is also at work in you believers. (1 Thess 2:9–13)

Paul sees the reception of the gospel as clearly bolstered by his own conduct amongst those in Thessalonica. Yet, for Paul, this conduct bolsters neither his own claims to be a master orator, nor his ability to peddle his own philosophy. Instead, his conduct bolsters his belief that he has actually communicated the word of God.[32]

---

both their private and public lives. Rhetoric should thus be used not for any type of persuasion, but only for "pointing to what is just." Plato, "Gorgias," 112.

31. Gregory the Great, *The Book of Pastoral Rule* (Crestwood, NY: St. Vladimir's Seminary Press, 2007), 207.

32. For Augustine, the confluence of prayerful speech is that the audience is affected by God. The human agency exerted by such speech is used by God toward God's purposes: "So the benefits of teaching, applied to the soul through human agency, are only beneficial when the benefit is effected by God, who could have given the gospel to man even without human authors or intermediaries." Augustine, *On Christian Teaching*, 123. As will be examined below, this hints at the type of ultimate good derived from the practice of proclamation. The "work" of conversion is ultimately the work of God; the missionary receives the unique joy of having participated in this work, of acting in accordance with God's will and desire. Prayer is the site in which the missionary asks that their speech remain in accordance with God's will.

The development of character aids in the ability of the missionary to persuade their audience. Because the proclamation of the gospel involves an invitation to assent to a belief that cannot be proven with analytic precision, and because it involves an invitation to believe amidst a host of competing worldviews and ideologies, the listener must adjudicate among a host of various arguments for and against Christianity. Judgments about the character of the one presenting the arguments are one of the ways in which listeners may adjudicate. The ethos of the messenger impacts the effect of the message they are communicating: "Consequently, the authority of a particular argument is closely connected to how the audience evaluates the person who offers that argument."[33]

Prayer, Imagination, and the Audience

While prayer begins with a dialogue with God, in which the missionary is persuaded by God and formed by God, it proceeds to extend outward, from dialogue between the self and God to dialogue about the self, others, and God. The missionary begins to pray for others and to ask God for guidance and direction on where to proclaim the gospel and the audience who will receive the message. In so doing, they imagine themselves engaged in dialogue with specific people.

The imagination plays a central role in the way we craft our discourse and how we adapt this discourse to an audience. As human beings who inhabit a world of language, we are formed not only through our communicative relationships with others, but also through the conversations we have with others in our minds. Kenneth Burke describes how imaginative discourse shapes the arguments one crafts and, in turn, effects a change in the person crafting the arguments: "In studying the nature of the object, we can in effect speak for it, and in adjusting our conduct to its nature as revealed in the light of our interests, we in effect modify our own assertion in reply to its assertion."[34] We imagine an interlocutor or a group of people, and we have a conversation with them in our minds. If it is an argument, we craft arguments that we believe will win over our audience. We visualize the assent to such arguments. Such imaginative construals precede all intentional actions, for

---

33. Cunningham, *Faithful*, 101.
34. Kenneth Burke, *A Grammar of Motives* (Berkeley: University of California Press, 1969), 237.

"one cannot just intend the act without imagining what it might look like as an accomplished fact."[35]

The assertion here is that this imaginative construal is something that is intentionally performed in prayer by the missionary. According to Gilbert Ryle, imaginative acts are not merely the operation of sense impressions,[36] but are their own discreet activities. As a discreet activity, specific acts of imaging can be performed with better or worse accuracy. Ryle gives the example of humming a tune in one's mind—such humming is not merely the accessing in the mind of some past musical performance, but it is its own mental event which can be performed with better or worse accuracy.[37] Part of preparing for a speech or discourse involves such imaginative acts, and one can prepare for such engagements through "giving the speech in their mind." Those who are new to public speaking, for instance, may be surprised at how much more difficult the speech was to say aloud than it was to speak in their mind. Part of one's growth will entail the closure of this gap.

In addition, the assertion that such imaginative construals should take place by the missionary in the context of prayer is an affirmation that God is present and at work in such acts. In prayer, the Holy Spirit penetrates our cognitive faculties, directing them toward both audience and argument.[38] In prayer, the missionary opens themselves up to an awareness of those around them with whom the Holy Spirit may be calling them to go and share the gospel. In so doing, they begin to imagine themselves proclaiming the word, convincing others to assent to such proclamation. They imagine their

---

35. O'Donovan, *Finding*, 187.

36. Ryle believes this common misconception is in part due to language. We use the phrase "one pictures the mountain" to refer to the mental act of imagining a mountain, which leads us to think that one has simply accessed a picture from their memory. The brain in this misconception is rendered akin to a computer hard drive—storing sense data that can be accessed by the individual at any point: "Imaging is not only not any sort of observing of anything; it is also not having a sensation of a special sort. Seeming to hear a very loud noise is not being in any degree deafened, nor is seeming to see a very bright light being in any degree dazzled." Gilbert Ryle, *The Concept of Mind* (London: Hutchinson, 1969), 255.

37. Ryle, *The Concept*, 269.

38. This is not to say that the Holy Spirit takes over for us, but rather it restores our agency, creating the opportunity to participate in God's work. According to Oliver O'Donovan, the Holy Spirit "confirms and restores us as moral agents, which is to say, as the subjects of our actions … in confirming us as subjects, he teaches us how, within this age of eschatological judgment, we may act. To do this he does not take over our subjecthood; he enables us to realize it." O'Donovan, *Resurrection*, 106.

interlocutor joyfully receiving this message, and, even though such reception is far from certain, it prompts the missionary to action.

There is in prayer an act of imaginative discourse in the mind of the missionary in which the missionary attempts to gain an accurate assessment of their audience, discovers and tests arguments, and deciphers how to proclaim the gospel in a way that honors God and respects their interlocutors. All this is done in prayer, open to the workings of the Holy Spirit. That this process is open to the Holy Spirit means that the missionary is open to godly intervention into this process. The Spirit may surprise with ideas and directives heretofore not considered by the missionary.

Luke's narratives of visions in the book of Acts show this relationship between the Holy Spirit, prayer, and missional directive. Throughout the book of Acts, Luke portrays the apostles as those who are in tune with and led by the Spirit. The Spirit manifests itself during times of prayer and, at other times unspecified by Luke, through creating pictures and scenarios that inspire and direct the apostles toward the who and where of their proclamatory endeavors.[39]

For Ananias it is a vision to seek out Paul (Acts 9:10–11), for Paul it is a vision to remain in Corinth to continue proclaiming the gospel (Acts 18:9–10), and for Peter, as will be shown below, a vision will guide the way in which his proclamation is adapted (Acts 10). Visions are best seen as one of the ways in which the Spirit is manifested through the activation of the image-making faculties of the minds of the disciples. Such activation is meant to further the mission of the church, directing the disciples to continue proclaiming the gospel.

This link between the Holy Spirit, visions, and proclamation is rarely commented upon. Yves Congar's magisterial work on the Holy Spirit, for instance, draws immediate connections between the reception of the Holy

---

39. Throughout the book of Acts, Luke portrays the apostles as those who are in tune with and led by the Spirit. The Spirit manifests itself during times of prayer and at other times unspecified by Luke. Visions are best seen as one of the ways in which the Spirit is manifested through the activation of the image-making faculties of the minds of the disciples. Such activation is meant to further the mission of the church, directing the disciples to continue proclaiming the gospel.

Spirit and the mission of the apostles in the book of Acts.[40] Congar also acknowledges the potential for the Holy Spirit to enable visions but does not draw the connection between this and mission.[41] The connection is taken up, however, by some Pentecostal theologians, most notably in the sermons and writings of Maria Beulah Woodworth-Etter. For Woodworth-Etter, one of the signs of the Holy Spirit at work within the church is the manifestation of visions and ensuing signs, which include the growth of the church.[42] This connection is used both as a framework to interpret the various visions in the book of Acts and also as a direct exhortation to her contemporaries to receive the Holy Spirit. Woodworth-Etter's exhortations utilized Proverbs 29:18 as leitmotiv: "Where there is no vision, the people perish."[43]

While I would not claim that the kind of ecstatic visions Woodworth-Etter may have in mind are essential to the experience of all Christians or essential for the growth and health of the church, her work does highlight the connection between vision, the Holy Spirit, and proclamation. While such visions might be more mundane—it may simply be the imagining of a quiet conversation between two friends—they are important for helping to direct the actions of the missionary and qualify the way they conduct such actions.

Prayer is thus indispensable to the practice of proclamation. Through it both the missionary and their message are molded by God. Through prayer, the sharing of this message with particular people is made possible. Through prayer, the missionary is given confidence and boldness, trusting that their words may be acceptable to God. Such boldness and confidence spurs the missionary to action. But, before the moment of speech, they must learn more about their interlocutors.

---

40. Yves Congar, *I Believe in the Holy Spirit* (New York: Crossroad Publishing Company, 1997), 44–47.

41. Congar's most explicit mention of visions pertains to their experience in regard to the proper interpretation of Scripture and the connection between visions and apocalyptic prophecy. See Congar, *I Believe*, 67, 121–22.

42. Maria Beulah Woodworth-Eller, "Sermon on Visions and Trances," in *Reader in Pentecostal Theology: Voices from the First Generation*, ed. Douglas Jacobsen (Bloomington, IN: Indiana University Press, 2006), 27.

43. Woodworth-Eller, "Sermon," 27.

PREPARATION

Empowered by the Holy Spirit, the missionary thus proceeds to prepare for their interactions with their audience. The purpose of such preparation is to better understand the intended audience and adapt their message accordingly. This is the logical next step after the missionary's imaginative encounter: once such an encounter is visualized, care is taken to discern how the imagined audience wrought through prayer might accord with the actual audience in reality.[44] As we will see, what will separate the practice of proclamation from other forms of persuasion and argumentation is that the adaptation of the message to the intended audience includes not only the missionary's human interlocutors, but also God.

Rhetorical scholars often affirm the interdependence of arguments and knowledge of the audience to which such arguments are directed. As Perelman and Olbrechts-Tyteca put it, "Knowledge of the audience cannot be conceived independently of the knowledge of how to influence it."[45] As we learn more about a person, we learn about their likes and dislikes, what motivates and moves them. David Zarefsky makes a similar assertion in that the discernment of the audience in a sense dictates the boundaries through which responsible argumentation may occur.[46]

Thus, the missionary begins the process of acquiring knowledge about their intended audience which, in the process, helps to better discern which aspects of the gospel proclamation will resonate more resoundingly. The acquisition of such knowledge will vary based upon the type of audience and the particular situation. If the missionary is moving to another country, they may learn some general information about the people living there: their language, history, prominent religious beliefs, etc. This may be done knowing full well that these are merely generalizations—cultures are a great deal more porous and heterogenous, and, hence, the missionary must know that their audience is a composite, "embracing people differing in character, loyalties, and functions."[47] However, such knowledge provides a starting point

---

44. Perelman and Olbrechts-Tyteca, *The New Rhetoric*, 23.

45. Perelman and Olbrechts-Tyteca, *The New Rhetoric*, 23.

46. David Zarefsky, *Rhetorical Perspectives on Argumentation: Selected Essays* (Cham, Switzerland: Springer International Press, 2014), xvi.

47. Perelman and Olbrechts-Tyteca, *The New Rhetoric*, 21.

for helping to determine which aspects of the Christian message will most resonate with their audience.[48]

The discovery of the audience presents the missionary with the range of justifications for the Christian faith. This should not be cause for alarm from Christians worried that the selection of justifications may compromise the Christian faith.[49] Choosing one point to emphasize does not necessitate a

---

48. As will be explained below, the discovering of the available means of persuasion and the adaptation of the message to the audience is highly contextual, and as such, attempts to give an exact, step-by-step process risks overgeneralization.

49. There is a parallel here with Christian political discourse within pluralistic societies, like most modern liberal democracies today. Here, the Christian attempts to discover the available arguments through which particular Christian political positions will be persuasive to those who do not share the Christian faith. If one desires such engagement, a question remains regarding the extent to which the Christian grounds for such positions may be carried into the public square.

Some advocates of political liberalism take the approach that such positions must be scrubbed clean of their religious overtones. A generous reading of such a view is what Christopher Eberle calls "justificatory liberalism." Eberle construes liberalism here not as the complete privatization of all religiously held beliefs, but rather a liberalism that constrains citizens to "privatize only that subset of his religious convictions constituted by religiously grounded claims for which he lacks a corroboratory public justification" (78). One can make religiously motivated moral claims on society, but only if such claims can be justified using corroborating secular arguments. Such secular arguments should be grounded in secular moral claims, such as freedom, equality, and due process. Christopher J. Eberle, *Religious Conviction in Liberal Politics* (Cambridge, UK: Cambridge University Press, 2002).

Appeals to public religion to politically persuade run counter to the logic of liberal political persuasion, as they are public justifications expressed in religious terms. The fear is that such appeals must at the least disrespect those that don't hold such religious convictions, and at the worst be the grounds for religious coercion. Public religious appeals are appeals that cannot be shared with those who hold different faith commitments, and thus hold the potential to force citizens to accept beliefs that are beyond common reason.

A different yet equally negative critique of public religion comes from a large group of contemporary American Protestant theologians. For these theologians, attempts at such political engagements intrinsically cloud Christian moral reasoning and enable the people of the church to take upon themselves a providential rule of history that is only to be possessed by God. The predominance of this view amongst Protestant theologians is due in large part to the impact of John Howard Yoder and Stanley Hauerwas on modern political theology. Their work elucidated a specific way in which the church relates to political powers. Both assert that, although Christianity does not advocate a specific political form, it is necessarily compromised when it colludes with empire. Instead, the position of the church is to accept the temporal authority of rulers granted through God's providence, speaking a corrective voice yet resisting the temptation to take such authority into their own hands: "Christian witness does not provide any foundations for government, either practically or philosophically, but that the Christian rather accepts the powers that be and speaks to them in a corrective way." Stanley Hauerwas, "Democratic Time: Lessons Learned from Yoder and Wolin," *Cross Currents* 55, no. 4 (2006): 539.

The position of Yoder and Hauerwas is important for understanding the change that may occur within the person crafting arguments for the public square and for understanding that such changes may bring about the compromise of the Christian faith in the interest of winning political arguments. There are, however, drawbacks to such an approach. First is whether such

rejection of another. For instance, the Pauline Epistles are filled with non-contradictory explanations and images of the significance of the cross (adoption, redemption, salvation, etc.).[50] The use of various images is context-specific to the audience of the epistles.

In a similar fashion, the missionary may discover which of these images best resonates with their interlocutors, that they may "touch the hearts of his audience with the same common doctrine but by distinct exhortations."[51] This helps to explain the appropriate emphasis on translation and intercultural studies within the field of missiology. For Andrew Walls, because Jesus the incarnate Word took on flesh in human history, the spread of the Christian gospel must also be rendered intelligible in specific times and places:

> At the heart of the Christian faith is the Incarnate Word—God became human. The divine Word was expressed under the conditions of a particular human society; the divine Word was, as it were, translated. And since the divine Word is for all humanity, he is translated again in terms of every culture where he finds acceptance among its people. ... The Word has to be translated in terms of specific segments of social reality.[52]

---

a strict separation of the ecclesial from the governmental powers is actually attainable: We are born already immersed in a web of commitments and influences, both ecclesial and political. An awareness of this entanglement should place a check on any notion that we have somehow been successful in establishing a purely prophetic position vis-à-vis the ruling powers and principalities.

Second, their position seems to ignore the ways in which Christian prophetic witness to the political powers has benefited from a public awareness of Christianity. The "corrective voice" that the church is to speak to the powers and principalities can be more resonate to societies that have at least some understanding of the Christian roots of that voice. For instance, Martin Luther King Jr. used numerous biblical references in his "I Have a Dream" speech. Such references were direct persuasive appeals meant to effect public change that were persuasive in part because the audience had an awareness of Christianity, whether they practiced the Christian faith or not. This awareness enabled King to quote directly from Scripture without reference, lending an immediacy to his appeals. In this way, King's speech was persuasive in part because it was explicitly Christian. Any talk of a "Public Missiology" should acknowledge the relationship between proclamation and gathering and political discourse. The expansion of Christianity through mission creates a larger audience of persons who might be politically persuaded by explicitly Christian rhetoric. Proclamation creates the conditions by which Christians might speak enthymematically, and thus persuasively, to contemporary public and political issues.

50. For a detailed account of the various explanations and images used by Paul, see Alister E. McGrath, *What Was God Doing on the Cross?* (Eugene, OR: Wipf and Stock Publishers, 2002).

51. Gregory the Great, *Pastoral Rule*, 88.

52. Andrew F. Walls, *The Missionary Movement in Christian History: Studies in the Transmission of Faith* (Maryknoll, NY: Orbis Books, 2009), 47.

One can view this translation of the gospel message as way of bringing forth certain justifications for the Christian faith in light of new audiences. For Walls, this process of translation can add richness to Christianity.[53] The missionary emphasizes certain images of the cross or certain justifications for Christianity and, in the process, helps to articulate new and noncontradictory expressions of the Christian faith.

Furthermore, discovering the available means of persuasion should lead the person of good character to uncover the ways in which one could be manipulated and thus discover which arguments may be persuasive and yet off limits. Here lies an important distinction in Aristotle: the definition of rhetoric is *not* to persuade, but to discover the available means of persuasion,[54] what in Latin would be termed *inventio*. The goal of rhetoric is not to persuade, as one can do so through a host of immoral means, but rather to better understand how persuasion may occur. If rhetoric is a tool, then learning how to use this tool is as much about using it effectively as it is about using it properly. In learning how to wield an ax properly, I learn both how to more effectively cut wood and also how to avoid cutting my friend's hand.

While the discovery of the available means of persuasion may occur in one succinct action—for instance, if the missionary is preparing to give a speech—the discovery of the available means of persuasion may occur over a longer period of time, particularly in regard to an ongoing friendship. For instance, if a friend self-identifies as a Marxist, this may lead the missionary to be intentional about learning more about Marxism in general. Perhaps the friend experienced tragedy in their life, in which case the missionary may learn more about how the Christian message best speaks to tragedy.

There need not be anything nefarious in the acquisition of such knowledge. Learning more about another person—their beliefs, passions, likes, and dislikes—can be a way of expressing care and interest in them. A loved one may appreciate that that their lover has taken the time to learn about their affection for flowers and built a garden in response to such a discovery. David Zarefsky presses this point further, suggesting that the audience itself

---

53. Walls, *Missionary Movement*, 54.
54. Aristotle, *On Rhetoric*, 35.

imposes a field of acceptable arguments onto the rhetor, constraining and limiting that which can be discussed.[55]

COMMUNICATION

After prayer and a consideration of their audience, the missionary engages in persuasive communication. The desire of the missionary is not simply one of well-wishing. It is not simply to pray for the betterment of another. In prayer, the missionary imagines a conversation, one that ends in their interlocutor professing belief in the risen Christ. This desire, fueled by prayer, prompts a moment of action.[56] It is this moment of action that, in many ways, makes mission *mission*.[57] The missionary speaks in order to share their faith in Christ and the justifications for their faith with another: "to communicate something is to hold it as a common possession."[58] The desire is to impart what has been received by God with another so that the other might share in what has been given. Communication is the way in which the invitation to share in such common possession is offered.[59]

---

55. Zarefsky, *Rhetorical Perspectives*, 39.

56. As Aquinas asserts, when we love someone, an image of that person is imprinted on our mind, and the love of this image pushes the lover to act toward the beloved (*Summa Theologiae*, I, q. 37). Giles Emery summarizes: "When we love someone, our beloved is 'engraved' in our heart, like a weight of love that pulls us and draws us to our beloved" (152). Thus, in prayer, the missionary imagines their interlocutor, loves this image, and is compelled to action to proclaim the gospel out of this love. See Emery, *The Trinity*.

57. It is at this communicative act that the traditional language of Trinitarian missions coincides with the modern definition of mission, for just as the Trinitarian missions refer to the activities of God, in which God is revealed as Father, Son, and Holy Spirit, so that humanity might be rescued, missionaries take the decisive and deliberate action to make this news known. See Emery, *The Trinity*, 25–27.

58. Oliver O'Donovan, *The Ways of Judgment: The Bampton Lectures, 2003* (Grand Rapids: Eerdmans, 2008), 244.

59. While the context in which this act of communication can vary, it is important to note that this conception of proclamation assumes at least some degree of intentionality. This is not to say that "antecedent probabilities" cannot be established through other means, just that missionary proclamation involves prayer and preparation for purposeful persuasion. Amidst ongoing friendships, for instance, the topic of religion and Christianity may arise naturally, in which case one could hope to be prepared to speak as well as they can. Proclamation involves, however, the seeking out of intentional conversation, prompted by and at the direction of the Holy Spirit. While such intentional conversation may be more or less formal, it does require what Douglas Ehninger calls a degree of "intellectual and moral tension," a tension that arises due to the acknowledgment that what is being offered by the missionary requires a change in the worldview of the other. See Douglas Ehninger, "Argument as Method: Its Nature, Its Limitations and Its Uses," *Speech Monographs* 37, no. 2 (1970): 104.

As mentioned above, preparation may aid in the process of discerning how such communication may proceed, but, because the conversion of each individual is unique, such preparation must meet the reality of the communicative event. There can be no definitive "pre-packaged word." Proclamation involves a performance, and the missionary must develop skills which allow them to faithfully adapt their proclamation to suit each situation. Here, J. L. Austin's description of the relationship between illocution and perlocution is helpful. The *way* we say something (illocution) impacts what is brought about as a result of our speech (perlocution).[60] The missionary thus learns the best ways to use words in order to illicit a response from their interlocutors.

Adaptation to the Audience

The adaptation of the gospel proclamation already begins in the discernment of the available means of persuasion. The missionary begins to assess how to present the gospel in a way that will be intelligible and how to craft the message in a way that will resonate with their audience. Such adaptation proceeds through the actual verbal communication of the gospel message. The speaker refines their message internally up until the moment of communication and continues to adjust this message based upon the response of their interlocutors.

That missionaries adjust to their circumstances is evident in even a cursory reading of the book of Acts. Peter and Paul do not give identical speeches to different audiences, but they adjust their messages based upon time and place. Paul's speech before the synagogue in Antioch situates the gospel within the history of Israel, beginning with the exodus out of Egypt (Acts 13:17). His speech before the Areopagus, however, begins with a reference to the altar inscription "To the unknown God," and makes no reference to Israel (Acts 17:23). Both speeches end with a word concerning impending judgment for those who do not receive the message.

---

60. Kevin Vanhoozer points out how Austin's description of this relationship places an emphasis on the performance of the speaker in the act of communicating, not simply on the words in which the speaker is uttering: "Austin's all-important notion of illocution requires us, I believe, to bring to the fore the speaker's (or author's) role in saying or writing something." Kevin J. Vanhoozer, *Is There a Meaning in This Text?: The Bible, the Reader, and the Morality of Literary Knowledge* (Grand Rapids: Zondervan, 1998), 209.

This contextualization is evidence of the need to adapt message to audience.[61] The presentation of the gospel is not the presentation of self-evident truths that necessarily bring one to assent, but the presentation of justifications that invite acceptance over matters that are inherently unprovable.[62] Thus, interaction with an audience drives the speaker to adapt, for "arguments that in substance and form are appropriate to certain circumstances may appear ridiculous in others."[63] An argument that the Christian church is the continuation of the history of God's people which began in the Israelite patriarchs may seem to the pagan statesman in the Areopagus odd, inconsequential, or even ridiculous.

---

61. I have already mentioned above the need to adapt the message before a proclamative encounter. In noting that this adaptation to the audience continues throughout this encounter is to stress the need for contextualization. Stephen Bevans suggests different models that have been used by missionaries as they encounter people of other faiths and cultural traditions (translation, anthropological, praxis, countercultural), while also asserting that such models are not necessarily mutually exclusive. Bevans, for instance, suggests that a modified version (drawing somewhat on the anthropological model) of the countercultural model best suits the contemporary North American missional context. See Stephen B. Bevans, "Living between Gospel and Context," in *Confident Witness—Changing World: Rediscovering the Gospel in North America*, ed. Craig Van Gelder (Grand Rapids: Eerdmans, 1999).

My point in mentioning a contextualization that occurs both before and during a proclamative encounter pushes the necessity of adaptation a bit further. The missionary can and should work to understand the particular milieu in which they labor, and also how to go about contextualizing the gospel in light of their discoveries. However, such pre-encounter labors must always be taken with a grain of salt, since the experience of working with actual individuals tends to challenge, if not shatter, our preconceived cultural assumptions: the missionary who learns about the rampant individualism and consumerism of North American culture might encounter an austere college student who would rather travel home to be with family on weekends than partake in bacchanalias on campus. (My use of the example of a college student is intentional, since all too often descriptions of the "North American cultural context" are simply caricatures of twenty-something well-educated urbanites.)

Because of the particularity of actual persons, the missionary needs to develop specific skills and virtues to know how to adapt one's language during a performative encounter: one must develop the skill of adapting and arguing on the fly, as well as the ability to discern in the moment which arguments may in fact compromise either the integrity of the missionary or the missionary's message. This coheres with my construal of proclamation as a virtuous practice: because proclamation is a non-repeatable practice, because it needs to be performed new in each situation, it will be impossible to fully contextualize the gospel message before each encounter.

62. Zarefsky, *Rhetorical Perspectives*, 41. By using the term "inherently uncertain," I do not mean that the one who assents to the Christian faith experiences something like a radical and perpetual uncertainty about their belief. Rather, the claim is simply that Christianity cannot be "proved" through something akin to a mathematical syllogism. If this were the case, the scope of assent to the Christian message would resemble more the scope of assent to the proposition that 2+2=4. See the above discussion on Newman and conversion.

63. Perelman and Olbrechts-Tyteca, *The New Rhetoric*, 25.

In their speech, the missionary attempts to persuade another to assent to a belief in the resurrected Christ and a profession of Jesus as Lord, and because such assent comes about not through demonstration but the "cumulation of probabilities,"[64] the content of the missionary's proclamation will vary according to circumstance: the goal is to establish "antecedent probabilities," to set forth a range of justifications for the Christian faith, any number of which may be persuasive to varying degrees.

Testimony

What sets Christian proclamation apart from some other forms of persuasion that attempt to gain assent through the establishment of antecedent probabilities is the priority it places on *testimony*. Christian proclamation is tied to the facticity of a historical event: the resurrection of Christ. This tethers the desire to gain assent to an event in which one can both hear and experience. Paul Ricoeur states that such testimony has a "quasi-empirical meaning":

> I say quasi-empirical because testimony is not perception itself but the report, that is, the story, the narration of the event. ... The witness has seen, but the one who receives his testimony has not seen but hears. It is only by hearing the testimony that he can believe or not believe in the reality of the facts that the witness reports.[65]

For Ricoeur, the fact that such testimony is rooted in a claim to experience an event that the interlocutor can only hear and not see renders said testimony "to the service of judgment."[66] Testimony must reach out for justifications that promote the validity of the story and the veracity of the one proclaiming it. In short, testimony does not nullify the need to establish antecedent probabilities, but rather strengthens the need for it.

And so the missionary proclaims Christ's death and resurrection as a witness who traces their assent back to the testimony of the disciples, and they invite an assent to something that may be heard but not seen but is nevertheless true assent and true belief: "Blessed are those who have not seen and yet have come to believe" (John 20:29). They marshal a host of contextual

---

64. Newman, *Grammar*, 190.

65. Paul Ricoeur, *Essays on Biblical Interpretation*, ed. Lewis Seymour Mudge (Philadelphia, PA: Fortress Press, 1985), 123.

66. Ricoeur, *Essays*, 123.

arguments—evidence of personal change, historical evidence,[67] the life of a community, judgments on evil, etc.—in order to win assent to a belief that is rooted in the historical particularity of the resurrection of Christ. While such arguments may take the form of logical arguments (for instance, the extraordinary improbability of a worldwide religious movement spread primarily through non-violence over the course of three centuries), they need not be limited by such justifications. The systematization of belief often comes *after* assent, not before it. The creeds, for instance, are a response to the reception of the apostle's testimony, not the primary means of earning assent.

That such persuasion is linked to a historical event also helps to exert a control on acceptable forms of adaptation. The significance of the event may be interpreted in various ways by various audiences (indeed, it must be, as the narrative itself must be intelligibly described)[68] but never denied in the interest of conversion. If the missionary can only persuade someone to become a Christian through a modification of the Christian message stripped of the resurrection, then they choose instead to accept the rejection of the message. To modify in such a way would strip Christianity of its meaning: "It is not possible to testify *for* a meaning without testifying *that* something has happened which signifies this meaning."[69] Here lies perhaps the conflation of the Greek term for "witness," *martyr*, with its reference to the Christian who has been murdered for their belief.

Adaptation to God

The adaptation of Christian proclamation is not only limited by its testimony to the historical event of the resurrection, but is also limited by the fact that such proclamation occurs before God as an audience. The missionary is simultaneously speaking to their interlocutors and to God, and, as such, they adjust their speech so that the words on their lips may be acceptable to God.

---

67. N. T. Wright's *The Resurrection of the Son of God* is perhaps the best example of a highly particular argument for the resurrection. Wright does not claim that his book "proves" that the resurrection is correct, but rather that, if one allows for the possibility that God exists and that miracles are possible, than the resurrection rises to the level of probability according to what one believes to be the standard of historical accuracy amongst historians.

68. "Narrative can never be separated from description. If the proclamation is to be understood and received, its implication for the understanding of world, human life, and action must still be accounted for non-narratively." Oliver O'Donovan, *Entering into Rest* (Grand Rapids: Eerdmans, 2017), 175.

69. Ricoeur, *Essays*, 133.

The missiologist Lesslie Newbigin states that a confession that "Jesus is Lord" is a "claim regarding the entire public life of mankind and the whole created world."[70] For Newbigin, the missionary who declares this in public appeals to God as authority, and, as such, it is God who authorizes proclamatory discourse: "I make this confession only because I have been laid hold of by Another and commissioned to do so. It is not primarily or essentially my decision. ... I am simply the messenger entrusted with this responsibility to deliver the message."[71] Fealty to this commission opens up the possibility that such a message will clash with other public, universal claims. Hence, in adapting their proclamation before God, the missionary must be prepared for this proclamation to be received as a word of judgment by their interlocutors.[72] Such words of judgment may take the form of direct prophecy: during his extended proclamation, Stephen appropriates the prophecy of Isaiah in judgment upon the Jewish leaders who have rejected Jesus (Acts 7:49–50). The judgment may also be implicit: the disciples are often persecuted based simply on "reports" of their activity. Paul's speech before the Areopagus is a particularly compelling example of a speech that is simultaneously highly contextualized for both the audience and God. Paul's speech is florid and respectful of pagan piety. Yet it also a blatant call for repentance in the face of impending judgment (Acts 17:30–31). The response from the audience (some believe but most scoff) is perhaps what should be expected from discourse that is at once meant to be highly persuasive yet ultimately unyielding in its central tenets.

While the adaptability of proclamation to suit God as audience may entail a word of judgment being pronounced, the effect may also work in reverse. The missionary may discover in the course of persuasive discourse that their own fealty to the gospel is in question. For instance, in declaring that the

---

70. Lesslie Newbigin, *The Open Secret: An Introduction to the Theology of Mission* (Grand Rapids: Eerdmans, 1995), 16.

71. Newbigin, *The Open Secret*, 17.

72. It is this understanding of proclamation as that which is performed before God that can help navigate the challenges of Christian political discourse in pluralistic societies, as detailed in the footnote above. In proclamation, the missionary presents arguments for the Christian faith, celebrating the times in which such arguments are resonate, and accepting whatever negative consequences may arise as a result of its rejection. Christian political witness may take place in a similar manner. The Christian is called to witness to political powers, celebrating the instances in which such powers are responsive and risking persecution when such witness is met with hostility. It is in this willingness to accept persecution where some of Yoder and Hauerwas's fears of collusion with empire might be allayed.

gospel is "good news for the poor," they may be convicted of their own lack
of charity to those in need.

Peter's proclamation of the gospel to Cornelius in Acts 10–11 is the most
vivid example of how the missionary is changed in both prayer before God
and discourse before God. Roman centurion and gentile Godfearer Cornelius
is called by God to send for Peter. On the way from Joppa to Caesarea to proclaim the gospel to Cornelius, Peter stops and prays. In prayerful preparation
for this missionary encounter, Peter receives a vision and the command to
kill and eat the various four-footed animals. He is perplexed by this vision
yet proceeds to meet with Cornelius and proclaim the gospel, and Cornelius
believes. What is fascinating about this passage is how Peter's attitude toward
the gentiles, and his interpretation of this vision, is affected *through* this
discourse. It is through this discourse that Peter learns the meaning of his
vision: that God shows no partiality and that the Holy Spirt has "been poured
out even on the Gentiles" (Acts 10:45). Upon his return to Jerusalem, Peter
is questioned regarding his ministry to the gentiles, and it is here that he
is able to recount his vision and the meaning he has discerned through his
discourse with Cornelius (Acts 11:1–18).

Thus, in the act of intentional persuasion, missionaries themselves
become open to change. Their interlocutors may present issues that force
the missionary back into prayer and a reassessment of their beliefs, where
they might hear a word from God that effects a change in their own understanding of the Christian faith. Proclamation entails a risk on the part of
the rhetor. Douglas Ehninger's characterization of argument (as opposed to
correction) as a "person risking" enterprise is also applicable to Christian
proclamation:

> By entering into argument in any but a playful mood, a disputant
> opens the possibility that as a result of the interchange he may be per-
> suaded of his opponent's view, or, failing that, at least may be forced
> to make major alterations in his own. In either case, he will emerge
> from the interchange with a different pattern of conviction, values,
> and attitudes than he held when he entered it, and to this extent will
> be a different "self" or "person."[73]

---

73. Ehninger, "Argument," 104.

For the missionary, proclamation is interchange with both God and another, and it entails the possibility that either or both may challenge their own views. Whether major changes occur or not, the missionary is left a different person after the exchange.

RESPONSE

The missionary continues to speak, adjusting their message to suit audience and God, until the encounter has ended, which may occur for a number of reasons. For speeches to larger crowds, the speech may simply finish with an invitation to repent and be baptized, which is a natural ending point. For personal discourse, the conversation may be cut short for other reasons—one of the interlocutors must leave for another meeting, the conversation moves to other topics, etc. Such encounters may end with a number of different outcomes: as noted in chapter three, interlocutors may accept, reject, or modify the message, or the matter may be left unresolved.

When proclaiming the gospel, the missionary invites a response, which reaffirms the aforementioned assertion that the penultimate goal of proclamation is conversion. This is what is "aimed at" by the missionary, and so the missionary gives space for their interlocutor to respond. I have already given account of conversion, a response in the affirmative to the act of proclamation, above. It is important to highlight here, however, those responses to proclamation that do not end in conversion and, relatedly, to stress how the acceptance of these responses by the missionary affirms and validates the personal agency of their interlocutor.

If, as Newman argues, conversion to Christianity is an assent based upon a cumulation of probabilities that is not syllogistic, and if such acts of assent are unique personal events, then it follows that acts of proclamation should not be able to guarantee a response in the affirmative. While the missionary may aim at conversion, the result might be simply an establishment of a probability in the mind of their interlocutor, a probability that may or may not lead to some act of assent in the near or distant future.

The act of proclamation thus invites a response, and while the missionary may hope that this response brings about an adherence to the Christian faith, they must be open to the possibility that it will not. An antecedent probability might be established, one in a host of others that may or may not eventually bring assent. To affirm the possibility of the rejection of their message is to affirm the personal agency of their audience.

Rather than simply reiterating what has been said above concerning conversion, it is appropriate here to emphasize the dynamics of human agency within the context of response. By lending space to their audience for a response, the missionary allows for what Charles Taylor calls "strong evaluation" to take place.[74] According to Taylor, there are certain fundamental evaluations that human beings make that contribute to the core of one's own identity. Identity is not simply a list of properties or descriptions, such as someone's family background or capacities, but rather those properties or descriptions that the individual *chooses* to value as part of their identity.[75] The fact, say, that one is born in the United States does not predetermine one to be patriotic; however, the one who passionately identifies as an American has chosen to make this fact a fundamental aspect of their identity.

Taylor makes this assertion in part to rebut both determinism and a notion of radical choice. Radical choice theorists posit that fundamental decisions, including a decision to believe in a religion, can be purely made in the abstract. However, one cannot purely step out of one's own background. There is no "disembodied ego" capable of complete removal from circumstance.[76] On the other hand, background does not determine identity. We are not simply products of material circumstance. Being born in the United States does not mean that one has to identify as an American. Likewise, for religious adherence, one can be born into a Catholic or Protestant household yet choose the degree to which such facts become core parts of one's identity. The sacrament of confirmation is meant in part to create space within individuals born into such households in order to enable core evaluations concerning their religious identity.

As individuals are presented with the gospel in the act of proclamation, they are thus given space to evaluate the claims and arguments being made. The missionary might have introduced new information to the respondent—of the reported details of Christ's life, death, and resurrection—or they may

---

74. Taylor, *Human Agency*, 1, 28.

75. Taylor, *Human Agency*, 34.

76. Taylor, *Human Agency*, 35.

have brought up arguments that challenge the respondent to re-evaluate their current commitments.

The respondent thus exerts their own agency in accepting, rejecting, or modifying the claims of the missionary. It has already been mentioned above how the multitude of responses to acts of proclamation evidence the variety of ways in which individuals receive and appropriate the gospel proclamations, sometimes (in the case of "hybrid identities") to the dismay of the missionary.

In leaving space for their interlocutor to evaluate and respond to their proclamation, the missionary allows for the possibility for their message to be rejected or for the matter to be left unresolved. We see in the book of Acts a range of responses, from a mixture of mild interest and indifference in Paul's dialogues in Athens (Acts 17), to a harsh rejection in the stoning of Stephen (Acts 7), to a "hybridization" in Acts 14:14-18, with Paul and Barnabas equated with Zeus and Hermes. Such a range of responses testifies to the ways in which personal agency is exerted by the recipients of gospel proclamation and to the apostles' willingness to accept this rejection and refrain from more forceful methods of obtaining assent.[77]

While their interlocutor may respond by rejecting or dismissing their proclamation, there are as well times in which this proclamation results in that which fulfills the vision of the missionary which was birthed in prayer: the reception of the gospel message and the confession of Jesus as Lord. Here, the labor of the missionary, as much as their proclamation is in and within the Holy Spirit, can be said to contribute to but not cause conversion. Claims to pure causality would render such proclamations as tautologies and the

---

77. While the apostles accept this rejection, this does not mean that such an acceptance is met with enthusiasm. The missionary's response to such rejection may be polite, or it may prompt a word of judgment. Note, for instance, the peculiar action of "shaking the dust off one's feet," an action commanded by Jesus and fulfilled by Paul and Barnabas in Acts 13:51. Carl Holladay describes this action as "a gesture of mocking contempt, as 'testimony against one's detractors'" (282). Jesus's instructions are to perform this act in the face of rejection, with the assurance that those towns that refuse the disciples face a judgment worse than Sodom (Luke 10:11-12). This gesture is a communicative act of *deferred* judgment. Jesus comforts the disciples with the exhortation not to take their rejection personally by insisting on a future judgment whose time and place is determined by God. See Carl R. Holladay, *Acts: A Commentary* (Louisville, KY: Westminster John Knox Press, 2016), 282. What makes this judgment different from forms of coercion is that it is *unenforceable* by the missionary; they cannot issue a fiat demanding acceptance. In this way, they are able to express disappointment and maintain disagreement yet honor the "principle of free choice that may be properly called 'assent.'" Ehninger, "Argument," 103.

methods of such conversion discoverable and applied through mechanistic means. However, if proclamation simply establishes probabilities which may contribute to a personal and unique act of assent on the part of the listener, the missionary can delight in having had a part to play in such assent and acknowledge that their place in the story of the convert will be that of a side character.[78] The missionary's words become the words of John the Baptist: "He must increase, but I must decrease" (John 3:30).

But the work of the missionary does not end there, since the Christian act of assent is simultaneously an assent to a life lived in the body of Christ, the church. Here, Peter's exhortation to "repent and be baptized," and Jesus's words to go and baptize are significant. As such, the missionary gathers those who receive the invitation to follow Christ into the church. While the act of gathering will be considered as a virtuous practice in its own right, the practice of proclamation is not complete with the response of the interlocutor: the missionary must finish their act by returning to prayer.

RETURN TO PRAYER

It is in prayer where the missionary is first prompted to go and speak, and it is to prayer that the missionary must return when they have finished their speaking. In this return to prayer, the missionary continues their discourse with God, this time reflecting upon the proclamative encounter and assessing their actions before God.

Humility

Gregory the Great ends his *Pastoral Rule* with an exhortation for the preacher to turn back to God in humility after they have spoken. The speaker, who has performed their task admirably, suiting sermon to audience, will face a danger if such speech is successful: prideful conceit. The speaker is tempted to confuse the works done by God through them as works done solely by them: "When the mind disregards the supernal Ruler, it seeks praise on its

---

78. This does not mean, however, that assent replaces existing friendships between the missionary and their interlocutors. Such conversions may in fact strengthen the bond between two friends, as Christ now becomes the grounds through which future friendship is predicated. Redemption in Christ Jesus affects the entirety of ourselves, including our social relationships, so the redemption of our friend will thus recontextualize and reconstitute this friendship, establishing Christ as its center. See McFadyen, *The Call*, 114–15.

own merits and begins to confer on itself every good that it has received for the purpose of being a herald for the real Giver. Moreover, it desires to spread abroad a good opinion of itself and it desires to be admired for all of its qualities."[79]

For the missionary, success brings with it the temptation to take credit for such success at the expense of God. This is particularly dangerous for the practice of proclamation, since its penultimate goal is to persuade another to change their views. If this goal is mistaken as the ultimate goal, proclamation becomes about winning—the achievement of victory due to a mastery of eloquence. If the missionary cedes to this temptation, then the critiques of Foss and Griffin—that the goal of rhetoric is the "rush of power" for the victorious rhetor[80]—are indeed valid.

Throughout the practice of proclamation, there is an emphasis on the ways in which the missionary conforms to God—in prayer before they speak, in speech that is directed both to the audience and to God, and finally in reflective prayer.

So in returning to the cloister of their mind after communicating the gospel, the missionary begins to seek humility in prayer: "Thus, it is necessary that when we are flattered by a wealth of virtues, we must turn the eye of our mind to our infirmity and allow it to humble itself."[81] The purpose of such prayer is to acknowledge one's indebtedness to God for every good work. The acknowledgment of our own infirmity paves the way for a moral examination of the communicative action just performed (see below) before entering into rest.

The Ultimate Goal of Proclamation: Delight and the Glory of God

"Rejoice always, pray without ceasing, give thanks in all circumstances; for this is the will of God in Christ Jesus for you" (1 Thess 5:16–19). The missionary closes their proclamatory act with a moment of rest and delight. The

---

79. Gregory the Great, *Pastoral Rule*, 210. John Chrysostom makes a similar point in stating that those charged with teaching the word must strive for both eloquence and a "contempt of praise." One must strive to develop the skills of eloquence and remain faithful to the word which they are charged to speak, yet at the same time they must guard against the temptation to become addicted to the applause of their audience. John Chrysostom, *Six Books on the Priesthood*, trans. Graham Neville (Crestwood, NY: St. Vladimir's Seminary Press, 1984), 128.

80. Foss and Griffin, "Beyond," 3.

81. Gregory the Great, *Pastoral Rule*, 211.

Sabbath is a time not merely for the cessation of activity but for the active reflection on the goodness of God: God rests on the seventh day not because of exhaustion, but simply to delight in the goodness of his creation. Human Sabbath mirrors this rest—it delights in God for what God has done in creating, sustaining, and redeeming life.

And so the missionary actively delights in what God has done through the act of proclaiming the gospel. They delight in the opportunity to speak about the resurrection, they delight in convincing others of its validity to the best of their ability, they delight in the responses to the affirmative, and they even delight in their fidelity to the gospel in the face of its rejection.

To participate in God's mission is to participate in the fullness of God. Delighting in the act of proclamation sediments God's goodness in the soul of the missionary, and because God's goodness is an infinite and inexhaustible plenitude,[82] it spurs the missionary on to further proclamatory actions. Gregory of Nyssa draws the connection between the limitlessness of virtue and the continual striving for its attainment: "In the case of virtue we have learned from the Apostle that its one limit of perfection is the fact that it has no limit. For that divine Apostle, great and lofty in understanding, ever running the course of virtue, never ceased straining toward those things that are still to come."[83] According to David Bentley Hart, Gregory believes that the practice of virtue, because it is the participation in the inexhaustible, fosters in the soul an even greater desire to experience God's beauty:

> And such is the action of every soul that loves beauty: drawn on forever by a desire enkindled always anew by the beauty that lies beyond the beauty already possessed, receiving the visible as an image of God's transcendent loveliness, but longing all the more to enjoy that beauty face-to-face, the soul experiences ceaseless delight precisely in that its desire can know no final satiety.[84]

In delighting in participation in God's mission of proclaiming the gospel to all the ends of the earth, the missionary experiences God's glory, a glory that, because it is inexhaustible, spurs in the missionary a desire to experience

---

82. David Bentley Hart, *The Beauty of the Infinite: The Aesthetics of Christian Truth* (Grand Rapids: Eerdmans, 2007), 195–96.

83. Gregory of Nyssa, *The Life of Moses*, 30.

84. Hart, *The Beauty*, 195.

more of it through the continual proclamation of the gospel.[85] As Herbert McCabe says of a virtuous practice, the discovery of its internal goods leads to "an enlargement of the capacity for experience."[86] To discover the good of proclamation enlarges our world, creating in us a greater capacity to experience the fullness of life in Christ.

The performance of the practice of proclamation thus draws one closer to God and creates a desire to want more of God's glory in performing this action with greater skill and frequency. The *performance itself*, not the response, is what spurs this greater desire. In the early chapters of Acts, Luke often narrates the end of proclamative discourse with a statement coupling some form of rejoicing and a continuation of preaching and teaching: after Peter and the apostles are beaten for witnessing Christ, they rejoice and continue to teach and preach Jesus as the Christ without ceasing (Acts 5:42). A similar account follows Peter and John's release from council inquiry, in which the disciples were "all filled with the Holy Spirit and continued to speak the word of God with boldness" (Acts 4:31 NIV). In both acceptance and rejection of the Christian message, there is rejoicing and a rejoinder to continue spreading the gospel.

THE PRACTICE OF PROCLAMATION

This chapter has set out to describe the Christian act of proclamation as a virtuous practice that resonates with the proclative performances by the apostles in the book of Acts. Throughout I have referred at times to the ways in which this conception of proclamation relates to the three key dimensions stated at the beginning of the chapter. In conclusion I will briefly summarize how this description of proclamation as virtuous practice fulfills each of these three key dimensions.

---

85. According to Jean-Louis Chrétien, the act of witness itself is inexhaustible and so calls forth continual proclamation: "The uncircumscribable nature of Christ's self-testimony calls unceasingly for witnesses, not one of whom exhausts it, though this does not make their testimony fragmentary." Jean-Louis Chrétien, *Under the Gaze of the Bible* (New York: Fordham University Press, 2015), 102.

86. McCabe, *The Good Life*, 48.

PROCLAMATION AS DISTINCT, COMPLEX,
COHERENT, AND PERFORMATIVE

Proclamation is a virtuous practice that is distinct, complex, coherent, and performative. Intentional persuasive speech has itself been considered a distinct practice for centuries—even the thinnest renderings of rhetoric describe it as speech that can be performed well or poorly.[87] Christian proclamation is further distinguished first by its content—the resurrection of Jesus Christ and the invitation to follow him as Lord—and second by its audience, which is both a human audience and God.

Proclamation is also coherent and performative. It begins in prayer, proceeds through the engagement in time in unique communicative encounters with others, and ends in prayer. This means that each engagement in proclamation is a non-replicable event that requires the missionary to artfully adjust to new circumstances; the ability to do so well will in part be due to the skills and virtues which they have developed.

This construal of proclamation is also sufficiently complex. As mentioned in the preceding sections, proclamation entails the performance of several discreet yet interrelated activities—prayer, discernment, communication— that must be coordinated together in order to be effective. Proclamation is a skill which can be performed better or worse, and one in which mastery requires practice and the development of the virtues, such as fortitude, temperance, and prudence. In addition, proclamation is the type of complex practice that is easy to learn yet hard to master. Like soccer, which can be learned by three-year-olds but mastered only by a select few professionals, proclamation is something that can be performed by new Christians (e.g., the woman at the well) and mastered by skilled professionals (e.g., St. Paul). This is important, as it shows that proclamation is something that can and should be performed by any Christian regardless of education or length of adherence. The offer to participate in the ongoing mission of God is extended to all, and the gift of experiencing the unique joys of proclaiming the gospel are offered to all. Yet, for some, proclamation may become part of one's vocation. For the missionary, proclamation is part of their role in the life of the church,

---

87. See, for instance, Cunningham's description of the nineteenth-century low point of rhetorical studies, in which eloquence was the only remaining aspect of the definition of rhetoric. Even in this thin definition of rhetoric as eloquence, there is still an emphasis on the ability to perform speech with varying levels of skill. Cunningham, *Faithful*, 19–24.

and they are devoted to its mastery. Such mastery affords the missionary the ability to be an authoritative teacher, apprenticing others who seek a similar vocation. In addition, this mastery becomes a source of inspiration for all Christians who from time to time engage in proclamation. The star basketball player may become a teacher and coach, interacting personally with younger players as they learn their craft. Yet she may also be an inspiration, her picture adorning the walls of aspiring youth.

This helps to explain the perceived oddity of the inauguration of the diaconate in the book of Acts. Because of the complexity of the practice of proclamation, the apostles are unable to devote their time to its exercise and still sufficiently tend to the poor. So, deacons are appointed so that the apostles may devote their time to honing their craft, the preaching of the word. The complexity of these activities leads to the emergence of distinct vocations, one devoted to proclamation, the other to service to the poor. Nicholas Afanasiev sees the emergence of these vocations as affirming both the universal ministry of all Christians on account of the Spirit being poured out on the whole church, as well as the work of that same Spirit in calling individuals to perform specific functions within the life of the church.[88] Such specific vocations are necessarily complementary with the various other functions performed within a church in which all have been given the same Spirit. However, there is not a strict division of labor. The Holy Spirit is capable of calling individuals to perform specific tasks at specific times that may not be directly related to their vocation.[89] This is evidenced by Luke's immediate portrayal of the first deacon, Stephen, engaging in skillful and persuasive

---

88. Nicholas Afanasiev, *The Church of the Holy Spirit* (Notre Dame, IN: University of Notre Dame Press, 2007).

89. Afanasiev, *The Church*, 17. In his assessment of ministry in the New Testament and early Christianity, Nicholas Afanasiev makes several important points in this regard. First, there is the notion that the deacons in Acts 6 might have functioned also as the leaders of the church in Jerusalem, in which case the division of labor is more explicitly over the expansion of the church through the mission of the apostles. In this case, the split would be over mission and pastoral ministry. Whether these deacons functioned more as presbyters is still debatable, but in either case there is still evidence of a kind of soft division of labor between mission and other activities in the life of the early church.

Afanasiev further examines the role of ministry as described in the New Testament, arguing that ordination to specific ministries is meant for enactment of specific tasks rather than the creation of separate classes of people within the church: "The difference between a person who has a particular ministry and a person who does not have such a ministry is not ontological but functional. ... There can be no non-charismatic members in the Church, just as there can be no members who do not minister in it." Afanasiev, *The Church*, 16.

oratory. Stephen's ordination to the deaconate does not preclude the exercise of proclamation, nor does Paul's apostleship preclude his advocacy for the struggling church in Jerusalem.[90]

PROCLAMATION AND THE BOOK OF ACTS

As the references to the book of Acts above have attempted to show, this conception of proclamation fits with the missionary conduct of the disciples in Luke's second volume. An additional note should be stated in regard to how this conception addresses the strengths and weakness of the construals of mission as growth and dialogue. Proclamation is a practice in which one can improve, and thus there is certainly room for the missionary to attempt to develop skills that help them to better understand their audience and the available means of persuasion. The well-crafted orations of Peter and Stephen, and the clear examples of Paul adapting his message to suit various audiences, clearly demonstrate the exercise of missionary skill. Furthermore, Luke's portrayal of these acts of proclamation clearly show that the numerical success of these ventures is not necessarily dependent upon the excellence of their performance. The results of these acts are varied: mass conversions, modest numerical success, and complete and violent rejection. These examples show that there are limits in how far the disciples are willing to adapt their message and that they prefer martyrdom to coerciveness.

PROCLAMATION, MORAL REFLECTION, AND ETHICS

The act of proclamation is a deliberate action—the missionary deliberates before speaking and deliberates after speaking. In doing both, they distinguish proclamation as an intelligible and serious action,[91] one that can be

---

According to Afanasiev, there are various ministries performed within the church, and one could classify certain ministries as higher or lower (in the sense that a bishop is "above" the congregation). Yet, "no one can act without or apart from the others" (17). Afanasiev's description of higher and lower functions could perhaps indicate what will be asserted below: that some may be able to perform their functions better than others and that there are ways in which those called to perform such functions may improve upon the performance of their Spirit-given tasks.

90. Here is at least a partial explanation for the selection of proclamation and gathering as preeminent missional practices. Their selection is not meant to deny the legitimacy of the church's service to the poor, but rather to strengthen it, as it is meant to show that proclamation and service are best thought of as discrete, complex practices which may be aided by the demarcation of separate vocations, yet such activities are still basic enough to be engaged in by all Christians.

91. O'Donovan, *Self*, 33.

performed well or poorly. Such reflection can be along the lines of practical reflection—did the initial discernment of the various means of persuasion for the audience actually fit with the reality of the situation at hand? Which arguments resonated with the audience? Which responses to questions were incoherent? In such reflection, one replays key moments in their mind, imagining better performances: "I should have said this at that moment!" Such reflection may be the grounds through which the preparation for future acts of proclamation will begin. In this way, the missionary hones their skills, learning how to better perform their tasks in future encounters. As a chess player may analyze previous games to learn from their mistakes, as athletes watch game film in order to improve for ensuing contests, the missionary reflects on their act of proclamation, discerning what went wrong, what went right, and the ways in which they may improve.

It is in the context of such practical reflection that limited room may be made for the various skills and techniques of the mission as growth model. The missionary may use various fields of research in order to better discover the available means of persuasion that will make their proclamation more resonant in future engagements. For instance, missiological research may aid in understanding some cultural particularities, or testimonies of converts may help the missionary discover which aspects of the Christian message resonated with specific people in specific places. However, such knowledge is chastened by several factors. First, because the process of assent to the Christian faith is not syllogistic, such research should not be seen as providing any sort of *guarantee* of future success. If the presentation of the gospel takes place within unique places, and the process of assent, as Newman contends, is deeply personal and multiform, then such research must be seen only as a potential aid. In this way, it is similar to athletic training: practice may help with future athletic performances, but it does not guarantee athletic success. Second, such research, when placed within the context of an overall performance of the practice of proclamation which includes prayer, must hold up under moral scrutiny. In examining the available means of persuasion, one may also discover which means of persuasion might be inappropriate. Evidence of success in the mission field may be evidence of the discovery of forms of mission practices that the missionary deems inappropriate as they compromise either the Christian message or the agency of the other.

This assertion regarding the scrutinizing of proclamative practices suggests that this process of reflection must be both practical and moral. In moral reflection, the missionary assesses whether they were faithful to the message they were proclaiming and whether their actions bestowed upon the audience the opportunity to clearly understand this message and freely respond in the affirmative or the negative. In this way it acknowledges the reality that proclamation is a *moral* action capable of drawing us closer to, or farther away from, God. Darlene Weaver emphasizes Aquinas's notion that all human action is moral action, as human action involves deliberation and choice. Thus, morality cannot be separated from human action: we act for particular ends, which is why "what" we do always involves a "why" and "what for."[92] To say that human actions are moral actions is to deny that morality can be treated as a separable component of human life. There is a temptation to think of proclamation as an intrinsically good act, one approved of by God simply because it discloses to the world the reality of the resurrection. Here, the morality of the act of proclamation is assumed by its performance, neglecting serious reflection upon the way it was conducted. In moral reflection, we examine not only the ends sought in proclamation, but the means taken toward that end. Here, the missionary questions the ways in which they may have been overbearing or perhaps misconstrued Christianity in the interest of assent.

Finally, reflection affords the missionary an opportunity to reassess their own beliefs, discovering the ways in which this encounter with another may refine their own faith. In the process of presenting the justifications for the Christian faith, the missionary may receive questions from their interlocutor that cause a reevaluation of their own beliefs: the devout Muslim in the midst of Ramadan may challenge the missionary's lack of emphasis on fasting, the Marxist may unearth in the missionary's beliefs unhealthy collusions between faith and money, or the care an atheist exhibits for their parents may convict the missionary who rarely visits the nursing home. In these ways, the missionary acknowledges the reality that persuasion is a two-way street, and that their dialogue was not simply a pretext for monologue.

---

92. Darlene Fozard Weaver, *The Acting Person and Christian Moral Life* (Washington, DC: Georgetown University Press, 2011), 107.

CONCLUSION—THE ULTIMATE
GOAL OF PROCLAMATION

MacIntyre's notion of a virtuous practice involves activities that have unique goods that are internal to their performance. There are unique goods that one obtains through the virtuous practice of proclamation. This is the ultimate goal of those who engage in this practice—the partaking in God's glory. This end should not be underemphasized. There is unique joy in speaking about Christ and his resurrection, a joy that can fill the soul regardless of its reception. The great sin of the missionary movement in the colonial era was its collusion with empire, a collusion evidenced in forced baptisms that stripped proclamation of its persuasive and invitatory tones. The great sin of the missionary movement today is the rendering of proclamation as banal. On the one side are those who submit proclamation to the powers of market efficiency, with the missionary striving for a managerial effectiveness that rivals corporate CEOs. Here the inspiration is from books such as *Good to Great* that narrate the market success of companies such as Kimberly-Clark and Gillette. If missionaries seek to draw inspiration from companies that produce shaving cream and bathroom tissue with masterful efficiency, they should not be surprised to find that their endeavors are equally as mundane.

On the other side are those who view proclamation as an uncomfortable action that is either avoided or performed begrudgingly. But there are limits to the degree in which our obligations will drive our actions. Our loves are greater drivers of our will, and those who proclaim Christ as an outflow of their love of God will find a greater abundance of joy in disclosing the gospel as *good* news, and a greater spur toward future missionary actions.

While there is intrinsic joy in the proclamation of the gospel regardless of its reception, there are occasions in which interlocutors respond in the affirmative to the Christian message, affording the missionary an opportunity to experience the joy of gathering such individuals into a worshiping community. It is imperative that we now turn to an assessment of gathering as virtuous practice.

6
—

GATHERING

The previous chapter stated that the penultimate goal of the practice of proclamation was the assent of an individual to the Christian faith, which immediately raises the question as to what happens after such assent occurs. The formation of new worshiping communities has long been considered the proper response of the missionary to conversion and is thus the second major activity performed by the missionary. Missionaries do not leave isolated individuals in the wake of their proclamation, disconnected in their new faith. Rather, they leave communities that gather together regularly to worship God the Father, Son, and Holy Spirit.

In the book of Acts, new converts are gathered together to form new worshiping communities centered upon Jesus Christ. Luke presents vivid descriptions of such communities, each given immediately after an event of proclamation (for instance, Acts 2:43–47; 4:32–34). Yet Luke's descriptions, vivid as they are, are tantalizingly brief. While he gives detailed accounts of acts of proclamation, there are no such accounts of gathering in Acts: Luke instead simply describes as fact the existence of new worshiping communities. The movement is from proclamation to conversion to church. Gathering is the middle step required to establish these churches, and a lack of its full-fledged description in Acts invites significant missiological inquiry: Why do missionaries gather converts into a church community? What are the essential activities of these churches? And how does the missionary go about forming these churches?

This chapter answers these questions, filling in the connective tissue between the proclamation of the gospel and the establishment of church congregations. It does so by describing the complex activity of gathering as a practice which fosters virtue in the missionary and glorifies God. It begins first by tracing the connections between proclamation and gathering in order to show how gathering is essential to the task of mission. From there, it examines the three major activities involved in the gathering of new worshiping communities, which unfold in a series of triads:

1. In order to establish place and the sacraments, the missionary engages in *inculturation*.

2. In order to establish language and the word, the missionary engages in *translation*.

3. In order to establish authority and ministry, the missionary engages in *delegation*.

Following this assessment is an examination of the goal of gathering, which is the delight in communion. The chapter concludes by showing how this description of gathering fits the stated goals of my conception of mission as virtuous practice.

PROCLAMATION AND GATHERING

Human beings are intrinsically and necessarily social, born into a network of relationships not of their choosing which imprint an indelible mark on their individual personhood. Who we are as individuals is honed through a lifetime of interactions with others, and the deprivation of such interactions risks our erosion as human beings. Children deprived of any social encounters will physically die within a few years. Solitary confinement is considered a nearly maximal form of punishment for the hardened criminal. Scripture states simply that "it is not good that the man should be alone" (Gen 2:18). The separation of humankind from God that results from sin radiates outward, fracturing the relationships between all human beings, beginning first with animosity between Adam and Eve and extending to the first murder perpetuated by Cain.

So God begins the work of salvation through the formation of a people through the descendants of Abraham, with the theme of gathering continuing to be interwoven into the tapestry of salvation history as depicted throughout Holy Scripture. Israel is constituted as a people through the giving of the Ten Commandments and the day of assembly (Deut 9:10—Septuagint *hēmera ekklēsias*), with the tabernacle becoming simultaneously the place where Israel gathers and the place where Israel meets God. In lieu of the destruction of the first temple, the Israelites long for God to gather their people together once again. Gerhard Lohfink points out that for Isaiah, Jeremiah, and Ezekiel, the hope of the scattered Israelites is for God to restore their community by gathering them together once again. Therefore, gathering "even becomes a soteriological *terminus technicus* in these prophetic books; that is, it is a fixed term for the bringing of salvation. 'Gathering Israel' often parallels 'help,' 'liberate,' 'rescue,' 'heal,' and 'redeem.' "[1] As the faith of the Hebrews is intrinsically social, the restoration of Israel and salvation for the Hebrew people must entail their gathering together once again.

This is why the coming of salvation by God through the incarnation of Jesus Christ involves the gathering of a people. Jesus's earthly ministry begins with the calling of the twelve disciples and the pronouncement of the kingdom of God. The number twelve, an obvious parallel to the twelve tribes, symbolizes the restoration of the scattered people of Israel through the person of Jesus. The twelve are "the beginning and center of growth for the renewed, eschatological Israel."[2] However, the gathering of the twelve is not simply for symbolic purposes; it also signifies that the coming salvation is intrinsically social.

This connection between salvation and gathering extends in Scripture through the events following Jesus's resurrection as portrayed by Luke in the book of Acts. Pentecost symbolizes the gathering of the scattered people of the world as a kind of reversal of Babel, bringing together those separated by language for the sake of inaugurating an age of the restored people of God on mission to bring news of this restoration to the world:

> Pentecost should be seen as the initial fulfillment of an eschatological vision in which the Jewish remnant scattered throughout the world returns to Jerusalem for the reconstitution of God's people. Once this occurs, the reconstituted or restored people of God would then reverse this centripetal movement and extend God's mission outward—centrifugally—to the world.[3]

As mentioned above, Luke goes on to structure the book of Acts in a way that shows the link between the proclamation of the good news of Jesus's

---

1. Gerhard Lohfink, *Does God Need the Church? Toward a Theology of the People of God*, trans. Linda M. Maroney (Collegeville, MN: Liturgical Press, 2014), 52.

2. Lohfink, *Does God Need the Church?*, 131.

3. Holladay, *Acts*, 94–95.

resurrection and the gathering of the people of God. To assent to a belief in Jesus as Lord and Savior entails the entrance into a community that embodies this salvation. Kavin Rowe summarizes this connection in Acts succinctly:

At least according to Acts, the universal Lordship of Jesus is not only about the heart but also about the formation of a particular public— the two, in fact, are inseparable: repentance and salvation entail a socially noticeable way of life. Put differently, the Christian mission's proclamation of the good news was simultaneously a summons to church.[4]

PROCLAMATION AND GATHERING AS
JOINT MISSIONAL ACTIVITIES

The previous section highlighted the connection between the proclamation of the good news and the summons to church as consistent threads throughout Scripture, and thus any construal of mission that seeks accordance with Scripture must take seriously this connection. If contemporary Christian missional practices should demonstrate a fittingness to the missional practices of Scripture, it is imperative that the proclamation of the gospel also be a summons to gather. This assertion would challenge forms of mission that proclaim a personal salvation but do not also include a serious attempt to gather new converts into a new or existing church. The sidewalk evangelist distributing tracts without any attempt to integrate their audience with a local congregation is one example of this kind of mission. A more widespread example is the manifold proclamations mediated through digital communications. Here, the gospel is promulgated through pixels and compressed audio, implicitly encouraging a faith that is equally disembodied, with the convert (at best) taught to self-select a church at their individual discretion. In these cases, a split is rendered between proclamation and gathering, between personal and communal salvation.

There also exist forms of mission that seek to gather individuals together without the proclamation of the resurrection of Jesus Christ. Chapter two highlighted this potential problem with the mission as growth model: if numerical growth is the goal of mission, then missionaries can start new

---

4. Rowe, *World*, 126.

churches through gathering existing Christians from other congregations. The proclamation of the gospel to non-Christians is not necessary and may even be a hindrance to numerical success, as more Christians may be in the market for a new church than non-Christians.

The mission as dialogue paradigm could also be construed as an attempt to gather together individuals for the purpose of developing relationships and establishing community without the shared belief in Jesus Christ. Twentieth-century missions in Africa could at certain times and places be characterized by the desire to develop community without Christ, with a push to establish schools, hospitals, nonprofit agencies, and governments rather than churches. Lamin Sanneh describes this kind of gathering without proclamation as the promotion of civilization without Christianity, a kind of "ecclesiastical Peace Corps."[5] Sanneh chronicles the frustrations of Vincent Donovan as he discovers that, after years of missions work in East Africa, his order had built several hospitals but no converts. Donovan construes this work as the work of civilization making, with the constant deferral of the Christian message under the auspices that natives were not sufficiently cultured (i.e., westernized) to become full Christians.

For Donovan, such mission was a denial of the power of God to enable those of other cultures to accept the gospel, gather together, and build a community as they saw fit. We have seen earlier a similar critique of the mission as dialogue paradigm—that it denies the agency of individuals to accept or reject the Christian message under the auspices of Western conceptions of pluralism, justice, and religious toleration.[6] This can leave the work of the missionary to gather for the sake of development, which can just as easily be the promotion of Western cultural values:

> I would still hold today that missionaries are sometimes confused in their role and in their handling of development. To assume that Western, i.e., American forms of development, both economic and agricultural (the latter often associated with toxic pesticides), are the most suitable forms for all Third World countries is a bit presumptuous, to say the least. And even for those programs of development

---

5. Lamin O. Sanneh, *Disciples of All Nations: Pillars of World Christianity* (Oxford, UK: Oxford University Press, 2008), 235.

6. See Milbank, "The End," 181–85.

that prove beneficial for peoples in foreign missionary countries, for the extraneous missionaries to take the leading role as the agents of change is to confuse the respective places of the evangelizer and the empowered evangelized.[7]

Donovan's response was to center mission on the transmission and translation of the gospel and the establishing of new congregations that were fully indigenous: "The final missionary step as regards the people of any nation or culture, and the most important lesson we will ever teach them—is to leave them."[8] We will discuss Donovan and his response further below.

While the aforementioned examples show the challenges involved in an approach to mission that does not take proclamation and gathering as essentially interrelated, the connection between proclamation and gathering is not controversial for many throughout Christian history: a missionary is simply one who preaches the gospel and establishes new churches. The question that remains is *how* such gatherings should be conducted, as well as the contents and purposes of actions performed in these gatherings. The remainder of this chapter will be devoted to unpacking the activities involved in the missional practice of gathering.

GATHERING AS VIRTUOUS PRACTICE

Just as the previous chapter construed Christian proclamation as a discreet practice, the purposeful exercise of which develops virtue in the missionary as they partake in the glory of God, so too can gathering be considered a type of virtuous practice. It encompasses a collection of skills in which the missionary can improve and which enable opportunities for the missionary to grow in character and glorify God. Just as proclamation is a discreet yet complex activity, with several actions, the practice of gathering is a coherent and complex activity: the establishment of a new congregation and the gathering of converts into this community.

---

7. Vincent J. Donovan, "Response to Reflections on Christianity Rediscovered," *Missiology* 18, no. 3 (1990): 277.

8. Vincent J. Donovan, *Christianity Rediscovered* (Maryknoll, NY: Orbis Books, 2003), 121.

What are the essential activities needed to constitute a new church? We can take as a starting point Luke's description of the first Christian church in Acts 2:41–47:

> So those who welcomed his message were baptized, and that day about three thousand persons were added. They devoted themselves to the apostles' teaching and fellowship, to the breaking of bread and the prayers.
>
> Awe came upon everyone, because many wonders and signs were being done by the apostles. All who believed were together and had all things in common; they would sell their possessions and goods and distribute the proceeds to all, as any had need. Day by day, as they spent much time together in the temple, they broke bread at home and ate their food with glad and generous hearts, praising God and having the goodwill of all the people. And day by day the Lord added to their number those who were being saved.

We can trace within this description several components of the worshiping community that have come to define the essential marks of a local congregation: there is the gathering together of Christians in a particular location and the celebration of the sacraments (the breaking of bread), there is the teaching of the contents and language of the faith by the apostles through the explication of Scripture (at that time, the Old Testament), and there is the assertion of some degree of authority granted to the apostles for the appropriate oversight of this community. These marks can be summarized as sacraments, word, and ministry. These marks are most vividly seen in the various definitions of the church during the Reformation. Article Nineteen of the Thirty-Nine Articles of Religion, for instance, gives a succinct definition of the church: "The visible Church of Christ is a congregation of faithful men, in which the pure Word of God is preached, and the Sacraments be duly ministered according to Christ's ordinance, in all those things that of necessity are requisite to the same."[9]

---

9. While authority is implicit in the phrase "duly administered," its necessity is explicitly reinforced in the ensuing article, which states that "the Church hath power to decree Rites or Ceremonies, and authority in Controversies of Faith."

While these essential components of the church are generally shared by most Christian denominations, there are great differences in how each of these marks are defined. For instance, the number of sacraments and the degree to which ministry includes oversight above the local

Gathering is the activity which establishes churches that bear these marks. It is the verb which precedes the noun of the church. My conception of gathering as virtuous practice proceeds by expanding upon these marks of the church, addressing the following missiological questions:

- *Why does the missionary gather?* The controlling metaphor of new birth in Christ is key to understanding the necessity of gathering. As a child needs a home, a community to learn language, and the ability to take on responsibility as they grow, the new Christian needs a worshiping location, a linguistic community, and the ability to exercise authority and responsibility within that community. The missionary thus gathers in order to establish *place, language, and authority.*

- *What does the missionary gather?* As described in Scripture, the church demarcates place through the sacraments, inculcates language through the word, and enables authority through the affirmation of ministry. Thus, the missionary gathers churches that bear the marks of *the sacraments, the word, and ministry.*

- *How does the missionary gather?* In order to perform the act of gathering well, the missionary needs to develop the skill of inculturation to establish place, translation to establish language, and delegation to establish authority. Thus, the missionary gathers through *inculturation, translation, and delegation.*

The next three sections proceed through this series of triads, beginning with the establishment of place and the sacraments, which necessitates the skill of inculturation. Second, it addresses the establishment of language and the word, which requires the skill of translation. And, last, it details the establishment of authority and ministry, which requires the skill of delegation.

---

congregation vary between denominations. This study will not delve deeply into these differences. The emphasis will instead be on how the missionary establishes churches that bear these marks. However, my own ecclesial commitments as an Anglican clergyman evince a particular understanding of Scripture, the sacraments, and church authority that will be evident from time to time, though the hope is that my elucidation of gathering is easily adaptable to various denominations and polities.

Included in Luke's description of the church in Acts 2 is the goal of such gatherings: the sharing of a common life together in Christ. My definition of gathering will thus end with an examination of its goal, which is the establishment of communion.

ESTABLISHING PLACE: THE SACRAMENTS AND INCULTURATION

Gathering requires the meeting of human beings at specific times and places in order to encounter the living God. Humans are corporeal beings, possessing bodies which occupy time and space. Mind, body, and soul cannot be separated, and our understanding of ourselves is thus linked to the experience of our body in time: "To the question 'Who am I?' it is highly unlikely we could provide a response without prior meditation on another question: 'Where am I?' "[10] According to Jean-Yves Lacoste, place "furnishes us the coordinates of existence."[11] It is that which our bodies navigate, and it is our interactions within place as well as the reflections on these interactions which provide the opportunity for meaning in human life.

While place furnishes us these coordinates, it also imposes on us limits. Our bodies cannot be in two places at once, and our bodies cannot fully abstract ourselves from our place without "losing all conceptual grasp of who we are."[12] Thus, there is a type of paradox in our experience of place. On the one hand, it provides us with a degree of stability: for those residing in one locale, they may wake up with familiar surroundings each day, freeing them to think and do other things. On the other hand, place may also be a source of anxiety: place precedes our existence, and we cannot completely control it. In a sense, it takes control of us:

> When the analysis retraces the dawn of experience up to the simple discovery that I am, and that I am in the world, then it encounters nothing of import if not the realization of a pure limitation: the world is not ours; on the contrary, its reality takes possession of us and determines us, and it is we who in the first place must submit to its authority.[13]

---

10. Jean-Yves Lacoste, *Experience and the Absolute: Disputed Questions on the Humanity of Man*, trans. Mark Raftery-Skehan (New York: Fordham University Press, 2004), 7.

11. Lacoste, *Experience*, 8.

12. Lacoste, *Experience*, 10.

13. Lacoste, *Experience*, 12.

Place thus provides us both with stability and anxiety, a sense of comfort as well as a sense that the world is not entirely in our control.

For those who assent to Christian proclamation, they are considered by St. Paul as "new selves" in Christ. This new self in Christ is, however, still a bodily self, and it is through the body that Christians encounter Christ throughout their lives. Location thus cannot be abandoned by the Christian, but instead must be renewed and restored so as to become the place through which one meets God. Because there cannot be a separation between the self and the body, conversion cannot be a purely mental phenomenon: "The encounter between man and the Absolute in no way overlooks location."[14] Scripture does not overlook the importance of location for encountering God, as evidenced most vividly in the construction of the tabernacle. Here, Moses is given highly specific details concerning every aspect of its construction, with the tabernacle becoming both the dwelling place of God and the meeting place for God and Israel. Gathering, place, and the encounter of the living God are thus intricately interwoven.

Although Christ's resurrection enabled salvation to extend beyond the cultural boundaries of the Israelites, it did not emancipate people from their bodies. The corporeal center of worship was no longer the physical materials of the tabernacle and (later) the temple in Jerusalem, but the physical body of Christ made manifest in the gathering of the local church. Because such gatherings take place within a world that is still sinful, there was an acknowledgment that to be Christian required a renewed and restored place. And so the early Christians took ordinary places—often the atriums of wealthy converts—and demarcated them as sacred through liturgical actions, the reading of Scripture, and the celebration of the Eucharist. The first half of worship followed the liturgical form of the synagogue, with the Scriptures now being shown to point to their fulfillment in Christ. The second half of worship appropriated the Passover sacrifice meal, with the celebration of the Eucharist in remembrance of Christ's sacrifice on the cross.[15] In performing such actions, they created space through which their members might encounter Christ and furnished coordinates for Christian existence.

---

14. Lacoste, *Experience*, 21.

15. See Gregory Dix, *The Shape of the Liturgy* (London: Dacre Press, 1970), 36–37.

Thus, the missionary must establish a place for those who assent to their gospel proclamation, creating space in which the new convert may live out their new life in Christ. They consecrate certain times and places as sacred, as places which differ from the ordinary. They establish place by enculturating liturgy: enacting rituals and rites that demarcate a particular place in time as a place through which God may be encountered. Louis-Marie Chauvet calls the enactment of such rituals a "symbolic rupture":

> A ritual always involves a symbolic rupture with the everyday, the ephemeral, the ordinary. A church, a temple, a high place, a sacred wood, or simply the space around a tree or in the center of the village square, whether it be permanent or temporary—the place of religious ritual is always "consecrated," that is, set apart, taken out of its ordinary status as a neutral space by a symbolic marker of some kind.[16]

Chauvet describes the "borderline nature" of these rites: because they appropriate the ordinary for extraordinary purposes, they are always in a liminal position.[17] They are meant to move people from the ordinary to the extraordinary, and, as such, they must occupy an appropriate symbolic distance between the two extremes.[18] If the symbols and rites used are too foreign to the gathering of Christians, they risk becoming inaccessible. Chauvet calls this "hieratic liturgy"—it is liturgy that is so frozen that it is isolated from the people gathered so that they "no longer evolve along with the culture and no longer tolerate any spontaneity of expression."[19] Here, the performance of such rites becomes a formality for those gathered, done out of obligation or from unexpressed and subconscious social benefit. For example, one may attend mass out of obligation, out of the desire to be a "good Catholic" or a "good Christian," and not have any idea why the priest washes their hands before the Eucharist or the meaning, history, or significance of singing the *sanctus*. A social norm is performed, a ritual observed, but God is not experienced. It is from this that the colloquial expression "dead liturgy" or "dead ritual" is derived.

---

16. Chauvet, *Symbol*, 330.
17. Chauvet, *Symbol*, 331.
18. Chauvet, *Symbol*, 331.
19. Chauvet, *Symbol*, 332.

At the other end, there is what Chauvet calls the trivialization of the liturgy.[20] Here, symbols, rites, and rituals lose their ability to point to the transcendent, becoming instead the reification of secular space. Here, God is equally inaccessible, and the place of the world will continue to impose itself on us. Churches are no longer distinguishable from the world and will begin to take on worldly ideologies:

> Trivialized under the excuse of being "relevant"; employing only everyday language, gestures, and objects; often drowned in a verbiage of explanation and moralistic sermonizing, rites become no more than pretexts for doing something else. People's ideologies are given free rein and often become in their turn more rigid than the constraint of the ritual programming they wish to combat.[21]

If the gathering of Christians differs in no way from ordinary existence, the life of those gathered will in no way differ from that of the non-Christians in their midst. If the church service is catered to represent a pop concert, one should not be surprised if the worldview of its members more closely resembles that of the average concertgoer.

For Chauvet, the appropriate symbolic distance must be pastorally negotiated. The pastor must create a place that is both accessible to parishioners and demarcates such space as a special location through which God is encountered. The missionary likewise must embark on a similar project, oftentimes starting from the very first gathering of new Christians through the process of inculturation. Such a process is essential and, to some extent, unavoidable. Andrew Walls states that the very nature of conversion implies a "turning what is already there; it is more about direction than about content"[22] and thus does not necessitate the adoption of a foreign culture, but a turning of culture to Christ. For Walls, the notion of inculturation is linked with the incarnation of Christ. The historical reality of God becoming flesh validates his creation as good, and thus the new convert does not take on a foreign body, but instead redirects their own body toward God's glory. Since

---

20. Chauvet, *Symbol*, 335.
21. Chauvet, *Symbol*, 335.
22. Walls, *Missionary Movement*, 79.

this body occupies a particular place, such conversion must also necessitate a turning of one's own social location toward the glory of God.

And so the process of conversion continues from the turn of the person toward God to the turning of one's location toward God through the establishment of specific rites and symbols. The missionary does not, however, create symbols and rites from scratch—they start with the fundamental rituals inherent in Scripture: baptism and the Eucharist. In regard to the Eucharist, Gregory Dix argues that its essential shape has gone relatively unchanged for the majority of churches throughout Christian history even as it has adapted to varying languages and contexts:

> That standard Shape has everywhere remained unchanged for more than eighteen hundred years, overlaid yet never refashioned. But within that rigid framework the eucharist has adapted itself perpetually with a most delicate adjustment to the practical conditions and racial temperaments and special gifts of a multitude of particular churches and peoples and generations.[23]

It is the "delicate adjustment to the practical conditions" which can be considered a skill which must be developed in the missionary. They must understand deeply the acts of baptism and the Eucharist as well as the cultural particularities of the group of new Christians that they are gathering together, from there discerning the delicate adjustments that make these Christian practices meaningful while retaining their definitive shape. It requires a deep understanding of the people they are gathering, the place in which they inhabit, and the symbols which they are called to perform. Out of this understanding comes decisions regarding the various rites and symbols with which this new gathering participates in the worship of God. For Roland Allen, the drive to understand the sacraments and the drive to enculturate them should be mutually linked: "High sacramental doctrine should make men eager ... to prove the sacraments for Christians, and to remove all hindrances which prevent men, anywhere, from using them."[24]

---

23. Dix, *The Shape*, xi.

24. Roland Allen, *The Spontaneous Expansion of the Church: And the Causes Which Hinder It* (Grand Rapids: Eerdmans, 1962), 51.

To take a rather minor example: Should a missionary and Catholic (or Anglican) priest who is establishing a new congregation wear a chasuble? A flat assertion or denial would bespeak some form of ignorance. This ignorance may take either conservative or liberal forms: Liturgical conservatives might insist on incorporating chasubles in the name of tradition alone. Liberals are more likely to encourage the missionary to jettison anything that could be seen as an outdated curiosity, out of step with the times or cultural sensitivities. Instead, the missionary should seek to understand why a chasuble is worn and how it contributes to the creation of symbolic distance and sacred space. In this case, the discovery that a chasuble was simply the most ornate and expensive fabric worn—that it demarcates both the specialness of worship and the opulence with which one worships—should cause the missionary to seek ways in which local formal dress may similarly demarcate worship as a special occasion.

We see in this discernment process how missionaries must exercise a kind of practical judgment, or prudence. While becoming educated on the various church practices, symbols, and rites is highly important, and discussion with their converts regarding their own specific symbols and practices is equally important, at some point a decision must be made. The symbol or action is adapted in some way with the hope that, in so doing, the congregation may fully enter into God's presence in worship. The establishing of place requires an ongoing process of such decisions, some great and some small. Every aspect of gathering new converts together for worship is scrutinized, with the missionary aiming to establish a space that is both consecrated for worship yet accessible so that one can fully enter into worship.

If done well, these decisions can be seen in hindsight not as mere syntheses of tradition and culture, nor as the discovery of a divine golden mean, but as a contribution to the enrichment of the Christian tradition. According to Andrew Walls, since the incarnation involves the assumption of the entirety of humanity, the more fully the church incorporates the full humanity of persons in various cultural locales, the more fully it lives into its identity as the body of Christ. This process of inculturation "brings a church more culturally diverse than it has ever been before; potentially, therefore, nearer to that 'full stature of Christ' that belongs to his summing up humanity."[25]

---

25. Walls, *Missionary Movement*, 81.

ESTABLISHING LANGUAGE: THE WORD AND TRANSLATION

The previous section described the necessity of place as a result of the essential corporeality of human beings. This point can be pressed further in the assertion that human beings are not only essentially corporeal, but also essentially social. The principal act through which human beings socialize is communication, primarily linguistic communication. A strain of modern philosophy, indebted to Martin Buber, is quick to point out the essential sociality of human beings: one only recognizes oneself as an "I" through an interaction with a "You." Alistair McFadyen presses this point further, arguing that "the sense of oneself as a subject, a person, is not individually but socially acquired."[26] Communication can be conceived as those interactions from which a "unique personal identity is sedimented."[27] It is, in a sense, a kind of two-way bridge in which we are able to understand the other as well as better understand ourselves as active subjects. The preeminent form of such communication comes through language. Thus, there is a correlation between the self, the community, and language: the individual self requires a linguistic community in order to grow as a person.

Alasdair MacIntyre describes the need for such communities in order for human beings to flourish *qua* human beings. Human beings are, like other animal species, born necessarily dependent on others. What separates human beings from other animal species, however, is the necessity of language and linguistic instruction for their development as persons. For MacIntyre, it is not simply language that separates human beings from other animal species, since other animals, particularly dolphins, have a somewhat complex language. Rather, the development of language is necessary for human beings to articulate evaluative judgments. Human beings must learn a language in order "to articulate, to reflect upon and to evaluate those different types of tacit or explicit judgments about goods which furnish them with their reasons for acting."[28] We have a desire to know "who and what and where we are."[29] Human beings need language and teachers to help them grow into individuals capable of making these sorts of judgments and self-evaluations. One

---

26. McFadyen, *The Call*, 70.

27. McFadyen, *The Call*, 70.

28. Alasdair C. MacIntyre, *Dependent Rational Animals: Why Human Beings Need the Virtues* (Chicago: Open Court Press, 2011), 67.

29. O'Donovan, *Entering*, 163.

is born dependent upon communities to learn language and upon teachers to help them grow into individuals that are able to evaluate and reflect well.

It is with this that one can begin to see the need for the establishment of a linguistic community within Christianity. Throughout the New Testament, conversion is referred to in terms of birth and growth. There is a consistent theme of new birth by the Holy Spirit. This spiritual birth is from "above" (John 3:3), enabling Christians to be children of God "who were born, not of blood or of the will of the flesh or of the will of man, but of God" (John 1:13). For Paul, conversion is an end to the old self and the taking on of the new self in Christ (Rom 6).

The Christian convert experiences a new birth in Christ through the Spirit, and this new birth, much like a biological birth, also necessitates a linguistic community for its proper development. Here is in part the significance of John's description of Jesus as the Word of God: Jesus is not only the very speech of God, and thus the way through which God may be known, but he is also the center of a new and redeemed linguistic community: "We can compare the coming of Jesus to the coming of a new language ... Jesus is the word, the language of God which comes to be the language of man."[30] The church gathers around Jesus the Word of God who heals the effects of sin which create distortions in relationships while also becoming the center through which redeemed communicative relationships may take place.[31] "To communicate is to embrace a structure of meaning in which the particular is located within the common,"[32] and for Christians, the Word of God, Jesus Christ, is this particular that is the locus of its commonality.

And so the missionary must not only communicate the gospel in order to persuade another of the Christian faith, they must also help to create the structures through which the new convert might learn the language of the Christian faith so they might grow into Christian maturity. As the missionary bears responsibility for their new birth, they also bear responsibility for immersing the new convert in their new linguistic world.

---

30. McCabe, *What Is Ethics?*, 129.

31. McFadyen, *The Call*, 142.

32. O'Donovan, *Entering*, 48.

The Content of Translation: Holy Scripture

The gathering of this linguistic community primarily involves the skill of translation: the ability to take a given set of material and render it intelligible to a particular audience. I will thus proceed to describe how the missionary performs this act of translation considered in a broad sense. Translation is not limited to discreet language, say Spanish to English, but rather it should be considered as all attempts to render intelligible ideas and concepts that were heretofore unintelligible.

An act of translation begins with the material to be translated. The teacher begins with a language that is foreign to their students. Holy Scripture is the language of the Christian faith and the *lingua franca* of the church, and so the missionary thus immerses the new convert in the language of faith. For this reason, from its very inception, the gathering of the church involved the public reading and explication of the Scriptures, a Christocentric adaptation of the common practice of the Jewish synagogue.

Jean-Yves Lacoste describes the process of the interpretation of Scripture as the forging of a third language, which "'fulfils' the language of Jew and Greek and yet is a 'hard' language, tying the future of mankind to the fate of a single crucified man."[33] Though the Christian does not have to learn a new language (say, Greek or Hebrew) when becoming a Christian, they nevertheless have to learn the content of the Christian faith as one who is learning a new language. The goal of translation is to enable converts to "make a home" in the world of this language.[34]

The content of the missionary's teaching is partially fixed by the canon of Scripture. The canon provides the "constant" that must be translated in a new "context." Fidelity to the canon is simply the expression of the desire of the missionary to teach the language of the Christian faith and not some other language. For instance, the Spanish teacher does not use a German textbook. We may expound on this analogy of teaching further: by choosing a select canon of material, the teacher places themselves within a particular tradition that is defined in part by that canon. By selecting specifically Spanish textbooks, the teacher is acceding to the particular linguistic tradition of

---

33. Jean-Yves Lacoste, "More Haste, Less Speed in Theology," *International Journal of Systematic Theology* 9, no. 3 (2007): 263.

34. Lacoste, "More Haste," 263.

the Spanish language—they are choosing to be a Spanish teacher and not a German teacher. In a similar way, by selecting the canon of Scripture as the content of their teaching, the missionary is placing themselves within the tradition of Christians that has been defined through their fidelity to this canon.[35]

The missionary, by selecting as the content of its translation the canon, is inviting and acknowledging God as "a member of the linguistic community."[36] Kevin Vanhoozer asserts that, in the recognition of the canon, the church recognizes the authority of the Holy Spirit both in authorizing these particular texts and drawing these texts together as a unified discourse.[37] When the missionary chooses to ground the gathering community in the language of Scripture, there is an acknowledgment of the continual work of the Holy Spirit to work through these particular texts.

The Skill of Translation

The act of translation involves selection and transmission, and so the missionary must begin by deciding which aspects of Scripture to emphasize and how to render Scripture intelligible for their audience. As we will see, these acts of translation can fit easily into an understanding of gathering as a virtuous practice, as they require a degree of skill and hold the potential to promote virtue in their practitioners.

In order to understand how this act of transmission occurs and how it involves the development of specific skills, it is helpful to turn again, as was done in the previous chapter, to the field of rhetoric. The practice of translation is akin to the proclamation of the gospel—it involves the understanding of content and audience and the marshalling forth of persuasive arguments based upon such understandings.

---

35. Translation is grounded in Scripture not only because the canon defines the content of the Christian faith, but also because Scripture itself is divine communication. The reason the missionary translates and transmits Scripture is not just because it is the foundational document of the linguistic community, but also because they believe that God acts within this linguistic community through Scripture. Scripture is itself "a divine performance, a mode of divine communicative action whereby the triune God furthers his mission and creates a new covenant people." Vanhoozer, The Drama, 176.

36. Vanhoozer, The Drama, 177.

37. Vanhoozer, The Drama, 177.

Wayne Booth's article concerning the use of rhetoric in teaching is an adroit examination of the process of translation. Here, Booth describes rhetoric as "the art of 'putting it across.' "[38] Rhetoric is the art of effectively transmitting material in a way that is intelligible and persuasive for an audience of students. For Booth, teachers should seek to develop the skill of the "rhetorical stance," which involves the discovery of "the available arguments about the subject itself, the interest and peculiarities of the audience, and the voice, the implied character, of the speaker."[39] Effective teachers are able to understand thoroughly the various arguments that undergird a particular subject while also having a thorough understanding of their interlocutors. Teachers err when they emphasize one of these two poles at the expense of the other. Booth labels an emphasis only upon the subject matter as the "pedantic stance" and an emphasis merely upon the audience as the "advertiser's stance."

The act of translation is the art of "putting it across." The missionary takes the subject matter of the Christian faith and attempts to render it intelligible amidst the cultural peculiarities of their audience of new converts. What is required is a thorough understanding of the Bible and the arguments and explanations for the various subject matters presented in Scripture. For instance, when attempting to explain the significance of Jesus's changing of water into wine at Cana (John 2), the missionary should seek to discover the plurality of ways in which this passage has been understood: that wine may connote the heavenly feast, the blood poured out on the cross, and the wine at the Eucharist table. They should understand the significance of Jewish purification rites, which the water was intended for. They should seek to understand the significance behind the restrictiveness of the revelation to the servants and the disciples.

However, the purpose of such knowledge is not that it should be rotely transmitted to their converts. The missionary cannot simply give out a spreadsheet of biblical meanings and expect the transmission of the Christian message any more than a geometry teacher may hand their students the

---

38. Wayne C. Booth, "The Rhetorical Stance," *College Composition and Communication* 14, no. 3 (1963): 139.

39. Booth, "The Rhetorical Stance," 141. Since the character of the speaker was covered in the previous chapter, and Booth largely brackets questions of ethos in this article, the ensuing will focus largely upon the first two aspects of Booth's conception of "The Rhetorical Stance."

Pythagorean theorem and walk away. Instead, they must seek to understand their audience so as to make such explanations resonate.

And so the missionary seeks to understand their audience: What images connote festivity, or purification, or sacrifice? What existing conceptions of Jesus might this story amend? How does this story compare with other known accounts of miracles? What is most resonate about this story: the pleading of a mother to her son, the exhibition of hospitality, or the revelation of Jesus's glory?

The missionary must take all of this into consideration, not only attempting to render the passage intelligible, but also showing how this story might affect the lives of their audience. Such a presentation is a unique event in time and space and, as such, "only partially amenable to systematic teaching."[40] The missionary who has honed the skills of translation through years of practice learns the subtle ways in which their presentation of the material will need to shift with the changes to their audience. Booth uses as his example the way in which a teacher's lesson may resonate with the 1 p.m. class but fall flat with the 2 p.m. class.

The missionary who establishes churches in parts of the world that have little to no experience with Christianity must try to explain the various aspects of Scripture and the Christian message in ways that resonate with their audience. The translation of Scripture into native languages is the most visible exercise of such skill. The history of overseas missions presents a whole host of examples of effective and ineffective acts of translation. Lamin Sanneh showcases the various ways throughout modern missionary history that such translation has been done effectively and poorly[41] and gives examples from his own West African upbringing. For Sanneh, the difficulty in effective translation can be summarized by his own experience with a translation of John 1 in Bakau: the interpretation of John the Baptist as "John the Swimmer" added a "cosmic impression" to the story, while the translation of the Word of God as the "palaver of God" offended nearby Muslims, creating an obstacle to the gospel transmission.[42]

---

40. Booth, "The Rhetorical Stance," 140.

41. See Sanneh, *Translating*, 192–210.

42. Sanneh, *Translating*, 193.

Translation occurs whenever the missionary attempts to explain some aspect of Scripture or any Christian concept, even if such explanation is occurring between people who have the same native language. The convert, for instance, does not instantly understand the Trinity by simply reciting the creed in their native tongue. Here we may take our cue from Wittgenstein's assertion that the meaning of words is determined within the world in which they are used. For Wittgenstein, words only have meaning within the social context in which they are learned. Language is learned through our interactions with others, which places a priority on teaching.[43]

While a Christian epistemology cannot completely adopt Wittgenstein's philosophy of language, as it misses the transcendent capacity of language,[44] his point is important for understanding the importance of teaching as an act of translation, particularly within mission in the North American context. The meaning of the phrase "Jesus is Lord and God" is not instantaneously intelligible to the new convert, even if the missionary and convert speak the same language. The missionary must teach, through various expressions, examples, illustrations, metaphors, etc., what the words "Lord" and "God" mean within the linguistic community of the church. The goal of such teaching is to bring about the adherence of an understanding of these words that is both intelligible to the student and in accordance with how these words have been understood within the Christian community throughout space and time. It is a continual teaching that *this* means *that*. This is equally important amongst missions between people who share a common language: it should

---

43. "In the course of this teaching, I shall shew him the same colours, the same lengths, the same shapes, I shall make him find them and produce them, and so on. ... I do it, he does it after me; and I influence him by expressions of agreement, rejection, expectation, encouragement. ... Imagine witnessing such teaching. None of the words would be explained by mean of itself." Ludwig Wittgenstein, *Philosophical Investigations*, trans. G. E. M. Anscombe (Oxford: Basil Blackwell, 1958), 83.

44. Wittgenstein's insistence that the meaning of language is not deeper than its social intelligibility would seem to contradict the role of the Christian understanding of the operation of the Holy Spirit within the life of a believer. The illumination of the Holy Spirit draws the believer into a real relationship of love and knowledge of God through Jesus Christ. This can bring about a true, though always incomplete, knowledge of God, as Luther famously stated. Here there is a break (or breakthrough) with Wittgenstein—the Holy Spirit enables the words we speak about God to be truly correspondence with a transcendent reality. At a more general level, Charles Taylor makes the simple assertion that many human beings hold to the belief that language possesses the possibility of opening up "contact with something higher or deeper (be it God, or the depths of human nature, desire, the Will to Power, or whatever)." Taylor, *A Secular Age*, 758.

be not assumed that terms such as "God" and "Lord" are commonly understood within the broader society.

Superb acts of translation have the ability to transcend mere adherence to the understanding of subject matter, potentially yielding new insights into the Christian faith. This has been noted earlier by Lamin Sanneh in his account of how the translation of John the Baptist as John the Swimmer yielded new "cosmological" insights. Exquisite acts of translation "achieve a communicative constancy [with the original conceptual content] that preserves and sometimes even develops our understanding of the original."[45] The most skillful translators not only successfully communicate the content of Scripture but also unearth insights that provide greater depth of understanding of Scripture.[46]

---

45. Vanhoozer, *The Drama*, 132.

46. Kenneth Burke's notion of poetic realism, as opposed to scientific realism, is helpful in understanding how such an expansion of understanding is possible. For Burke, the reality of character (which can be a person, or subject, or anything that is distinct) is made known through the putting forth of a variety of perspectives through which, with justice, that character might be perceived. The more complex a character, the more perspectives may be given to further one's understanding of it. For instance, an object that we do not fully understand compels us to "deliberately try to consider it in as many different terms as its nature permits: lifting, smelling, tasting, tapping ... dividing, matching, contrasting, etc." (422). For Burke, "characters possess degrees of being in proportion to the variety of perspectives from which they can with justice be perceived" (422). The more complex the character, the greater variety of perspectives that exist. For instance, there are far more numerous justifiable perspectives for an individual human being than there are for an individual rock. Thus, when one can provide a new perspective on a particular character, it is able to aid in its understanding without necessarily contradicting other perspectives. See Kenneth Burke, "Four Master Tropes," *The Kenyon Review* 3, no. 4 (1941).

For the Christian, the knowledge of God is inexhaustible from the vantage point of human beings. Thus, exquisite acts of translation on the part of the missionary have the ability to add to the various noncontradictory perspectives on God, plunging the inexhaustible depths of the knowledge and love of God. For the missiologist Andrew Walls, Christianity itself rests on a divine act of translation: "the Word of God became flesh" (26). God becomes flesh within a specific time and place so that he might be made known. In every act of translation, the missionary participates in the divine movement of translation, making Scripture intelligible in new times and places and thus rendering greater understanding of the Christian God: "New translations, by taking the word about Christ into a new area, applying it to new situations, have the potential actually to reshape and expand the Christian faith" (29). My addition to this assertion is to posit that translation may not be limited to interactions between two discreet languages but occurs whenever the missionary attempts to explain Scripture to an audience of new converts. See Walls, *Missionary Movement*, 26–42.

Translation and Structures of Immersion

Effective translation enables the convert to inhabit the world of Scripture and successfully live within the linguistic community of the church. The goal is not simply the mastery of a new language, but that such mastery enables one to flourish within a new linguistic community, just as the goal of learning Spanish is to live and flourish within Spanish-speaking communities.

We can here extend the aforementioned Pauline analogy of conversion as a new birth. Upon birth, a parent takes responsibility for the education of their child, which involves the inculcation into a linguistic community. Yet the goal of such teaching is not rote memorization, but rather the flourishing of the child as they grow into adulthood. One of the most fascinating aspects of early childhood development is the ways in which children learn a new language without the aid of formal education. Simply by being surrounded by conversations and by being spoken to before verbal response is possible, the child learns their language. From here formal education is added in order to further develop and refine the linguistic capabilities that formed through these simple acts of immersion.

Similarly, the missionary bears responsibility for the convert's new birth in Christ by teaching them the language of the church, yet the point of such teaching is that the new convert may become an adult capable of living out their faith in new and unique situations. This requires both their immersion in the language of Christianity and formal instruction. The emphasis of the missionary is on the creation of these structures of immersion, through which a whole host of Christian words are communicated to the new convert, both directly and indirectly. The new believer hears the words of Scripture, the creeds, and formal and informal prayers. They are invited to respond to what they hear in Sunday school and in Bible studies, etc. In these ways, even without any formal catechesis, the new believer learns the language of Christianity.

In gathering a new congregation, the role of the missionary in this teaching capacity may vary, but at the minimum they must set up some structures that ensure the continued growth of individuals into a linguistic community. We have already mentioned one such historic structure: the public reading and explication of Scripture within corporate worship. Other structures may vary according to context. For some churches, this may mean a rigorous education program, for others, a Bible study. What is important is that these structures mediate the language of the Christian community and aid in the growth of individuals within this community.

As they grow in their faith, the new convert begins to rightly participate in the drama of redemption through faithful performance of the canonical script of the Bible. It is at this point that the missionary begins to step back from their role as teacher and starts delegating authority of the gathered congregation to these new converts.

GATHERING TO ESTABLISH AUTHORITY:
THE SPIRIT AND DELEGATION

In a passage from *The Spontaneous Expansion of the Church*, Roland Allen lists the key activities that a missionary must do once they have gathered a group of new converts. Allen's list serves as a summary of the virtuous practice of gathering: the missionary must hand over to new converts the creeds, the Gospels, and the sacraments, which I have addressed above in the establishment of language and place. Allen continues to address two other points that should follow these activities: the appointment of ministers and the exiting of the missionary.[47] For Allen, these final activities are the key to the missionary enterprise, and the reluctance of missionaries to successfully delegate authority is viewed by Allen as the key hindrance to the expansion of the church. These activities I will consider together as the establishment of authority through the acknowledgment of the reception of the Holy Spirit amongst new converts, which requires the exercise of the skill of delegation.

The Content of Authority: Self-Effacing, Exhaustive, and Immediate

Authority is the capacity to evoke action: it "calls a form of action into being."[48] One possesses authority if they are able to get someone else to do something. While authority is often thought of, particularly in contemporary discourse,

---

47. Allen, *The Spontaneous Expansion*, 146–50.

48. O'Donovan, *Resurrection*, 122. It is important to note that in my selection of the term "authority," I am intentionally avoiding the similar term "power." The terms are similar, as the various translations of the Greek *exousia* can attest. However, the selection of authority is in keeping with the more common translation of *exousia*, as evidenced in the key passage of Matthew 28:18, as well as keeping with the more common term for "power" in the New Testament, *dynamis*. In addition, "authority" is used due to the problematic nature of the term "power" in contemporary discourse, which often evokes the exercise of willful control over unwilling subjects. In preferencing authority, I am following a distinction used by Max Weber in his use

as simply the exercise of power and domination, this does not necessarily have to be the case. As Oliver O'Donovan points out, modern misconceptions of authority are often due to the reduction of authority to political authority, which can be construed as "a reason for acting without reasons."[49] Here, one is forced to act for no other reason than that some exterior authority has commanded them to do so. Few would pay their taxes if such payments were optional and voluntary: the reasons for freely giving money to the federal government are simply not compelling for most people.[50] Instead, one pays their taxes under the threat of force: we pay because we don't want to go to jail.

But there are much broader ways of conceiving of authority. Beauty, for instance, has the ability to elicit movement, as it "bids all things to itself."[51] For Dionysius, the superabundant beauty of God draws human beings back toward unity with God.[52] We are drawn toward that which is beautiful, and this movement is sparked by our desires rather than coerced in contradiction to our desire. Similarly, authority need not be tied to the threat of force in order to be legitimate. Matthew 7 depicts the amazement of a crowd following the teachings of Jesus, acknowledging that "he taught them as one having authority, and not as their scribes" (Matt 7:49). Authority in this instance compels action without coercion, and is tied to the person who reveals something that is recognized as true: "The disclosure of a fragment of reality that shines through something said or done commands our attention and belief, and so shapes our action. To recognize authority is to discern a reality accessed through what is communicated to us."[53]

For Christians, all authority rests in God. God is the source of all authority as he is the source of all being and all action: God *authorizes* existence.

---

of "authority" as the ability to elicit action in another in which the recipient acknowledges such exercise as legitimate.

49. O'Donovan, *Resurrection*, 121.

50. In the United States, it is important to note that one can donate at any time to the Treasury, which can be done through a voluntary overpayment of taxes. The fact that so few Americans do this shows that the principal reason for paying taxes lies in the government's threat of force.

51. Pseudo-Dionysius, *Pseudo-Dionysius: The Complete Works* (New York: Paulist Press, 1987), 76.

52. Pseudo-Dionysius, *Pseudo-Dionysius*, 7.

53. O'Donovan, *Finding*, 84.

However, God also grants a limited authority to his creation, so that human beings may possess a true authority in the world while also acknowledging God as ultimate authority: "God, in creating, has effected not only other beings, but other powers, yet without in any way diminishing his own sovereign being and power."[54]

A Christian understanding of authority is best seen within the context of the divine economy. All authority on heaven and on earth has been given by the Father to the Son (Matt 28:18). As authority has been given to the Son, the Son remains the source of all human authority. The Father and the Son send the Holy Spirit to the disciples, who is not a separate source of authority but rather makes the believer aware of the authority of the Son. The Spirit's authority is always relative to Christ.[55] For the Christian, Jesus is the source of authority, yet Jesus enables people through the Holy Spirit to share in this authority. This is summarized in Matthew 28:18-19: "All authority in heaven and on earth has been given to me. Go therefore and make disciples of all nations, baptizing them in the name of the Father and of the Son and of the Holy Spirit, and teaching them to obey everything that I have commanded you."

There are three key facets of authority that are thus important for understanding it within the context of mission. First, authority is *self-effacing*. Authority is Christocentric—it is always tied to the person and work of Jesus Christ. For the early Christians, the authority of the disciples is tied to their witness to the resurrection of Christ, which becomes shortly after their deaths the testimony to Christ in Holy Scripture. For example, John 15 showcases the direct correlation between remaining in Jesus through obedience to his commands and the bearing of fruit (John 15:4). Authority, the capacity to elicit change in others as manifested here in the metaphor of fruit, is directly tied to abiding in Christ. Thus, the exercise of authority by the apostles in the book of Acts continually references Jesus Christ. Acts 8:4-14, for instance, ties the proclamation of Christ by Philip directly to the healing of the sick and possessed. In addition, Peter directly invokes the name of Christ to heal a beggar (Acts 3:1-10). The reception of the Holy Spirit by Jesus thus enables

---

54. O'Donovan, *Resurrection*, 124.

55. See Emery, *The Trinity*, 38-39.

the disciples to exercise real authority that is nevertheless tethered to and dependent upon the authority of Christ.

Second, authority is *exhaustive*. Authority is continually handed over: first from the Father to the Son, then from the Son to the disciples through the Holy Spirit. This is seen throughout the Gospel of John, particularly in the Farewell Discourses and in the granting of the Holy Spirit: "'Peace be with you. As the Father has sent me, so I send you.' When he had said this, he breathed on them and said to them, 'Receive the Holy Spirit. If you forgive the sins of any, they are forgiven them; if you retain the sins of any, they are retained'" (John 20:19-23). The reception of the Holy Spirit enables the disciples to go into the world with the power to baptize and forgive in Jesus's name. Thus, we see here a continual descent of authority—authority is always given so that it can in turn be given away. The link here between Christ's statement regarding his authority and the power of the disciples to go and baptize is crucial, for it is in baptism that new converts receive the Holy Spirit and are thus given authority. In essence, Jesus grants the disciples authority to hand over authority.

Third, authority is *immediate*. The handing over of authority by the missionary begins *at the moment of conversion*. The new convert is given authority when they are given the Holy Spirit. This is seen most vividly at Pentecost, where the disciples go from being people in hiding to people who proclaim the gospel and heal the sick. As the missionary begins to gather together new converts to form a congregation, they immediately begin to discover the ways in which they might equip new believers to exercise authority as full members of the body of Christ.

This immediate vesting of authority is evidenced sacramentally, for at least some denominations, by the immediate partaking of the Eucharist by those baptized. Such a practice, particularly emphasized within the Orthodox tradition, is meant to show that the newly baptized person fully participates in the life of common worship from the beginning of their new birth in Christ. For Nicholas Afanasiev, the participation in the Eucharist is not only a sign of the full inclusion of new members into the life of the church, but also an act that both symbolizes and actualizes their full participation as *ministers* in the church. The newly baptized are here concelebrants of the Eucharist, joining with the ordained clergy in exercising their sacerdotal ministry: "The participation of the newly baptized in the eucharistic assembly, which completes the charismatic act of his reception into the Church, brings into the open the nature and characteristics of the ministry unto which every member of the Church is ordained."[56] Afanasiev here draws the connection between the Holy Spirit, the authority of Christ, and the immediate authority of the new believer: the charismatic act of baptism is completed in the immediate celebration of the Eucharist, in which the newly baptized is authorized to celebrate Christ.

Mission can thus be considered a great dispersal and expansion of the authority of Christ through the power of the Holy Spirit at work in the lives of new converts. Authority within the context of contemporary mission should be seen as the continuation of this dispersal. Authority is thus for the missionary *self-effacing, exhaustive, and immediate*. In preaching, teaching, healing, exorcising, etc., the missionary continually points to the fact that their authority to accomplish such tasks is dependent upon Jesus Christ. At the same time, they are constantly looking for ways to immediately hand over this authority to those who become Christians and are assembled within the church.

From the outset, the missionary looks for ways to hand over responsibility for the day-to-day tasks of the gathering congregation to newly baptized Christians. In so doing they *authorize*—grant the exercise of authority to— new converts. Put bluntly, the missionary gives the new convert something to do and empowers them to do it with some degree of autonomy. In so doing they acknowledge that the newly baptized have received the Holy Spirit and that the Spirit has given them gifts which should be exercised. The missionary's responsibility is one of recognizing these gifts and aiding in their visible expression within the newly formed local congregation.

Because authority is given to each new Christian, the missionary should help to hand over this responsibility to every person in the new congregation. This is perhaps some of the reasoning behind the various "lists" of spiritual gifts that are given by St. Paul. Such lists are not intended to be exhaustive but rather demonstrate how each new Christian has a role to play within the church, as each body part has a role to play in the functioning of a body.

The uniqueness of each individual means that the ways in which such authority is established will look different in various local contexts, as the

---

56. Afanasiev, *The Church*, 34.

various "lists" vary in Paul's letters. Formal authority, most visible in the ordination of indigenous leadership, should not be seen as opposed to a looser
arrangement of informal ministries, but rather the manifestation of true
authority having been handed over. The establishment of local ministers
can be seen as the natural result of this handing over of authority. As new
converts are given responsibility for the life of their congregation, particular needs arise that call for the establishment of more formal orders and
ministries.

We see this with the establishment of the deaconate in the book of Acts
(Acts 6:1–7). Here, the appointment of these "minsters of the table" is in direct
response to a local need: the adequate distribution of food to widows. In
response to this need, the office of the deaconate is formed, with the simple
requirement that those called to this more formal ministry be of "good
standing, *full of the Spirit* and of wisdom" (Acts 6:3, emphasis mine). Oliver
O'Donovan draws the remarkable connection between the establishment of
these seven deacons and the focus of the disciples on "serving the word."[57]
O'Donovan sees in this the beginnings of the ministry of oversight, which
manifests itself eventually in the establishment of local elders, as being tied
directly to the authority of Christ. The local demands of the community
create a situation that calls for both the greater exercise of local authority and
a greater need to ensure that such authority is grounded ultimately in Christ:
"The function of this increasingly devolved responsibility was to secure the
normativity of the apostolic Gospel for each place, mediating between the
universality of the word and the contingency of localities."[58] This devolved
responsibility is described vividly in the opening chapter of Paul's letter to
Titus. Paul describes how he has left Titus "behind in Crete for this reason, so
that you should put in order what remained to be done, and should appoint
elders in every town, as I directed you" (Titus 1:5). Paul hands authority over
to Titus *in order that* Titus would in turn authorize ministry in each locale.

The delegation of authority by the missionary will thus involve aiding in
the raising up of local institutions of authority. These formal offices, and the
people that occupy them, emerge from within the local congregation yet are
always tethered to the universal gospel of Christ's death and resurrection

---

57. O'Donovan, *The Ways of Judgment*, 284–85.

58. O'Donovan, *The Ways of Judgment*, 286.

from which their offices are necessarily authorized. The culmination of this handing over of authority is in the formal ordination of presbyters, local ministers who will be entrusted with the oversight of the newly gathered congregation as well as ensuring its continued fidelity to the gospel.

The Problem of Authority in Mission

The immediacy of this handing over of authority cannot be overemphasized. According to Roland Allen, the key hindrance to mission lies in what we might call a false gap in authority. Missionaries wait too long to hand over authority and local ownership of the congregation, depriving new converts of their rights to establish self-governing churches that take on their own responsibility for continuing the work of evangelization. Why is the immediacy of the authority of Christ jettisoned? Allen posits that, under the fear of the new convert turning to heresy, the missionary adopts a lengthy process of Christian education that prevents the new convert from ministering until their teachers are sufficiently assured of their educational competency. Here, new converts are taught a continual reliance on outside teachers, and missionaries are taught to "expect nothing out of our converts."[59] Furthermore, once converts begin to exercise their authority, foreign missionaries quickly send outside teachers and money to ensure their "intellectual advancement," in the process teaching new converts that they must continually rely on outsiders: "They learn to receive, they learn to rely on paid and trained men. The more teachers they have, the less they feel the need for exerting themselves to teach others."[60]

For Allen, the hesitancy of missionaries to establish local authority is rooted in a failure to trust in the workings of the Holy Spirit. The natural impulse of the new convert, filled with the Holy Spirit, is to zealously proclaim the gospel and minister within the local congregation. The missionary is fearful of such expression and, in reaction, sets up institutional barriers that deaden this natural zeal: "If new converts once receive the impression that they should express the natural instinct to impart a new-found joy, the divine desire for the salvation of others, only under direction, they are in

---

59. Allen, *Spontaneous Expansion*, 32.
60. Allen, *Spontaneous Expansion*, 33.

bonds, cramped and shackled."[61] Allen is even harsher in his critique, claiming that what the missionary fears most is "the expression of human self-will
and self-assertion."[62] In short, the missionary refuses to hand over what has
been received and, in the process, severely hinders Christian mission. They
in essence put a halt to the continuous outpouring of authority which began
with the giving of the Holy Spirit to the disciples. Such authority was always
centered upon Christ's authority which has been exhausted for humankind. Out of fear, the missionary halts this dispersal of authority—placing
themselves at the privileged center from which all authority must emanate.
Authority is stagnated under a veiled paternalism and concentrated not in
Christ but in the perceived wisdom of the missionary and their institutions.

It should be noted that such issues are not limited to overseas missions.
The establishment of so-called satellite campuses in some North American
evangelical churches is evidence of a special brand of paternalism. Here, the
entrusting of local teachers, and often local worship leaders, is eschewed,
and these "services" are provided for the local congregation through video
broadcast from the home church. Parishioners of these satellite campuses
are implicitly taught that the gifts of the Holy Spirit are not made manifest
in local contexts but are to be held in trust by a select group of professionals
whose talents are validated by the growth of their churches.

The Skill of Delegation

These aforementioned issues raised by Allen are not meant to suggest the
immediate abandonment of the new convert. The establishment of place and
language, in the form of the sacraments and the word, demonstrates that the
missional practice of gathering does not leave new converts empty-handed.
Instead, what is suggested is that the missionary develop the practical skill
of delegation, here defined simply as the passing on of authority from one
person to another. Three principal components are involved in this skill: the
discernment of fit (between person and task), the training in the task, and
the letting go of authority.

First, the missionary must discern what responsibilities are best suited
for the new convert. This begins with an imaginary construal of the convert's

---

61. Allen, *Spontaneous Expansion*, 15.

62. Allen, *Spontaneous Expansion*, 14.

flourishing within a particular role. The missionary contemplates the various activities performed by the newly established congregation, envisioning a particular person flourishing in a particular role. Such vision may involve practical discernment as well—an assessment of their various gifts, strengths, and weaknesses. The missionary then engages in a conversation with the convert, sharing this vision and calling them to begin entering into this particular task. Such a calling, however, may be accepted or rejected—it is finally a discernment between pastor and parishioner, and while the parishioner may be persuaded to engage in such activities, they retain the right to suggest alternative responsibilities.

Second, the missionary must train the convert in the task at hand. The most effective way to train is simply through imitation—the convert apprentices the missionary in the task at hand, first observing how the activity is performed, then gradually taking over the performance of that task. For instance, the convert observes the missionary teaching and preaching, then the missionary gives space for the convert to teach under immediate supervision, with the goal that such immediate supervision will quickly subside.

Finally, the missionary lets go. The convert becomes the point person for that particular activity, and the missionary no longer intervenes directly in the day-to-day practice of such activity. In so doing, they hand over responsibility and authority to the new convert, empowering them to exercise their gifts for the building up of the body of Christ. They "set up deep patterns of local response and initiative without the burden and handicap of foreign imposition."[63]

While the missionary may help each convert discover a particular role within the functioning of the local gathering, of the upmost importance is discernment of leaders to whom authority over the congregation is delegated. As mentioned above, the raising up of indigenous leadership is the natural consequence of the continual handing over of authority on the part of the missionary. For this reason, it is imperative that the leaders appointed must come from within the new gathering. These leaders are granted the same authority that was given to the missionary—the authority to proclaim the gospel, to teach, and to administer the sacraments. It is at this moment that

---

63. Sanneh, *Disciples*, 47.

the missionary's job is complete: all that has been given to them by Christ has been given to these new converts.

It should be noted that this handing over of authority is not an abandonment. While St. Paul established local congregations with indigenous leadership throughout his missionary ventures, he did not abandon these churches once he left. There remained contact with these churches, as evidenced most visibly in the writing of his epistles. Here there is a handing over of "direct personal government" while maintaining connection through various forms of communication.[64]

While there are a number of practical skills involved in delegation, the most important is discernment regarding when to walk away. The missionary must decide at a particular point to remove themselves from the day-to-day operations of the local congregation while maintaining both consistent communication and the possibility of intervening if serious issues arise. For Allen, such a skill can only be developed through experience, since each situation of gathering is unique and highly contextual:

> The man then who would guide such a Church as I have described and assist its education must obviously get out of the way to give it room; because if he stays, or if he leaves some one from outside in charge, it will plainly not have room to move. But he must watch over it and warn it by instruction when it is in danger of going seriously astray, or of falling heavily. The exact point at which such warning is necessary is a question of the most intimate delicacy; and it can only be solved by the instinct and insight of the educator with the watchful eye. It is impossible for any one else to judge, or to lay down any rule beforehand.[65]

The precise moment when the missionary should leave, and when they might in turn intervene again to give warning, cannot be predetermined. The missionary learns through practice how to better discern potential leaders, how to train them, and the precise moment to walk away.

---

64. Roland Allen, *Missionary Methods: St. Paul's or Ours?* (Grand Rapids, MI: Eerdmans, 1962), 87.

65. Allen, *Spontaneous Expansion*, 151–52.

While the precise moment when to walk away cannot be predetermined, this should not detract from the immediacy with which the missionary hands over authority. *The handing over of authority begins immediately but is completed at a point to be determined.* This is key. Allen's critique of Western missionaries in the nineteenth and twentieth centuries is that the handing over of authority is not immediate and that the point in which missionaries do walk away is forever displaced to an indeterminate future. In so doing, they stymie the work of the Holy Spirit that is operable in the life of the Christian at the moment of their conversion. If the missionary truly dispersed authority from the beginning, they would notice that the completion of this dispersal would most likely occur sooner than expected.

Allen's careful examination of the missionary movements of St. Paul highlights this point. Frequently, Paul would travel to a new area, preach the gospel, start a new church, and leave that church with its own indigenous leadership within one year. This was done without the vast educational materials existent today—Paul did not possess the New Testament, let alone a catechism or Bible study guide. This is perhaps the great irony today: that missionaries possess a seemingly infinite number of resources to aid in the training of local leadership, and yet such resources only seem to foster delegative paralysis. At its worst, the failure to hand over authority can calcify into a kind of two-tiered ecclesial structure, with "missions," "ministries," or "mission congregations" constituting a lower standing to their subservient churches.

THE GOAL OF GATHERING:
DELIGHT IN COMMUNION

It is with this stepping away that the missionary completes the act of gathering and the missionary practice as a whole. It is imperative to assess more fully the end goal of the virtuous practice of gathering, for the goal is not simply to walk away, but to leave behind a certain type of community. Stated succinctly, *the goal of the virtuous practice of gathering is to delight in the establishment of communion.*

Communion is the union of persons to God and each other through the power of the Holy Spirit, which enables such unity to become visibly instantiated as the body of Christ. The church is already established by Christ as his body, and the Holy Spirit "brings to human hearts God's love," drawing individuals into communion with God and each other in local manifestations of Christ's body.[66] For J-M.R. Tillard, communion emerges with the establishment of a local church which makes visible the content of the gospel proclamation. Communion is the concrete reality of the gospel message made manifest in the relationships of the local community. If the gospel proclaimed is one that speaks of lives reconciled to God, communion is the evidence of lives reconciled to each other. If the gospel proclaimed is good news to the poor, then the communion of the local congregation evidences relationships that extend toward the poor. Human beings do not create communion by such actions; rather, these actions are the visible fruit of the communion established by the Holy Spirt.[67]

Thus, for the missionary, their goal is to see the content of the gospel proclamation made visible in the lives of new converts within a newly gathered congregation. The goal is to see what they initially proclaimed to their audience brought to visible fruition. What begins as a picture in the mind of the missionary—a picture of their friend's conversion and new life in Christ— is displayed in their new life in communion. The word of God proclaimed by the missionary becomes flesh in the body of Christ gathered together by the missionary.

The gathering of this communion is itself fully the body of Christ. As Tillard puts it, the church universal is a communion of local communions. The church is "a communion of communions, appearing as a communion of local Churches, spread throughout the world, each one itself being a communion of the baptized, gathered together into communities by the Holy Spirit."[68] This point is crucial in regard to the missionary act of gathering: if the word is preached, if the sacraments are celebrated, if authority is handed down to local leadership, then what is gathered is a church, a local manifestation of the body of Christ. The missionary who gathers together converts in a nursing home, who establishes the preaching of Scripture and the celebration of the sacraments, who appoints leaders within the nursing home community

---

66. Dietrich Bonhoeffer, *Sanctorum Communio: A Theological Study of the Sociology of the Church* (Minneapolis: Fortress Press, 1998), 165.

67. Bonhoeffer, *Sanctorum Communio*, 182.

68. J.-M.R. Tillard, *Church of Churches: The Ecclesiology of Communion* (Collegeville, MN: Liturgical Press, 1992), 29. Tillard asserts that the celebration of the Eucharist is the act par excellence that constitutes each local gathering as a manifestation of the church universal.

to oversee its daily life, leaves behind a communion that is as much a church as Canterbury Cathedral. The difference is one of scope, not kind.

The delight that the missionary experiences is the delight in viewing from afar the communion they have helped to establish. In so doing, they give glory to God for the work he has done in establishing the body of Christ. We see this joy evidenced throughout Scripture in the life and writings of St. Paul, particularly in his interactions with the church in Ephesus. Paul had gathered this church together during his missionary journey, eventually appointing indigenous leaders upon his exit (Acts 19). Paul then returns to the church in Ephesus and begins to exhort their elders to shepherd the church of God, "of which the Holy Spirit has made you overseers" (Acts 20:28). Paul's message also comes with a warning against the inevitable rise of false teachers to challenge the leadership of the elders (Acts 20:29–30). Finally, the scene ends with one of the most intimate portrayals of communion in the book of Acts, with the elders praying, weeping, embracing, and kissing Paul (Acts 20:36–38). We see in these passages a vivid example of Paul establishing a church, handing over authority while maintaining communication, and finally delighting in what he has left behind.

This does not, however, mean that such a gathering is perfected by the missionary. While the missionary establishes place, language, and authority, they are not ultimately responsible for the long-term future of the new congregation. While they labor to the best of their ability, they do not ultimately control how a new gathering will proceed. The end goal of the missionary is not the long-term success of the congregation, but rather the mere establishment of place, language, and authority as evidenced in visible local communion. Other benchmarks of long-term sustainability, such as numerical benchmarks, budgetary goals, or the purchasing of property, are not grounded in Scripture and, as such, should be considered options left to the discernment of indigenous leadership.

The final act of the missionary is to take delight in the communion that is gathering locally which they have left behind. As they have entered into labor on behalf of God, they enter into rest in order to delight in the works of God. They delight in the relationships established, the ways in which converts continue to grow in their love in knowledge of Christ, and in the leaders faithfully appointed to oversee the congregation. While these moments to step back are certainly calls for reflection on the missionary's labor—the effectiveness of their work, an assessment of the potential ways in which they might improve, etc.—the primary purpose of stepping back is merely to delight and give thanks. This is most vividly seen in the opening chapter of Paul's first letter to the church in Corinth:

> I give thanks to my God always for you because of the grace of God that has been given you in Christ Jesus, for in every way you have been enriched in him, in speech and knowledge of every kind—just as the testimony of Christ has been strengthened among you—so that you are not lacking in any spiritual gift as you wait for the revealing of our Lord Jesus Christ. He will also strengthen you to the end, so that you may be blameless on the day of our Lord Jesus Christ. (1 Cor 1:4–8)

Paul is giving thanks for the church that he has helped to establish in Corinth and for the ways in which such a gathering has enabled the continued growth of its members. In addition, Paul asserts that this church has already been given every spiritual gift needed. Despite the numerous issues present in the church in Corinth, issues that Paul will address in his letter, the church nevertheless has everything it needs to continue to thrive. Paul is delighting in the church in Corinth, continually giving thanks for what has been accomplished. He is not giving thanks for the establishment of a perfect church, but a church that is equipped with everything it needs.

GATHERING AND THE GOALS OF MISSION

This chapter has sought to describe the missionary act of gathering as a virtuous practice that holds the potential to glorify God and promote virtue in those who engage in it. While this chapter has been devoted to unpacking the significance of the multitude of activities involved in this work, in closing it is appropriate to explain how this conception of gathering fits with the stated goals of my conception of mission as stated in chapter four. Throughout this chapter I have referenced various books of the Old Testament, the writings of St. Paul, and the book of Acts to support a claim that this construal of gathering fits well with the acts of gathering evidenced in Scripture, but in regard to how my conception of gathering fits with the other stated goals of this project, more needs to be said. This will be done first by showing how gathering meets the criteria for a virtuous practice, how it helps to address the problems of distinction and agency, and, last, how it enables moral reflection.

GATHERING AS DISTINCT, COMPLEX,
COHERENT, AND PERFORMATIVE

Chapter four described the various components of Alasdair MacIntyre's notion of a virtuous practice. My description of gathering conforms to this description in being distinct, complex, coherent, and performative. First, the act of gathering is distinct. What the missionary attempts to leave behind as a result of their activities is a distinct community that is centered upon Jesus Christ, defined spatially through the sacraments and linguistically through a focus on holy Scripture. These aspects help to define the establishment of a church as distinct and separate from other forms of community. The missionary is not simply applying the skills of community development but creating a distinct community whose common life is defined by word and sacrament. This distinctiveness also contributes to the unique joys which may be experienced by those who engage in this practice. The joy is not in seeing simply a community established, but a community that is in communion with God and each other, a community that is growing in their love and knowledge of God through Jesus Christ, and a community that has been given every spiritual gift needed to thrive.

The act of gathering is also complex and coherent. The complexity of this act is obvious: it involves three activities—inculturation, translation, and delegation—that each require a certain degree of skill and which can be improved upon through training and experience. Yet, the complexity of the act is limited in time by a clearly defined endpoint. The act of gathering ends when the missionary walks away, leaving structures in place to ensure the continual teaching and celebration of the sacraments, and ministers in place to directly oversee the new congregation. The appointment of leaders ensures that this practice has a terminal point from which the missionary may step back, assessing their work and delighting in what has been accomplished.

Finally, the act of gathering is performative. Throughout this chapter I have highlighted the various ways in which the act of gathering must be performed anew with each audience. Enculturating the sacraments requires sensitivity to the cultural particularities of converts, translation requires an understanding of the linguistic dynamics of the new gathering, and delegation requires the calling out of specific and unique individuals. This performative aspect means that, while one can improve upon the skills needed to effectively gather, the practice itself cannot ever be fully mastered.

DISTINCTION, AGENCY, AND VIRTUE

One of the purposes in using MacIntyre's notion of a virtuous practice for my conception of mission is that it helps to understand mission in a way that addresses the three perpetual problems in mission studies: distinction, persuasion, and agency. My conception of gathering as a virtuous practice helps to address this goal particularly in regard to issues concerning distinction and agency.

By characterizing gathering as an activity that has a beginning and endpoint and showing how proclamation and gathering together form the key missionary actions, I have sought to give a conception of mission that is distinct. Mission begins with the proclamation of the gospel, it continues in the gathering of new adherents to the Christian faith, and it ends in the departure of the missionary and the establishment of a self-sustaining local congregation. While other activities in the life of the Christian and the life of the church are certainly important, it is these activities that define mission. As mentioned earlier, it is in the cessation of either proclamation or gathering that mission loses its distinctive tone. To proclaim the gospel without establishing a congregation is to deny the essential bodily and social dimensions of Christianity. It is the promulgation of a gnostic faith, denying the incarnation of Christ. To gather without proclaiming the gospel is to establish a community without Christ. Such communities often run the risk of promoting a Western notion of civilization and cultural advancement and miss the ways in which mission entails the advancement of Christ and his kingdom.

The discussion concerning authority helps to address the problem of agency in mission. Chapter two assessed the problem of agency in regard to the mission as growth model. Here, the agency of individuals was usurped in the interest of technical missional efficiency. This purported mastery over others extends not only to the ability to predict with causal regularity the number of individuals who will join newly formed churches, but also to the roles and responsibilities of such individuals when they do join. The problem is that, by acknowledging the agency of new converts and their authority as equal members of the body of Christ, the missionary risks the cessation of numerical growth. And so the perpetual temptation of the missionary is to hold on to authority, denying full participation in the body of Christ for their new parishioners, all in the interest of maintaining control over a managed process of growth.

However, if the goal of gathering is delighting in the communion established, the missionary is free to risk the cessation of their authority in the interest of granting full participation in the common life of the church. The writings of St. Paul testify to the risks entailed in such delegation. The church in Corinth quickly fell into disarray upon Paul's departure, yet Paul shows no signs of regret for his decision to leave. Paul does not take back control of the congregations he planted once problems arise, but instead instructs, counsels, and rebukes, in the hope that the congregations *themselves* might amend their ways. He maintains his authority as an apostle to set things right yet entrusts those in the local church to put things in order (2 Cor 13). In so doing he acknowledges the ability and agency of those called to a life within the body of Christ.

GATHERING AND MORAL REFLECTION

A key component of my conception of mission is that it encourages both practical and moral reflection on the tasks performed by missionaries. The practice of gathering requires the skills of inculturation, translation, and delegation, and such skills are ones in which one might advance in their practical abilities. In regard to translation, for instance, the missionary can grow in their knowledge both of Scripture and the linguistic particularities of the context in which they labor, helping to enable better ways to communicate Christian teaching. Similarly, the missionary can learn how to better delegate in ways that both successfully bestow authority onto new converts while also setting them up to effectively discharge their new roles and responsibilities.

What is discovered in such a process is that, in order to obtain proficiency in such skills, the development of the virtues is required, particularly the virtue of prudence. There is no textbook for inculturation or translation. The unique particularities of each newly formed community mean that the challenges posed to the missionary are always unique. The section on inculturation has shown how even the most minute detail in gathering, including decisions regarding formal and informal dress, can have a profound impact on the development of the local congregation. What needs to be honed is the ability to take in new information and make appropriate and swift decisions

in accordance with what is good. Similarly, Roland Allen attests to the necessity of the exercise of prudence for deciding the precise moments when the
missionary hands over authority and walks away from their new work. Due
to ever-changing circumstances, such decisions cannot be made beforehand.

Vincent Donovan's writings are perhaps the best examples of such reflection. Recounting his work with the Masai, Donovan remarks upon what he
perceived as one of his greatest mistakes. When he was preparing converts
to receive the Eucharist, some of the male Masai asked that they not eat the
bread in front of the women. At the time, Donovan rejected this request for
fear that it would destroy the symbolic significance of the Eucharist as an act
of unity around a common meal. Upon reflection and the realization that this
rejection may have contributed to the relative dearth of Masai Christian men
as compared to women converts, Donovan simply states, "Perhaps I erred in
my practical judgment."[69]

Reflection, however, extends not only to the practical performance of
gathering, but also to its place within the life lived for the glory of God.
Reflection is ultimately done before God—it is an offering of one's labors
before God in the hope that such labors are holy and pleasing to him. There
can be in such reflections both repentance and delight: repentance for the
ways in which the missionary tampered the zeal of their parishioners in the
interest of bureaucratic control, and repentance for the ways in which they
mistook the peculiarities of Western civilization as essentials of Christianity.
Donovan's accounts are rare instances of a missionary willing to examine
himself before God for the often-agonizing judgment calls made in the interest of preserving the Christian faith while making such faith accessible.

Finally, there is in reflection before God delight in what has been performed by the missionary. The missionary does not delight principally in
the size and number of churches planted, but rather in the communion
established in part due to their labors. Donavan gives a vivid picture of
this delight in describing his flight from Africa upon the completion of his
seventeen-year missionary journey. On this flight, Donovan pictures what
he has left behind:

---

69. Donovan, "Response," 278.

The priests and brothers and sisters and lay people and Lutheran ministers and their wives, who had been my colleagues, were, right at that
moment, working on and walking around those very mountains I was
flying over. ... But maybe, most of all, as I looked down from the last
time, I remembered people like Ole Sikii making the painful climb,
foot by foot, up the volcanic side of Oldonyo L'Engai, on his lonely
quest to see the face of God. ... And Keti, with her baby strapped to
her back, walking happily over the green hills of Africa to bring the
gospel to Masai kraals that had never heard it. ... How liberating to
know that no matter who it is that plants, or who it is that waters, it
is God who makes things grow.[70]

Donovan's reflection on his work of preaching the gospel and starting new
churches is focused on the people he encountered and the lives that were
changed in part through God working through his labors. The community
established and the knowledge that indigenous peoples were carrying on
Christ's mission are particular sources of delight.

CONCLUSION: GATHERING AS THE
END AND BEGINNING OF MISSION

The image of a plane flight overlooking continued mission highlights how
gathering is both the end of the missionary's charge and the beginning of
new mission. The missionary leaves the newly gathered congregation fully
equipped to carry on the responsibilities of worship and to continue to proclaim the good news of Jesus Christ. While mission ends with the missionary walking away, each of the three tenets associated with the practice of
gathering serve to prepare the new converts for the continuing enterprise
of mission.

Authority and Ministry. Mission ends with the handing over of authority
to local ministers, just as the authority granted to the disciples to go and
make disciples has been handed down throughout generations of missionaries from one local congregation to the next. Having been granted the gift
of making disciples and having completed their task in the establishment
of a new congregation, the missionary extends authority to local ministers,

---

70. Donovan, *Christianity Rediscovered*, 147.

an authority that has never been their own, but always Christ's. They trust that new generations of leaders, evangelists, and missionaries will emerge from within these congregations to carry on the task of mission "to the ends of the earth" in the power of the Holy Spirit.[71]

Word and Language. The missionary also leaves this congregation with the language of the Christian faith, most vividly in an understanding of God's word in Holy Scripture. The structures developed in gathering the congregation, principally the public reading and exposition of Scripture, ensures that the new converts can grow in their understanding and articulation of Christian faith. In so doing the new convert is simultaneously equipped to begin to articulate this faith to those outside of the newly gathered community.

Communion and Sacrament. Finally, the newly gathered community manifests their common life together in Christ, which becomes a visible sign of the reconciliation of God with humankind. This visible manifestation stokes within the hearts of the new congregation a deep desire to gather others into this communion, and this desire for communion with Christ and his body only increases as it is further experienced. To borrow a phrase from Gregory of Nyssa, "there is no limit to the operation of love, since the beautiful has no limit ... whatever by its nature cannot admit anything worse will proceed towards the limitless and unbounded good."[72] To experience communion with Christ in his church is to experience that which is truly good and beautiful, sparking a desire to bring others into such communion. Tillard calls this the "dynamism of reconciliation":

> To become through the Spirit at baptism a member of the Body of
> Christ and to become identified with him through the Eucharist, is to
> enter into the dynamism of a reconciliation which wishes to be put

---

71. For Roland Allen, in handing over authority, the missionary trusts that the bigger issues that may come up within the life of the church in a particular area can only be handled once people are given ownership to handle the smaller concerns in the local congregation. Both the expansion of the church and the leaders equipped to shepherd such expansion emanate from the local congregation fully given the authority of Christ: "By exercising government in the small body, the real leaders of the church learn to govern and direct a church composed of many such little churches. ... By active evangelistic work in their own neighbourhood they learn to lead a mission in a whole province." Allen, *Spontaneous Expansion,* 152.

72. Gregory of Nyssa, *On the Soul and Resurrection,* trans. Catharine P. Roth (Crestwood, NY: St. Vladimir's Seminary Press, 2002), 81.

into action continually, to win the entire world so that the eternal design embraces every divine work.[73]

The celebration of the Eucharist becomes the sacramental act that both symbolizes and enacts communion, fueling a desire to gather others into this communion. This lies at the heart of what Ion Bria sees in Orthodox conceptions of mission, in which "the missionary structures of the congregation were built upon the liturgy of the Word and Sacraments."[74] The celebration of the liturgy radiates out from the church to the world, empowering the church to sanctify the entirety of their lives and witness to others the reconciliation they have experienced in this celebration:

> Renewed by the Holy Communion and the Holy Spirit, the members of the Church are sent to be authentic testimony to Jesus Christ in the world. The mission of the Church rests upon the radiating and transforming power of the Liturgy. It is a stimulus in sending out the people of God to the world to confess the Gospel and to be involved in man's liberation.[75]

In establishing place through the inculturation of the sacraments, the missionary is not simply bringing about local iterations of church traditions but is also creating space through which new converts encounter God and experience a common life with each other around Christ in the power of the Holy Spirit. In so doing they in turn enflame a desire for the newly gathered to proclaim the gospel and gather others into this transformed and reconciled community.

---

73. Tillard, *Church of Churches*, 48.

74. Ion Bria, "The Liturgy after the Liturgy: Mission and Witness from an Orthodox Perspective," in *Martyria/Mission: The Witness of the Orthodox Churches Today*, ed. Ion Bria (Geneva: WCC Publications, 1980), 69.

75. Bria, "The Liturgy," 68.

7

—

ENTERING INTO THE CRAFT OF MISSION: TRAGEDY, TRADITION, AND TELOS

The preceding three chapters developed my conception of mission as practices which promote virtue and further the practitioner toward their final end of partaking in the glory of God. The goals of this conception of mission were to address perpetual problems of mission studies in a way that both accorded with Scripture and enabled moral reflection. This view of mission was presented from the top down, beginning with an understanding of the relationship between God and creation, then describing the *telos* of humankind as the beatific vision, and ending with a description of the various actions involved in the virtuous practices of proclamation and gathering. This concluding chapter returns to and builds on these preceding chapters in order to consider how an individual might begin the process of learning the craft of mission and how this calling fits within the context of a life well lived. It is meant to give a bottom-up perspective on this model of mission, describing the practical steps to enter into mission and the conflicts and challenges that ensue when one enters into this tradition. In so doing it will summarize my conception of mission in a way that both recapitulates and enriches its core themes.

The chapter begins by showing how an individual begins their journey toward becoming a skilled missionary craftsman by entering into the tradition of mission, and how mission can be practiced by both amateurs and professionals. Second, I will show how one might experience growth in virtue, as well as how they might draw closer to God through the engagement in these missional practices. Such activities necessarily bring about questions regarding ultimate ends and what constitutes a life well lived, which will be the focus of the third section. However, since mission is but one of many practices in which one might partake, and because there are inevitable conflicts between competing practices in a single life, the fourth section will be devoted to examining the problem of tragedy. This book will end with a brief examination of three key biblical passages that sum up the work as a whole.

BECOMING A MASTER MISSIONARY: ENTERING INTO THE TRADITION OF MISSION

The past three chapters have articulated a conception of mission as a virtuous practice and explained in detail the various activities involved in the particular practices of proclamation and gathering. The assessment of these various parts highlighted the complexities of these practices, showing how their exercise requires continual performance and reflection upon past performances. It is meant to show that one can *advance* in their skills and abilities; one can improve upon these practices as one might improve upon other crafts,[1] such as chess, woodworking, or soccer.

In examining the virtuous practices of proclamation and gathering, I have sought to evaluate each of the various activities involved as well as provide the justifications for each of these activities. It has concerned what activities are involved and why they are included within each practice. While this assessment has sought to answer the what and the why, I have intentionally refrained from examining in too much depth the how. The reasons for this are plural: First, it simply lies outside the parameters of this study. To delve deep into the mechanics of public speaking, translation, prayer, and persuasion would be to greatly expand this book to an unwieldy breadth, in the process making it difficult for its core arguments to remain lucid. Second, the lack of "how-to" guidance is also due to the highly contextual nature of mission, which will always be somewhat resistant to a universalizing of best practices. I have mentioned above the profusion of how-to books on mission, evangelism, and church planting. Such books often promise results based on the narrative of success promulgated by their authors, yet such success is rarely replicable. Each individual and each community is unique, and so

---

1. I use the word "craft" as synonymous with the term "practice," though it is used to evoke more a sense of a kind of practice which has its own historical tradition. MacIntyre uses the terms interchangeably, preferring "craft" in *Three Rival Versions* and "practice" in *After Virtue*.

what should be sought after by the missionary should not be a book on how to win friends and influence people (with the gospel), but rather the seeking out of Christ within the particular tradition of mission. This leads to a final and most important assertion: that the way one advances in the craft of mission is not primarily through the obtainment of practical tips and tricks, but by entering into the tradition of mission as an apprentice to a master missionary.

In this regard, the practical advice is quite simple: if someone wants to master the practices of a missionary, they should find one who has mastered these practices and follow them as their student and apprentice. They should seek to find someone who has mastered the art of proclaiming the gospel and gathering new Christians into worshiping congregations. They should walk alongside them, imitating their actions, learning from their collected wisdom, accepting their praise and admonishment as they take their first steps in performing the acts of proclamation and gathering.

Such an assertion begs the question: How does one identify a master? By acknowledging their need to be taught, the novice acknowledges in humility their lack of knowledge. But, if they are lacking such knowledge, how could they identify one who has perfected such practices? This question is not new—MacIntyre traces its roots all the way back to Plato's *Meno*.[2] The answer is twofold: First is the simple assertion that human beings have within them potentialities given to them by their Creator, and such potentialities, if not inordinately damaged by sin, give people the ability to see such potential actualized in other human beings. God has created human beings to be dynamic, capable of growing and seeing the ways in which they have the potential to grow. Such ability is somewhat intuitive—we can watch a film of a Billy Graham crusade and recognize a gifted proclaimer of the gospel even if we can't necessarily identify why he is a gifted speaker or how he developed into a gifted speaker. The specific work of mission extends this assertion of innate capacities in that there is a belief that the reception of the Holy Spirit fosters in the convert the innate desire to share their faith with others.

Second, the engagement in such virtuous practices requires a commitment at the outset that is in many regards a leap of faith. The student does not know for certain that they are in the company of a master, yet at some

---

2. MacIntyre, *Three Rival Versions*, 63.

point they must commit to following, trusting and hoping that they are correct. Where the student winds up will in part be determined by this initial commitment: "A prior commitment is required and the conclusions which emerge as enquiry progresses will of course have been partially and crucially predetermined by the nature of this initial commitment."[3] Since human beings are necessarily dependent upon others, and human life is constrained by time and place, there can be no purely disengaged vantage point from which such commitments can be made. Simply put, we don't have any choice but to start from where we are. If one wants to master the craft of mission, they must trust that God has created them with the capacity to advance in such practices, and that their entering into such practices will yield a greater knowledge of mission that is certain without being complete.

By consenting to tutelage, the student enters into the specific tradition of missions and mission work. Like other crafts, it is imbedded in a tradition that extends back into a history which has shaped both the definition of the craft and the standards by which that craft has been superbly performed. The student thus enters into this tradition and takes their place within this tradition: "To share in the rationality of a craft requires sharing in the contingencies of its history, understanding its story as one's own, and finding a place for oneself as a character in the enacted dramatic narrative which is that story so far."[4] The missionary inherits their tradition, which includes faithful performances from women and men through various centuries and geographies, accepting their contributions to the tradition as well as acknowledging the ways in which they provide helpful examples of such faithful performances in various contexts.

Consequently, an emphasis on the history of missions should be a large part of the education of the missionary novice. The historical sections of Bosch's *Transforming Mission* and Bevans and Schroeder's *Constants in Context*, the work of Adrian Hastings, Andrew Walls, Lamin Sanneh, and Scott Sunquist, are all vital for understanding the history of specific missions as well as the ways in which various individuals helped to advance this tradition.

The missionary learns from their master through witnessing their actions, receiving their instructions, and critically reflecting on their own

---

3. MacIntyre, *Three Rival Versions*, 60.

4. MacIntyre, *Three Rival Versions*, 65.

experiences while engaging in missional practices. In doing so, they develop virtues. Chapter four outlined three of the virtues which the missionary might develop. Of particular importance for the advancement of mission within a particular tradition is the virtue of prudence, the "application of right reason to act."[5] The ever-changing temporal and cultural situations through which mission is performed quickly render how-to books obsolete. Prudence is required not only to perform mission well, but also to discern how to act in accordance with one's ultimate goal. It is developed not only through engaging in activity, but also in reflecting on previous actions. Alasdair MacIntyre situates the exercise of prudence within the context of perfecting a craft:

> To become adept at a craft ... one has to learn how to apply two kinds of distinction, that between what as activity or product merely seems to me good and what really is good, a distinction always applied retrospectively as part of learning from one's earlier mistakes and surpassing one's earlier limitations, and that between what is good and best for me to do here and now given the limitations of my present state of education into the craft and what is good and best as such, unqualifiedly.[6]

This project has attempted to show at various points the importance of moral reflection for the task of mission. The purpose of such reflection is to offer up one's actions to God, assessing their merits and the faithfulness with which they were performed: "The question bears on us whether our acts have constituted 'good works.' Are they accomplished? Can we be satisfied in them? May we offer them to God as a service that will acknowledge his working within us?"[7] One advances in the craft of mission through this continual reflection, learning to discern better from poorer practice, humble from selfish practice, faithful from unfaithful practice.

---

5. Aquinas, *Summa Theologiae* II–II, q. 47, art. 4.

6. MacIntyre, *Three Rival Versions*, 127.

7. O'Donovan, *Finding*, 41.

MISSION AND VOCATION:
PROFESSIONALS AND AMATEURS

Chapter four described the soft division of labor between deacons and apostles that emerges in Acts 6. Deacons are appointed so that those called to be apostles may focus on the task of proclaiming the gospel, yet such a focus does not preclude deacons from proclaiming the gospel themselves. We can describe this distinction as one between those called to the specific vocation of mission and those whom, though not called to that vocation, nevertheless participate in either of the missional practices of proclamation or gathering. Another way to characterize this distinction, which avoids the plurality of differing contemporary uses of the terms "apostle" and "deacon," is to characterize the work of mission as performed by professionals and amateurs.

The distinction between professionals and amateurs has obvious parallels to other traditions. One might seek to enter into the craft of the violin as a professional, attending a conservatory and joining a symphony as a full-time career. Or one might enter the craft as an amateur, practicing at home and occasionally performing in volunteer orchestras. Those who enter into the vocation of mission as professionals devote the majority of their working hours to honing their craft, which should involve extended periods of time apprenticing to a master missionary and often includes relocation to new territories with the explicit goal of proclaiming the gospel and starting new congregations. Though possessing jobs in unrelated fields, amateurs might still receive evangelism training (often from a professional missionary) but perform missional practices amongst friends and coworkers.

While it is more likely that professionals would become masters of a craft, this does not preclude the occasional amateur from achieving such heights. We can think of Albert Einstein's violin playing, or the famous streetball player Raymond Lewis, as examples of amateurs who nevertheless achieved mastery. Likewise, there are occasions in which amateurs may master the practices of mission though they are not engaged in full-time mission work. For instance, a mechanic who learns proclamation from a parent might expertly preach to his coworkers and gather new converts into a local church.

Those who pursue the craft of mission as professionals are afforded greater time to learn and perfect the practices of proclamation and gathering but also submit themselves to the teaching and scrutiny of experts in their craft. Luther's distinction between public and private proclamation of the word is important for understanding the necessity of this scrutiny. For Luther, the priesthood of all believers entails that the "Word of God is given to all Christians to proclaim,"[8] and the laity have an obligation to proclaim this word in their private interactions. However, the needs of the community require one or many to engage in the public proclamation of the word. This need for Luther is quite practical—the need for food, clothing, and shelter requires most to engage in secular labor, and such people do not have the time to devote to studying the word and preaching. Hence, a few should be chosen to devote their lives to study and public proclamation. However, because such work is public, it is open to the scrutiny of the church community, since the harm done by such persons is multiplied. Thus, the community has a right to rebuke such people for incompetence or a lack of Christian character.[9]

Since mission is a vocation that requires the public proclamation of the gospel to those outside of the church (similar to that of pastoral ministry), those who enter into the craft of mission as professionals open themselves up to a greater scrutiny than Christian laity who engage in mission. Such scrutiny begins with the entrance into vocation, which comes not through individual decision but rather from the discernment of a calling from God that is confirmed by the local church or missionary organization. Once admitted, the novice can be disciplined and removed from their profession. There may be occasions in which expert missionaries may recommend that such novices not proceed as professionals due to insufficient progress, incompetence, or a lack of Christian maturity. Such discernment can be extraordinarily difficult, as it involves potentially difficult conversations with novices whose desires do not match their calling or their abilities. It is important to note, however, that the demonstration of advancement in the practical abilities of proclamation and gathering are not necessarily tied to numerical growth. Superb performances of these practices might not yield favorable responses, but experts are those who have trained their eyes to bracket such factors, just as a virtuoso violinist can acknowledge a brilliant performance from a fellow virtuoso even amidst a drowsy audience. Meanwhile, the missionary who achieves great numerical success may be found to be deficient in Christian

---

8. Martin Luther, "Concerning the Ministry," in *Luther's Works*, vol. 40, *Church and Ministry* II, ed. Conrad Bergendoff (Philadelphia, PA: Fortress Press, 1975), 34.

9. Luther, "Concerning the Ministry," 35–36.

character and be asked to step away despite such success. It should be noted that the requirements for various vocations in 1 Timothy almost exclusively involve issues of character (1 Tim 3:1–13). The tradition of mission is refined through the purgative disciplining of its professionals—whether it be of the upright Christian who never develops practical proficiency, or the practical expert who fails to embody the gospel in their personal life.

Luther's assertion regarding the need for all Christians to exercise their priestly calling to proclaim the word distinguishes the craft of mission from other types of practices. The missional practice of proclamation is one which *all* Christians are called to perform at various times throughout their lives. Chapter one described Barth's assertion that witness to Jesus Christ is what defines a Christian as a Christian and what intrinsically unites them to other Christians in the church. To be a Christian is to point others to Jesus Christ and join with others in a community that makes manifest Christ's body on earth. All are priests, and all are called to offer their priestly sacrifices—of time, energy, reputation—toward glorifying God by proclaiming Christ.

Roland Allen sees the expansion of mission tied directly to "the unexhorted and unorganized activity of individual members of the Church explaining to others the Gospel which they have found themselves."[10] Allen does not mean that such proclamations should be ill performed, but rather that the role of ministers and missionaries should always be to help and encourage such performances rather than hinder them by requiring their professionalization. Mission is to be performed by all Christians, and churches should foster an environment that encourages its exercise without prompting. Professional missionaries are not the center through which all mission must flow but rather exist as models of mission done well and as teachers who aid in the performance of mission from all Christians, in the process expanding and enriching the craft of mission. There is a symbiotic relationship between professionals and amateurs in many crafts. The tradition of baseball, for instance, is bolstered not only by every spectacular World Series performance, but also by every pick-up game in an abandoned sandlot. Indeed, the performances of amateurs and professionals are mutually reinforcing: the sandlot pitcher is inspired by the World Series performance, thus striving for a future life in the major leagues. Similarly, the tradition

---

10. Allen, *The Spontaneous*, 7.

of mission is strengthened through the fostering of both superb professionals and its spontaneous expression amongst all Christians: the teenager is inspired by the stories of saintly missionaries to proclaim the gospel to their friends, which in turn fosters the hope of a career in the mission field.

GROWTH AND SANCTIFICATION

To speak of saintly missionaries raises questions regarding growth and sanctification within the context of the craft of mission. As one engages in practices, they learn what is good and best for the exercise of that activity at a particular moment, and eventually they begin to learn what is good and best unqualifiedly. Virtuous practices have a transcendent quality to them—they both help the practitioner better discern how to act so as to obtain their ultimate end while developing virtues which help them grow toward this end. In short, one who engages in these practices better understands their final goal and develops character that pushes them toward this goal. So, for instance, one can learn fortitude through practicing a particular sport, thus becoming a person who has the virtue of fortitude and can exercise this virtue in other activities, including schoolwork.

This is true as well for the virtuous practices of mission. While engaging in proclamation and gathering, the missionary can develop cardinal virtues such as temperance, fortitude, and prudence (see chapter four). These virtues, sedimented into the character of the missionary, can then be further exercised in other activities. The missionary who learns to forgo frivolous leisure activities to pray for their friends develops temperance and is thus better equipped to restrain similar impulses when the practice of parenting demands it. At one level, to conceive of mission in this way is to acknowledge that it affords the opportunity for individuals to grow, as Aquinas puts it, toward their natural ends.

There is, however, a deeper way of conceiving of mission that goes above and beyond MacIntyre's notion of a virtuous practice. This is one of the reasons why my conception of mission and virtue placed MacIntyre's concept of practice within a broader Thomistic moral theology, since the exercise of the practice of mission does not simply develop cardinal virtues toward a natural end of humankind but is a distinctly Christian activity that is infused with the Holy Spirit and thus affords the missionary the opportunity to grow in faith, hope, and love as they move toward their supernatural end. Chapter four highlighted, for instance, how the act of proclamation develops the virtue of faith: the missionary proclaims what they believe, and this external act affirms and strengthens their inward confession of faith.

We can speak of this kind of development in the life of the individual who engages in mission as sanctification. Chapter four had mentioned that, for Aquinas, God works in human actions as the source both of their existence and their free decisions. One way that Aquinas speaks of God's actions in the work of human actions is that of sanctifying grace.[11] Not only does God's grace infuse habits so that the cardinal virtues might be perfected, it is also a "constant presence on the wayfarer's journey."[12] Human beings have the capacity to act so as to cooperate with this grace, with God working as the source both of human existence and free will and providing divine assistance in ways that are not competitive with human action. Shawn Colberg states the implications for Aquinas's conception of sanctifying grace: "If all salutary human acts can be associated with God's presence and movement, the wayfarer's journey becomes itself an intimate movement into greater union with God."[13]

To situate mission within Aquinas's moral theology is to conceive of it as just these sorts of salutary human acts that can draw the missionary into greater union with God. As one enters into the craft of mission, learning from their teachers and the great tradition of missionaries before them, they proclaim the gospel and gather individuals in worshiping communities. But these actions are performed not just in the interest of becoming expert missionaries, but also as labors through which God might work. As such, they offer such activities up to God and ask retrospectively if these actions were performed so as to be holy and pleasing to God. It is a supplication, offered by the missionary in the hope that God might work through and in them, accomplishing what he will through their actions and sanctifying themselves in the process. "God's work of sanctification is to reveal his working in the

---

11. Aquinas defines sanctifying grace as "that through it a man is himself joined to God." Aquinas, *Summa Theologiae*, I-II, q. 111, art. 1.

12. Shawn M. Colberg, "Aquinas and the Grace of Auxilium," *Modern Theology* 32, no. 2 (2016): 210.

13. Colberg, "Aquinas," 210.

members and communities of the church, through experiences of living and acting in the faith of Christ."[14]

The purpose of mission when conceived of as the partaking in virtuous practices is thus much deeper and richer than what is offered by other models of mission. Mission work is not simply the occasion for God to show up, it is not simply the race to convert as many souls as possible, and it is not simply an opportunity to learn more about ourselves and others. Though it may include all of these facets, it is principally performed as works meant to honor God and move individuals closer to their ultimate end of partaking in his glory.

As one enters into the craft of mission, their progress can be charted to various degrees of tangibility. First, they learn the basics of proclamation and gathering. They learn how to pray for their friends and how to speak so as to testify persuasively to Christ's death and resurrection. Progress in these areas is relatively easy to see—prayer times can become more frequent and focused, conversations become more fluid, and the missionary finds themselves less often at a loss for words when sharing the Christian message. While engaging in these practices, the missionary also develops virtues that are perhaps noticed only after longer periods of time. Passions for frivolous pursuits might wane over time. Months or years later the individual may realize that such desires are non-existent, and that their temperate disposition may help them in other practices as well. The missionary may discover over time that their decision-making abilities have improved and that they are able to effectively receive, deliberate, and act on information with greater alacrity in other areas.

Sanctification, however, can be charted with less clarity, since it is not something that can be mapped out ahead of time. There can be no exercise books for sanctification, as there are for the violin. This is the case because sanctification is a work of the Holy Spirit and cannot be domesticated and controlled by human beings. Egregious maladies have occurred when missionaries are convinced, *a priori*, that their actions are enacting God's will.[15] Such claims deny the present reality of sin in the world, which clouds our

---

14. O'Donovan, *Entering*, 79.

15. See, for instance, a brief account of the role of Francis Xavier in the Goa Inquisition in Bindu Malieckal, "Early Modern Goa: Indian Trade, Transcultural Medicine, and the Inquisition," *Scripta Instituti Donneriani Aboensis* 26 (2015): 149–50.

judgments and obscures the oft-hidden selfish motives behind even the most ardently Christian activities. Moral reflection as it relates to the practices of mission has been stressed throughout the previous chapters, and its necessity in regard to sanctification is equally vital. Oliver O'Donovan sees the particular act of thanksgiving, done in reflecting on our actions, as key to recognizing the ways in which God has worked in and through us: "A thanksgiving that concerns itself with a work of God in our lives and communities is bound to be retrospective, for there is no other angle from which we may speak concretely about God's working within our own work."[16] Such acts of thanksgiving are not meant to paper over the frail inconsistencies in our labors or our mixed motives. While the act of moral reflection may involve confessing our sins and acknowledging our weakness, it can also acknowledge that God has worked despite our weakness: "The whole burden of thanksgiving is that sin, which blasphemes God and resists his working, has not been given the last word in the shaping of our lives. God has drawn our inconsistency under the control of his own consistency."[17]

My conception of mission embeds prayerful reflection as an integral component of the practice of proclamation. The purpose of including this in the definition of proclamation is to highlight not only the ability for the missionary to consider the ways in which they might improve on their practice or how they might further develop prudence so as to excel, but also, and most importantly, so that the missionary might give thanks to God. We can trace here three aspects of this act of reflection. First, the missionary repents of the ways in which they have fallen short in their task of mission. Perhaps they exhibited cowardice, shying away from difficult aspects of the Christian message for fear of personal rejection. Or perhaps, as was described in chapter five by Gregory the Great, they have taken undue personal pride in winning over their audience, delighting in a rush of power. Second, the missionary reflects on the ways in which they could improve upon their practice. For instance, questions arise that may prompt the missionary toward further study, and arguments may need refining. Lastly, they give thanks to God, in so doing acknowledging the possibility that, despite moments of sin, frailty, and inexperience, God might work in and through them in the acts of mission.

---

16. O'Donovan, *Entering*, 79.
17. O'Donovan, *Entering*, 85.

This process of reflection and thanksgiving entails unique acts, which again testifies to the fact that sanctification can never be turned into a replicable program. "Sanctification is a happening in which we are presently caught up, not yet complete and entire. The experience that bears witness to it unfolds from day to day, following life's unanticipated directions."[18] This does not mean, however, that evidence of sanctification is completely elusive, but rather that one must describe it narratively.[19] We speak not of people on the path of sanctification, but instead point to the lives of people who are sanctified, or saintly. We speak of sanctifying acts *a posteriori*, and we speak of sanctified lives *a posteriori*.

Because of the unique ways in which God works in individuals, and because such sanctification can only be seen retrospectively, what is needed if one is to enter into the tradition of mission is not a prepackaged plan of holiness, but examples of saintly missionaries. The study of the tradition of mission should include the recounting of the lives of missional saints. The recounting of these stories is not done in order to model best practices, but instead to train the novice to develop an eye for discerning good from bad missional performances, as well as inspiring them to continue to hone their craft. An appropriation of Augustine's hagiology in regard to virtue is helpful for illuminating this point. For Augustine, Christ is both the model and pathway to virtue, but he is also uniquely human and divine, sinless, and thus beyond perfect imitation. Human beings need examples whose acquisition of virtue, though partial, is at least attainable. The saints provide this example, but, unlike the hero worship of pagan philosophy, these saints are models precisely because of their humility and repentance before Christ.[20] They are models because they are sanctified persons.

Hence, my conception of mission and virtue calls for a recovery of a now faded literary genre, that of the missionary biography. Missionary biographies peaked in the English-speaking world in the nineteenth century, with stories of famous missionaries such as Charles Simeon, Henry Martyn, and

---

18. O'Donovan, *Entering*, 73.

19. O'Donovan, *Entering*, 73.

20. See Robert Dodaro, *Christ and the Just Society in the Thought of Augustine* (Cambridge, UK: Cambridge University Press, 2004).

William Carey.[21] The biographies of Henry Martyn in particular were highly popular and being used as influence for literary characters in the works of numerous Victorian-era authors such as George Eliot and Charlotte Brontë. These biographies depicted the lives of missionaries as ones of selfless renunciation in pursuit of a higher calling to a life of overseas mission. They gave a selective history that was meant to inspire those interested in the missionary calling but who were perhaps fearful of the sacrifices that mission entails. John Sargent states such a purpose in the introduction of his biography *The Memoir of Rev. Henry Martyn*:

> In making a selection from a mass of such valuable matter, it has been my anxious wish and sincere prayer that it might prove subservient to the interests of true religion. One principal object with me has been, to render it beneficial to those disinterested minsters of the Gospel, who, "with the Bible in their hand, and their Savior in their hearts," devote themselves to the great cause for which Mr. Martyn lived and died; and truly, if the example here delineated should excite any of those servants of Christ in similar exertion, or if it should animate and encourage them amidst the multiplied difficulties of their arduous course, my labor will receive an eminent and abundant recompense.[22]

Such biographies were meant to model the lives of saintly persons in the craft of mission and inspire other wayfarers. What is needed today are similar types of stories written within contemporary contexts. This should include the lives of masters of mission today. In this case, the definitive biography of Festo Kivengere, the so-called Billy Graham of Africa, might be the most important missiological text yet to be written.[23] But it should also include lives of saintly women and men who have engaged in mission with less notoriety. The purpose of such works, like the lives of the saints throughout Christian history, are meant to show how one can glorify Christ in a variety of different and unique situations.

---

21. Mary Ellis Gibson, "Henry Martyn and England's Christian Empire: Rereading *Jane Eyre* through Missionary Biography," *Victorian Literature and Culture* 27, no. 2 (1999): 421.

22. John Sargent, *A Memoir of Rev. Henry Martyn* (Boston, MA: Perkins and Marvin, 1831), 6.

23. Despite this moniker, only three biographies have been written on Kivengere, one of which is an authorized biography and one of which is a children's book. His life and work have remained relatively untouched by the field of missiology.

The parallel to the lives of the saints is important, since the purpose of such texts are not to give accounts of *successful* missionaries, but *saintly* missionaries. The lives of missionary martyrs, like Elisabeth Elliot's account of Jim Elliot in *Shadow of the Almighty*, give retrospectives on human obedience and God's sanctification which call not for replication, but rather inspire new and creative performances of mission in new and differing circumstances.

MISSION AND THE LIFE WELL LIVED

As one engages in mission, questions arise that go above and beyond the acts of mission themselves, for to reflect on these actions before God is to situate them within the context of one's overall life. For Alasdair MacIntyre, the engagement in practices becomes the starting point for an understanding of what it means to live a good life. We grow through engaging in the various practices afforded to us by our particular social and historical location, with the hope that the development of virtues helps to clarify our conception of the telos of life and moves us toward that telos:

> The virtues therefore are to be understood as those dispositions which not only sustain practices and enable us to achieve the goods internal to practices, but which will also sustain us in the relevant kind of quest for the good … and which will furnish us with increasing self-knowledge and increasing knowledge of the good.[24]

A Christian conception of the virtues in relationship to a conception of the good must qualify and amend MacIntyre's description. Stanley Hauerwas and Charles Pinches believe that MacIntyre's conception of the virtues is still too wedded to pagan conceptions of virtue and that he defends first virtue, then Christianity.[25] The Christian conception of the justification of the sinner through the grace poured out on the cross would seem to counter any assertion that the conception of the good can be discerned purely through human

---

24. MacIntyre, *After Virtue*, 219.

25. Hauerwas and Pinches, *Christians*, 68. It should be noted here again that MacIntyre later rejects a notion of telos that is purely socially determined, insisting instead that the telos of human beings is grounded in their specific nature. Hauerwas and Pinches's point is still relevant, however, since their claim is that, for Christians, the revelation of Christ actually reveals to Christians essential aspects of their nature. "There is an essential feature of our nature—a natural fact—that Christians claim is disclosed in a particular history." Hauerwas and Pinches, *Christians*, 120.

endeavor.[26] For Hauerwas and Pinches, Christianity's notion of the good is not teleological, but eschatological. The end of the human being lies in the resurrection, which fosters in the Christian principally the virtue of hope.

I concur with this assessment, as it is in line with the discussion concerning Aquinas's accounts of agency and the beatific vision as the goal of human beings as addressed in previous chapters. The good of human beings lies in the vision of God, and human beings can only become aware of this as their final end through the grace of God. It is through God's grace that we receive an awareness of our end, and it is through the gift of God's revelation in Holy Scripture that we can understand the Christian virtues of faith, hope, and love. As Hauerwas and Pinches state, a Christian understanding of sin and redemption, and the concomitant virtue of forgiveness, are universal claims about the nature of humanity that are nevertheless made known to the Christian through the particular event of Christ's death and resurrection.[27]

A Christian conception of virtue and the telos of humanity as eschatological thus qualifies MacIntyre's statement concerning the unity of the virtues and their relationship to a conception of the good. For Christians, the final end is given, not acquired. The distinctive virtues of the Christian community are not socially constituted, but rather given in Scripture and socially mediated by the Christian community throughout time.[28] With this in mind, the engagement in virtuous practices does aid one in the development of virtue, and the virtues developed transcend that of the particular practice. Knowledge of the end of humankind may be given through the grace of God, but it is through growth in virtue that this end becomes clarified.

The previous discussion of Gregory of Nyssa is vital for understanding how growth in virtue need not conflict with a notion of the good life as given by God. Gregory's examination of Moses's ascent on Mount Sinai is a model for growth in virtue. The goal of human life is represented as the cloud on

---

26. Hauerwas and Pinches, *Christians*, 114.

27. Hauerwas and Pinches, *Christians*, 120.

28. As mentioned earlier, Kevin Vanhoozer's *The Drama of Doctrine* is written in part to contradict Lindbeck's conception of doctrine as the product of the church by emphasizing the role of God as one who acts, and continues to act, through Holy Scripture. Doctrine is not embedded in the social practices of the church but is rather the dramatic and faithful performance of Scripture. My assertion here is that a Christian conception of virtue is akin to Vanhoozer's conception of doctrine. While mediated through the social practices of the church, it ultimately derives from the revelation of God in Christ and God's divine communication in Scripture. See Vanhoozer, *The Drama*, 83–112.

top of Sinai. The cloud represents both the givenness of God—God is present in a particular location—while simultaneously representing the invisible exhaustiveness of God: "The one who is going to associate intimately with God must go beyond all that is visible and (lifting up his own mind, as to a mountaintop, to the invisible and incomprehensible) believe that the divine is *there* where the understanding does not reach."[29] The object of our pursuit of virtue is given as a gift, yet this object transcends our understanding: "When ... Moses grew in knowledge, he declared that he had seen God in the darkness, that is, that he had then come to know that what is divine is beyond all knowledge and comprehension."[30]

Growth in virtue is thus a kind of purification which enables the soul to ascend the mountain and draw near to God as their telos. In so doing, they grow in their love and knowledge of God, in the process discovering more clearly the ineffable and exhaustive beauty of God which transcends all understanding. My assertion here is simply that the development of virtuous practices for the Christian—in particular here the missional practices of proclamation and gathering—help to enable this kind of growth in virtue. It provides both a path to growth in virtue and clarifies the ends to which the wayfarer strives.

Chapter three highlighted the ways in which the engagement in mission changed the beliefs of missionaries. The persuasive act of proclamation led to a revision of the message which they proclaimed, often causing missionaries to return to their home country with a fresh set of criticisms and challenges to the so-called "mother church." Another way to describe this phenomenon is that of a clarification of the ends to which mission transcendently points. Vincent Donovan's aptly titled memoir *Christianity Rediscovered* is a fascinating example of how the proclamation of the gospel and the gathering of new churches, when performed in humility and obedience to God, hold the potential to become moments in which one's ultimate end is clarified. A Spiritan priest who spent several years working with the Masai tribe of Tanzania, Donovan became highly critical of much of Western Christianity and their missionary ventures for all too often equating the spread of Christianity with the spread of Western civilization: "We have to

29. Gregory of Nyssa, *The Life of Moses*, 43.
30. Gregory of Nyssa, *The Life of Moses*, 95.

admit that Western Christianity has monopolized Christ, and has shackled Christ in the bondage of a single culture to such an extent that the Western Christ has become a stumbling block for the Holy Spirit."[31] For Donovan, the missionary must never presume to have the final word on the Christian faith and must be ready to discover Christianity anew through the responses of those to whom one proclaims Christianity. This willingness to have one's faith continuously clarified and chastened is endless and unceasing, part of the work of mission itself:

> Never accept and be content with unanalyzed assumptions, assumptions about the work, about the people, about the church or Christianity. ... The day we are completely satisfied with what we have been doing; the day we have found the perfect, unchangeable system of work, the perfect answer, never in need of being corrected again, on that day we will know that we are wrong, that we have made the greatest mistake of all.[32]

To engage in mission in this way is to ascend the mountain of the Lord, growing closer to God as we climb, purifying our hearts through faithful performances, and clarifying our vision of the summit to which we strive.

TRAGEDY

As one pursues the craft of mission, one can grow in their love and knowledge of God and see with greater clarity the end they are pursuing. But the practice of mission is but one of a host of practices in which one partakes. The life lived well, the life aimed toward one's telos, is not simply one of solitary vocation. The aforementioned examination of sanctification and saintliness points to this—we speak narratively, of entire lives lived well in pursuit of God. Once one situates mission as one of many virtuous practices which one can pursue in the quest to live a life that is holy and pleasing to God, then the question arises as to how the practices of mission relate to these other practices.

The relationship between practices is challenged and frustrated by human limitations. We are historical and socially contingent people, inheriting

---

31. Donovan, "Response."
32. Donovan, *Christianity Rediscovered*, 146.

a whole host of roles and responsibilities that are at best only partly our making: "We enter upon a stage which we did not design and we find ourselves part of an action that was not our making."[33] We cannot speak of a missionary in complete isolation. One can be simultaneously a citizen, a son or daughter, a parent, a pastor, and a missionary, with each of these roles having its own range of demands and responsibilities. Because the development of virtues transcends one particular activity, what we do in one practice affects what we do in others.

Because human beings are finite, limited in time and space, they cannot gain expertise in every practice, and because the roles and responsibilities of each individual are not entirely their own making, conflicts between goods can and do arise. The responsibilities of a parent might entail from time to time a scaling back of job-related goals, for example. In making such a determination, one may not be choosing between good and evil, but rather making a determination of the proper ordering of goods. In so doing, they accept that a life well lived involves tragedy. There are decisions that must be made in life that are not decisions between right and wrong, but ones in which "both of the alternative courses of action which confront the individual have to be recognized as leading to some authentic and substantial good. By choosing one I do nothing to diminish or derogate from the claim upon me of the other; and therefore, whatever I do, I shall have left undone what I ought to have done."[34]

For the missionary, this means that there are times in which they might have to settle for poorer performances of proclamation and gathering in the interest of other goods. Family responsibilities are a paradigmatic case in point. Time spent in the hospital tending to an ill spouse is time not spent in the mission field. Such a decision may yield growth in virtue as a result of performing well the responsibilities of a spouse, but it may not yield growth in one's mission.

The tragic result of competing vocations that comprise a single life well lived is nowhere better displayed than in the character of St. John Rivers in Charlotte Brontë's *Jane Eyre*. Rivers is portrayed as a man wholly devoted to God, unwavering in his belief of a near-future vocation in Christian mission,

---

33. MacIntyre, *After Virtue*, 213.

34. MacIntyre, *After Virtue*, 224.

and a paradigm of Victorian virtue.[35] St. John has carefully cultivated the specific virtue of temperance, for instance, in his rejection of the advances of Rosamond Oliver, and fortitude in the maintenance of a vigorous visitation schedule for the region's destitute. Such virtues prepare him for his calling to take upon himself the practice of Christian mission, and he pursues matrimony with Jane Eyre in the interest of finding a spouse suitable to such a calling. However, St. John refuses to acknowledge that the calling to marriage is as much a vocation as is the calling to Christian mission. He sees *only* a suitable missionary spouse; Jane is but a means to the end of successful mission. His inability to see sincere love and affection as vital to the marital vocation, and his unwillingness to entertain one iota of sacrifice to his missionary calling for the sake of a spouse, ultimately leads Jane to reject his proposal. This rejection is depicted by Brontë as being appropriate for both Jane and St. John—Jane receives an affectionate husband in Mr. Rochester, and St. John indefatigably proclaims the gospel in India. For Brontë, those unwilling to accept the ways in which the various practices and vocations may hinder each other in a single life should instead seek to be more singularly devoted in their vocation. Taking a spouse may help the missionary, but it may also create situations that require the sacrifice of missional goals. Those unwilling to accept this possibility should remain single.

There is a danger particularly amongst missionaries of denying the tragedy of such decisions. The belief is that in such cases there is a right or wrong decision, and God will reward those who make the right decision with overall material benefit. So the missionary who takes furlough to nurse their ill spouse is rewarded upon their return to the mission field with a greater numerical success for their correct decision. Such thinking unduly binds the workings of God and obscures the relatively simple empirical point that mission is often weakened when missionaries are not present. The various lamentations by Paul in his epistles speak to this point. Paul writes often to address issues in the churches that he has gathered that have emerged in his absence. Paul cannot be two places at once and acknowledges that one of the ramifications of this fact is that the churches he started may be lured

---

35. Rivers is most likely a composite character patterned after the stories of famous missionaries of that time, through whom Brontë would have been acquainted through her Anglican minister father. See Gibson, "Henry Martyn."

by false teachers (see 2 Cor 12–13, for example). Should Paul have remained permanently in Corinth to quell that church's frequent problems, or should he have spent more time, as he did, in Ephesus (1 Cor 16)? Such decisions are decisions between two goods, and that the gathering in Corinth may have been weakened by Paul's absence speaks to a tragic aspect of his mission.

When the missionary is faced with such decisions, they pray and make what they discern to be the best decision possible. In so doing, they trust that they will grow in virtue, grow in their love and knowledge of God, and grow as a person created in God's image, even if this means that some of one's subordinate desires may wind up being unfulfilled in this earthly life.

However, tragedy is not the defining characteristic of the Christian life or the life of the missionary. If the telos of human life is defined by the attainment of earthly goods, then the inevitable destruction of our earthly bodies in death bears an indelible and tragic stamp on human existence *in toto*. As mentioned above, the ultimate end for Christians, the partaking in the vision of God, is eschatological, given as a promise sealed on the human heart by the Holy Spirit. While tragedy is a mark of all life, it no longer *defines* the Christian life. Hope in the resurrection of the body and the vision of Jesus in the heavenly temple affirms both the tragedy of earthly life (since this goal is not given in the present) and the assurance that such tragedies will be swallowed up in the end of time. Our earthly sufferings, as Paul puts it, "are not worth comparing with the glory about to be revealed to us" (Rom 8:18).

CONCLUSION

—

I will end this work with brief examinations of three passages from Scripture that together summarize the major tenets of my conception of mission as virtuous practice. Rather than extended exegesis of these passages, they are offered as simple illustrations of the key aspects of my conception of mission and what I hope are core takeaways for those who choose to enter into the craft of mission.

PSALM 96

> Sing to the LORD a new song;
>> sing to the LORD, all the whole earth.
> Sing to the LORD and bless his Name;
>> proclaim the good news of his salvation from day to day.
> Declare his glory among the nations
>> and his wonders among all peoples.
> For great is the LORD and greatly to be praised;
>> he is more to be feared than all gods. (Ps 96:1–4)[1]

In the beginning of this psalm, intertwined seamlessly with exhortations to sing and declarative statements regarding the greatness of God when compared to idols, is the command to proclaim the good news of God's salvation.

The virtuous practice of proclamation is an act whose goal is to give glory to God through the act itself. Following the lines of the psalm, it is an act of praise. When the missionary proclaims the good news of salvation, they are persuasively speaking before an audience while simultaneously praising and honoring God with their words. Far from being a command

---

1. Translation from the 1979 Book of Common Prayer.

begrudgingly accepted by Christians, further still from a staid mechanistic program, the proclamation of the gospel is portrayed with a hymnic quality befit for the Psalter as it punctuates the end of the psalmist's melodic line. This book has sought to demonstrate the intrinsic and internal goodness of the missional act of proclamation, and I can see no better way to accentuate this point than to see proclamation as an activity caught up in a heavenly symphony.

LUKE 10:17-20

The seventy returned with joy, saying, "Lord, in your name even the demons submit to us!" He said to them, "I watched Satan fall from heaven like a flash of lightning. See, I have given you authority to tread on snakes and scorpions, and over all the power of the enemy; and nothing will hurt you. Nevertheless, do not rejoice at this, that the spirits submit to you, but rejoice that your names are written in heaven." (Luke 10:17-20)

Returning to Jesus after their first missionary venture, the seventy report astounding news: that their message has had sway even over the demons. As Jesus notes, their power over demonic forces is due to him—the authority of Jesus is vested in his followers as they faithfully proclaim the good news in his name. One would think that this statement, coupled with Jesus's first-person account of the fall of Satan, would be the key takeaway from this venture. Yet Jesus states that his followers should not rejoice in such things, but rather that their names are written in heaven.

My conception of mission and virtue has emphasized the effect that engaging in missional practices has on the one who performs them. These actions hold the potential to promote virtue and allow the individual to draw near to God. This growth in virtue can at times be discerned upon the terminus of mission activity in a moment of reflection. While one can acknowledge the marvels which may occur through performing the acts of mission, and indeed one should expect such marvels to occur for those given authority by Christ, the joy experienced in reflecting upon these actions is centered principally and simply on the fact that God has chosen to work in and through our faithful performances of mission.

ACTS 7:51–60

"You stiff-necked people, uncircumcised in heart and ears, you are forever opposing the Holy Spirit, just as your ancestors used to do. Which of the prophets did your ancestors not persecute? They killed those who foretold the coming of the Righteous One, and now you have become his betrayers and murderers. You are the ones that received the law as ordained by angels, and yet you have not kept it."

When they heard these things, they became enraged and ground their teeth at Stephen. But filled with the Holy Spirit, he gazed into heaven and saw the glory of God and Jesus standing at the right hand of God. "Look," he said, "I see the heavens opened and the Son of Man standing at the right hand of God!" But they covered their ears, and with a loud shout all rushed together against him. Then they dragged him out of the city and began to stone him; and the witnesses laid their coats at the feet of a young man named Saul. While they were stoning Stephen, he prayed, "Lord Jesus, receive my spirit." Then he knelt down and cried out in a loud voice, "Lord, do not hold this sin against them." When he had said this, he died. (Acts 7:51–60)

We return in closing to the figure who has been something of a near-leitmotiv for this work as a whole. This project is in many ways an attempt to make sense of Stephen as a person whom Scripture holds as an exemplar of the missional practice of proclaiming the gospel.

He is ordained to the service of the poor so that the apostles might focus on the distinct task of proclaiming the gospel, and yet he himself engages in the practice of proclamation as well. He gives a well-crafted speech intent on conversion which fails to increase the number of converts to Christianity. He engages in dialogue that is both caustic and persuasive. He is willing both to condemn those who reject the message of Christ and forgive those who stone the messenger of Christ.

Yet it is Stephen who is presented by Luke as the first great martyr of the church. He radiantly displays the virtue of fortitude in refusing to couch his testimony to Christ's resurrection, the virtue of hope in anticipating his heavenly reward, and the virtue of love in forgiving those who destroy his earthly body. Stephen is given as a reward for his missionary labors the highest of gifts, the vision of Jesus standing at the right hand of the Father.

The only other individuals in Scripture who received this gift were the select few who beheld the Taboric glory of Christ on the Mount of Transfiguration.

To enter into the craft of mission is to take one's place alongside Stephen. The promise to those who faithfully pursue such practices, directing their efforts toward honoring and pleasing God, is that their lives will also radiantly display virtue, and though those virtues which shine forth may be different from Stephen's, the reward will be the same.

BIBLIOGRAPHY

—

Aagaard, Johannes. "Mission after Uppsala 1968." In *Critical Issues in Mission Today*, 13–21. Grand Rapids: Eerdmans, 1974.

———. "Trends in Missiological Thinking during the Sixties." *International Review of Mission* 62, no. 245 (1973): 8–25.

Afanasiev, Nicholas. *The Church of the Holy Spirit*. Notre Dame, IN: University of Notre Dame Press, 2007.

Allen, Roland. *Missionary Methods: St. Paul's or Ours?* Grand Rapids: Eerdmans, 1962.

———. *The Spontaneous Expansion of the Church: And the Causes Which Hinder It*. Grand Rapids: Eerdmans, 1962.

Anderson, Gerald H. "The Theology of Mission among Protestants in the Twentieth Century." In *The Theology of the Christian Mission*, edited by Gerald H. Anderson. New York: McGraw-Hill, 1965.

Annas, Julia. *Intelligent Virtue*. Oxford: Oxford University Press, 2013.

———. *The Morality of Happiness*. New York: Oxford University Press, 2009.

Anscombe, G. E. M. "Intention." *Proceedings of the Aristotelian Society* 57 (1956): 321–32.

Aquinas, Thomas. The *"Summa Theologica"* of St. Thomas Aquinas. 22 vols. Translated by Fathers of the English Dominican Province. London: Burns, Oates, & Washbourne, 1920–1935.

———. "New English Translation of St. Thomas Aquinas's *Summa Theologiae (Summa Theologica)*." Translated by Alfred J. Freddoso. Updated July 31, 2021. https://www3.nd.edu/~afreddos/summa-translation/TOC. htm.

Aristotle. *Nicomachean Ethics*. Translated by Martin Ostwald. Upper Saddle River, NJ: Prentice Hall, 1999.

———. *On Rhetoric: A Theory of Civic Discourse*. Translated by George A. Kennedy. New York: Oxford University Press, 1991.

Augustine. *Confessions*. Translated by Henry Chadwick. Oxford: Oxford
University Press, 2008.

———. *The Enchiridion on Faith, Hope and Love*. Translated by J. B. Shaw.
Washington, DC: Regnery Publishing, 1996.

———. *On Christian Teaching*. Translated by R. P. H. Green. New York:
Oxford University Press, 2008.

———. *The Trinity*. Translated by Edmund Hill. Hyde Park, NY: New City
Press, 1991.

Baldi, Cesare. "The Mission of the Church." In *Catholic Engagement with
World Religions: A Comprehensive Study*, edited by Karl Josef Becker,
Ilaria Morali, Maurice Borrmans, and Gavin D'Costa, 280-303.
Maryknoll, NY: Orbis Books, 2010.

Balthasar, Hans Urs von. *Dare We Hope "That All Men Be Saved"?: With a
Short Discourse of Hell*. San Francisco, CA: Ignatius Press, 1996.

———. *The Theology of Karl Barth: Exposition and Interpretation*. San
Francisco, CA: Ignatius Press, 1992.

Barclay, John M. G. "Pushing Back: Some Questions for Discussion." *Journal
for the Study of the New Testament* 33, no. 3 (2011): 321-26.

Barth, Karl. *Church Dogmatics*. Vol. II. Edited by G. W. Bromiley and
Thomas F. Torrance. Edinburgh: T&T Clarke, 1957.

———. *Church Dogmatics*. Vol. IV. Translated by G. W. Bromiley. Edinburgh:
T&T Clark, 1961.

———. *The Humanity of God*. Translated by John Newton Thomas.
Richmond, VA: John Knox Press, 1960.

Bevans, Stephen B. "Living between Gospel and Context." In *Confident
Witness—Changing World: Rediscovering the Gospel in North
America*, edited by Craig Van Gelder, 141-54. Grand Rapids:
Eerdmans, 1999.

Bevans, Stephen B., and Roger Schroeder. *Constants in Context: A Theology
of Mission for Today*. Maryknoll, NY: Orbis Books, 2004.

Bitzer, Lloyd F. "The Rhetorical Situation." *Philosophy & Rhetoric* 25 (1992):
1-14.

Bizzell, Patricia, and Bruce Herzberg. "Introduction." In *The Rhetorical
Tradition: Readings from Classical Times to the Present*. Boston, MA:
Bedford Books, 1990.

Bone, Jennifer Emerling, Cindy L. Griffin, and T. M. Linda Scholz. "Beyond Traditional Conceptualizations of Rhetoric: Invitational Rhetoric and a Move toward Civility." *Western Journal of Communication* 72, no. 4 (2008): 434-62.

Bonhoeffer, Dietrich. *Sanctorum Communio: A Theological Study of the Sociology of the Church*. Minneapolis: Fortress Press, 1998.

Booth, Wayne C. "The Rhetorical Stance." *College Composition and Communication* 14, no. 3 (1963): 139-45.

Bosch, David J. *Transforming Mission: Paradigm Shifts in Theology of Mission*. Maryknoll, NY: Orbis Books, 1991.

Bria, Ion. "The Liturgy after the Liturgy: Mission and Witness from an Orthodox Perspective." In *Martyria/Mission: The Witness of the Orthodox Churches Today*, edited by Ion Bria, 66-71. Geneva: WCC Publications, 1980.

Brockriede, Wayne. "Arguers as Lovers." *Philosophy & Rhetoric* 5, no. 1 (1972): 1-11.

Brown, Raymond E. *The Gospel according to John*. Vol. 29-29A. Garden City, NY: Doubleday, 1966.

Buber, Martin. *I and Thou*. Translated by Walter Arnold Kaufmann. New York: Charles Scribner's Sons, 1970.

Burke, Kenneth. "Four Master Tropes." *The Kenyon Review* 3, no. 4 (1941): 421-38.

———. *A Grammar of Motives*. Berkeley, CA: University of California Press, 1969.

———. *Permanence and Change: An Anatomy of Purpose*. Berkeley, CA: University of California Press, 1984.

Chadwick, William. *Stealing Sheep: The Church's Hidden Problem with Transfer Growth*. Downers Grove, IL: InterVarsity Press, 2001.

Chauvet, Louis-Marie. *Symbol and Sacrament: A Sacramental Reinterpretation of Christian Existence*. Collegeville, MN: Liturgical Press, 1995.

Chesterton, G. K. *Orthodoxy*. New York: Barnes and Noble, 2007.

Chrétien, Jean-Louis. *Under the Gaze of the Bible*. New York: Fordham University Press, 2015.

Chrysostom, John. *Six Books on the Priesthood*. Translated by Graham Neville. Crestwood, NY: St. Vladimir's Seminary Press, 1984.

Cobb, John B. "Beyond 'Pluralism.'" In *Christian Uniqueness Reconsidered: The Myth of a Pluralistic Theology of Religions*, edited by Gavin D'Costa, 81–96. Maryknoll, NY: Orbis Books, 1990.

———. *Beyond Dialogue: Toward a Mutual Transformation of Christianity and Buddhism*. Philadelphia, PA: Fortress Press, 1982.

———. *Christ in a Pluralistic Age*. Philadelphia, PA: Westminster Press, 1975.

———. "Introduction." In *Death or Dialogue: From the Age of Monologue to the Age of Dialogue*, edited by Leonard J. Swidler, John Boswell Cobb, Paul F. Knitter, and Monika K. Hellwig. London: SCM Press, 1990.

———. "Introduction." In *The Dialogue Comes of Age: Christian Encounters with Other Traditions*, edited by John B. Cobb and Ward McAfee, 1–9. Minneapolis, MN: Fortress Press, 2010.

———. "Rethinking Christian Faith in the Context of Religious Diversity." In *The Dialogue Comes of Age: Christian Encounters with Other Traditions*, edited by John B. Cobb and Ward McAfee, 9–40. Minneapolis, MN: Fortress Press, 2010.

———. *Transforming Christianity and the World: A Way beyond Absolutism and Relativism*. Maryknoll, NY: Orbis Books, 2004.

Cobb, John B., and Ward McAfee. *The Dialogue Comes of Age: Christian Encounters with Other Traditions*. Minneapolis, MN: Fortress Press, 2010.

Cochran, Elizabeth Agnew. *Protestant Virtue and Stoic Ethics*. London: Bloomsbury T&T Clark, 2018.

Colberg, Shawn M. "Aquinas and the Grace of Auxilium." *Modern Theology* 32, no. 2 (2016): 187–210.

Collins, Jim. *Good to Great: Why Some Companies Make the Leap ... And Others Don't*. London: Random House, 2009.

Congar, Yves. *I Believe in the Holy Spirit*. New York: Crossroad Publishing Company, 1997.

Cornille, Catherine. "Soteriological Agnosticism and the Future of Catholic Theology of Interreligious Dialogue." In *The Past, Present, and Future of Theologies of Interreligious Dialogue*, edited by Terrence Merrigan and John R. Friday, 201–15. Oxford, UK: Oxford University Press, 2017.

Crisp, Oliver. *Deviant Calvinism: Broadening Reformed Theology*. Minneapolis, MN: Fortress Press, 2014.

Cunningham, David S. *Faithful Persuasion: In Aid of a Rhetoric of Christian Theology*. Notre Dame, IN: University of Notre Dame Press, 1990.

D'Costa, Gavin, ed. *Christian Uniqueness Reconsidered: The Myth of a Pluralistic Theology of Religions*. Maryknoll, NY: Orbis Books, 2004.

———. "Pluralist Arguments: Prominent Tendencies and Methods." In *Catholic Engagement with World Religions: A Comprehensive Study*, edited by Karl Josef Becker, Ilaria Morali, Maurice Borrmans, and Gavin D'Costa, 329–43. Maryknoll, NY: Orbis Books, 2010.

Davis, Ellen F., and Richard B. Hays. "Nine Theses on the Interpreation of Scripture." In *The Art of Reading Scripture*, edited by Ellen F. Davis and Richard B. Hays, 1–9. Grand Rapids: Eerdmans, 2003.

Descartes, René. *A Discourse on the Method of Correctly Conducting One's Reason and Seeking Truth in the Sciences*. Translated by Ian Maclean. Oxford, UK: Oxford University Press, 2006.

Dix, Gregory. *The Shape of the Liturgy*. London: Dacre Press, 1970.

Dodaro, Robert. *Christ and the Just Society in the Thought of Augustine*. Cambridge, UK: Cambridge University Press, 2004.

Donovan, Vincent J. *Christianity Rediscovered*. Maryknoll, NY: Orbis Books, 2003.

———. "Response to Reflections on Christianity Rediscovered." *Missiology* 18, no. 3 (1990): 276–78.

Dunn, William N., and David Y. Miller. "A Critique of the New Public Management and the Neo-Weberian State: Advancing a Critical Theory of Administrative Reform." *Public Organization Review* 7, no. 4 (December 2007): 345–58.

Dupuis, Jacques. *Christianity and the Religions: From Confrontation to Dialogue*. Maryknoll, NY: Orbis Books, 2002.

———. *Toward a Christian Theology of Religious Pluralism*. Maryknoll, NY: Orbis Books, 1997.

Eberle, Christopher J. *Religious Conviction in Liberal Politics*. Cambridge, UK: Cambridge University Press, 2002.

Edwards, Jonathan. *The Works of Jonathan Edwards*. Vol. 7, *Ethical Writings*. Edited by Paul Ramsey. New Haven, CT: Yale University Press, 1989.

Ehninger, Douglas. "Argument as Method: Its Nature, Its Limitations and Its Uses." *Speech Monographs* 37, no. 2 (1970): 101.

———. "Introduction." In *Elements of Rhetoric: Comprising an Analysis of the Laws of Moral Evidence and of Persuasion, with Rules for Argumentative Composition and Elocution*, by Richard Whately, ix–xxii. Carbondale, IL: Southern Illinois University Press, 2010.

Emery, Gilles. *The Trinity: An Introduction to Catholic Doctrine on the Triune God*. Washington, DC: Catholic University of America Press, 2011.

Flett, John G. *The Witness of God: The Trinity, Missio Dei, Karl Barth, and the Nature of Christian Community*. Grand Rapids: Eerdmans, 2010.

Foss, Sonja K., and Cindy L. Griffin. "Beyond Persuasion: A Proposal for an Invitational Rhetoric." *Communication Monographs* 62, no. 1 (1995): 2–18.

Frost, Michael, and Alan Hirsch. *The Shaping of Things to Come: Innovation and Mission for the 21st-Century Church*. Peabody, MA: Hendrickson, 2003.

Fulkerson, Richard. "Transcending Our Conception of Argument in Light of Feminist Critiques." *Argumentation & Advocacy* 32, no. 4 (1996): 199–217.

Gass, Robert H., and John S. Seiter. *Persuasion, Social Influence, and Compliance Gaining*. Boston, MA: Allyn and Bacon, 1999.

Gibson, Mary Ellis. "Henry Martyn and England's Christian Empire: Rereading *Jane Eyre* through Missionary Biography." *Victorian Literature and Culture* 27, no. 2 (1999): 419–42.

Gregory the Great. *The Book of Pastoral Rule*. Crestwood, NY: St. Vladimir's Seminary Press, 2007.

Gregory of Nyssa. *The Life of Moses*. Translated by Abraham Malherbe and Everett Ferguson. New York: Paulist Press, 1978.

———. *On the Soul and Resurrection*. Translated by Catharine P. Roth. Crestwood, NY: St. Vladimir's Seminary Press, 2002.

Guder, Darrell L. *Called to Witness: Doing Missional Theology*. Grand Rapids: Eerdmans, 2015.

Gunton, Colin E. *The One, the Three, and the Many: God, Creation, and the Culture of Modernity*. Cambridge: Cambridge University Press, 1993.

Hart, David Bentley. *The Beauty of the Infinite: The Aesthetics of Christian Truth*. Grand Rapids: Eerdmans, 2007.

Haslam, Nick. "Concept Creep: Psychology's Expanding Concepts of Harm and Pathology." *Psychological Inquiry* 27, no. 1 (2016): 1–17.

Hauerwas, Stanley. "Democratic Time: Lessons Learned from Yoder and Wolin." *Cross Currents* 55, no. 4 (2006): 534–52.

Hauerwas, Stanley, and Charles Robert Pinches. *Christians among the Virtues: Theological Conversations with Ancient and Modern Ethics.* Notre Dame, IN: University of Notre Dame Press, 1997.

Hays, Richard B. *The Moral Vision of the New Testament: Community, Cross, New Creation; A Contemporary Introduction to New Testament Ethics.* London: T&T Clark, 2003.

Hayward, Victor E. W., and Donald McGavran. "Without Crossing Barriers: One in Christ vs. Discipling Diverse Cultures." *Missiology* 2, no. 2 (1974): 203–24.

Herdt, Jennifer A. *Putting on Virtue: The Legacy of the Splendid Vices.* Chicago: The University of Chicago Press, 2012.

Hibbert, Richard Yates. "Negotiating Identity: Extending and Applying Alan Tippett's Model of Conversion to Believers from Muslim and Hindu Backgrounds." *Missiology* 43, no. 1 (2015): 59–72.

Hick, John. "The Next Step beyond Dialogue." In *The Myth of Religious Superiority: Multifaith Explorations of Religious Pluralism,* edited by Paul F. Knitter, 3–13. Maryknoll, NY: Orbis Books, 2005.

Hick, John, and Paul F. Knitter, eds. *The Myth of Christian Uniqueness: Toward a Pluralistic Theology of Religions.* Maryknoll, NY: Orbis Books, 1987.

Hirsch, Alan. *The Forgotten Ways: Reactivating Apostolic Movements.* Grand Rapids: Brazos Press, 2016.

———. *The Forgotten Ways: Reactivating the Missional Church.* Grand Rapids: Brazos Press, 2006.

Holladay, Carl R. *Acts: A Commentary.* Louisville, KY: Westminster John Knox Press, 2016.

Hunter, George G. "The Legacy of Donald A. McGavran." *International Bulletin of Missionary Research* 16, no. 4 (1992): 158.

Johnson, Keith L. "A Reappraisal of Karl Barth's Theological Development and His Dialogue with Catholicism." *International Journal of Systematic Theology* 14, no. 1 (2012): 3–25.

Johnson, Luke Timothy. *The Acts of the Apostles.* Collegeville, MN: Liturgical Press, 1992.

Kant, Immanuel. *Critique of Pure Reason*. Translated by Paul Guyer and
    Allen W. Wood. New York: Cambridge University Press, 1998.

Kelsey, David H. *The Uses of Scripture in Recent Theology*. Philadelphia, PA:
    Fortress Press, 1975.

Knitter, Paul F. *Jesus and the Other Names: Christian Mission and Global
    Responsibility*. Maryknoll, NY: Orbis Books, 1996.

Lacoste, Jean-Yves. *Experience and the Absolute: Disputed Questions on the
    Humanity of Man*. Translated by Mark Raftery-Skehan. New York:
    Fordham University Press, 2004.

———. "More Haste, Less Speed in Theology." *International Journal of
    Systematic Theology* 9, no. 3 (2007): 263-82.

Lewis, C. S. *The Screwtape Letters with Screwtape Proposes a Toast*. New York:
    HarperOne, 2015.

Lindbeck, George A. *The Nature of Doctrine: Religion and Theology in a
    Postliberal Age*. London: SPCK, 1984.

Littlejohn, W. Bradford. "Addicted to Novelty: The Vice of Curiosity in a
    Digital Age." *Journal of the Society of Christian Ethics* 37, no. 1 (Spring
    2017): 179-96.

Locke, John. "An Essay Concerning Human Understanding." In *The
    Rhetorical Tradition: Readings from Classical Times to the Present*,
    edited by Patricia Bizzell and Bruce Herzberg, 699-710. Boston, MA:
    Bedford Books, 1990.

Lohfink, Gerhard. *Does God Need the Church? Toward a Theology of the
    People of God*. Translated by Linda M. Maroney. Collegeville, MN:
    Liturgical Press, 2014.

Long, D. Stephen. "From the Hidden God to the God of Glory: Barth,
    Balthasar, and Nominalism." *Pro Ecclesia* 20, no. 2 (2011): 167-84.

———. *The Perfectly Simple Triune God: Aquinas and His Legacy*. Minneapolis,
    MN: Fortress Press, 2016.

———. *Saving Karl Barth: Hans Urs Von Balthasar's Preoccupation*.
    Minneapolis, MN: Fortress Press, 2014.

Lozano-Reich, Nina M., and Dana L. Cloud. "The Uncivil Tongue:
    Invitational Rhetoric and the Problem of Inequality." *Western
    Journal of Communication* 73, no. 2 (2009): 220-26.

Luther, Martin. "Concerning the Ministry." Translated by Conrad

Bergendoff. In *Luther's Works*, vol. 40, *Church and Ministry II*, edited by Conrad Bergendoff. Philadelphia, PA: Fortress Press, 1975.

MacIntyre, Alasdair C. *After Virtue: A Study in Moral Theory*. 2nd ed. Notre Dame, IN: University of Notre Dame Press, 1984.

———. *Dependent Rational Animals: Why Human Beings Need the Virtues*. Chicago, IL: Open Court Press, 2011.

———. *Ethics in the Conflicts of Modernity: An Essay on Desire, Practical Reasoning, and Narrative*. Cambridge: Cambridge University Press, 2016.

———. "Intractable Moral Disagreements." In *Intractable Disputes about the Natural Law: Alasdair MacIntyre and Critics*, edited by Lawrence S. Cunningham, 1–52. Notre Dame, IN: University of Notre Dame Press, 2009.

———. *A Short History of Ethics: A History of Moral Philosophy from the Homeric Age to the Twentieth Century*. New York: Macmillan, 1966.

———. *Three Rival Versions of Moral Enquiry: Encyclopaedia, Genealogy, and Tradition*. Notre Dame, IN: University of Notre Dame Press, 1990.

Malieckal, Bindu. "Early Modern Goa: Indian Trade, Transcultural Medicine, and the Inquisition." *Scripta Instituti Donneriani Aboensis* 26 (2015): 135–57.

Marion, Jean-Luc. *The Visible and the Revealed*. New York: Fordham University Press, 2008.

McCabe, Herbert. *The Good Life: Ethics and the Pursuit of Happiness*. London: Bloomsbury, 2005.

———. *What Is Ethics All About?* Washington: Corpus Books, 1969.

McFadyen, Alistair I. *The Call to Personhood: A Christian Theory of the Individual in Social Relationships*. Cambridge: Cambridge University Press, 1990.

McGavran, Donald A. "Loose the Churches: Let Them Go! An Essential Issue in Indian Evangelism." *Missiology* 1, no. 2 (1973): 81–94.

———. "My Pilgrimage in Mission." *International Bulletin of Missionary Research* 10, no. 2 (1986): 53–58.

———. *Understanding Church Growth*. Grand Rapids: Eerdmans, 1970.

McGrath, Alister E. *Luther's Theology of the Cross: Martin Luther's Theological Breakthrough*. Oxford: Wiley-Blackwell, 2011.

————. *What Was God Doing on the Cross?* Eugene, OR: Wipf and Stock, 2002.

McKenny, Gerald P. *The Analogy of Grace: Karl Barth's Moral Theology.* Oxford: Oxford University Press, 2013.

————. "Moral Disagreements and the Limits of Reason: Reflections on MacIntyre and Ratzinger." In *Intractable Disputes about the Natural Law: Alasdair MacIntyre and Critics,* edited by Lawrence S. Cunningham, 195–226. Notre Dame, IN: University of Notre Dame Press, 2009.

Meilaender, Gilbert C. *The Theory and Practice of Virtue.* Notre Dame, IN: University of Notre Dame Press, 1984.

Middleton, Vern, Charles H. Kraft, Paul E. Pierson, Alan McMahan, Brad Gill, Steve Wilkes, Jeff K. Walters, et al. "The Legacy of Donald McGavran: A Forum." *International Journal of Frontier Missiology* 31, no. 2 (2014): 61–72.

Milbank, John. "The End of Dialogue." In *Christian Uniqueness Reconsidered: The Myth of a Pluralistic Theology of Religions,* edited by Gavin D'Costa, 174–92. Maryknoll, NY: Orbis Books, 1990.

————. *Theology and Social Theory: Beyond Secular Reason.* Oxford: Blackwell, 2006.

Muller, Richard A. *Post-Reformation Reformed Dogmatics.* Vol. 2. Grand Rapids: Baker Academic, 2006.

Neill, Stephen. *Creative Tension.* London: Edinburgh House Press, 1959.

Newbigin, Lesslie. *The Open Secret: An Introduction to the Theology of Mission.* Grand Rapids: Eerdmans, 1995.

Newman, John Henry. *An Essay in Aid of a Grammar of Assent.* London: Oxford University Press, 1985.

Niebauer, Michael. "Dialogue or Proclamation? Communication Ethics and the Problem of Persuasion in Mission." *Missiology* 45, no. 3 (2017): 336–48.

O'Collins, Gerald. *Salvation for All: God's Other Peoples.* Oxford: Oxford University Press, 2008.

O'Donovan, Oliver. *Common Objects of Love: Moral Reflection and the Shaping of Community; The 2001 Stob Lectures.* Grand Rapids: Eerdmans, 2002.

————. *Entering into Rest.* Grand Rapids: Eerdmans, 2017.

————. *Finding and Seeking: Ethics as Theology.* Vol. 2. Grand Rapids: Eerdmans, 2014.

———. *Resurrection and Moral Order: An Outline for Evangelical Ethics*. Grand Rapids: Eerdmans, 1994.

———. *Self, World, and Time: Ethics as Theology*. Vol. 3. Grand Rapids: Eerdmans, 2013.

———. *The Ways of Judgment: The Bampton Lectures, 2003*. Grand Rapids: Eerdmans, 2008.

O'Meara, Thomas F. "Virtues in the Theology of Thomas Aquinas." *Theological Studies* 58, no. 2 (1997): 254–85.

Oborji, Francis Anekwe. *Concepts of Mission: The Evolution of Contemporary Missiology*. Maryknoll, NY: Orbis Books, 2006.

Ortner, Sherry B. "Fieldwork in the Postcommunity." *Anthropology and Humanism* 22, no. 1 (1997): 61–80.

Pascale, Richard T. *Managing on the Edge: How Successful Companies Use Conflict to Stay Ahead*. New York: Penguin Books, 1991.

Perelman, Chaïm, and Lucie Olbrechts-Tyteca. *The New Rhetoric: A Treatise on Argumentation*. Translated by John Wilkinson and Purcell Weaver. Notre Dame, IN: University of Notre Dame Press, 1969.

Peters, Thomas J. *Thriving on Chaos: Handbook for a Management Revolution*. New York: Knopf, 1987.

Pieper, Josef. *Prudence*. London: Faber and Faber, 1960.

Pinches, Charles Robert. "Human Action and the Meaning of Morality: A Critique of Jean Porter on Action and Aquinas. " *Pro Ecclesia* 12, no. 2 (Spring 2003): 133–58.

Plato. "Gorgias." In *The Rhetorical Tradition: Readings from Classical Times to the Present*, edited by Patricia Bizzell and Bruce Herzberg, 61–112. Boston, MA: Bedford Books, 1990.

———. "Phaedrus." In *The Rhetorical Tradition: Readings from Classical Times to the Present*, edited by Patricia Bizzell and Bruce Herzberg, 113–43. Boston, MA: Bedford Books, 1990.

Porter, Jean. *The Recovery of Virtue: The Relevance of Aquinas for Christian Ethics*. Louisville, KY: Westminster John Knox Press, 1990.

———. "The Subversion of Virtue: Acquired and Infused Virtues in the *Summa Theologiae*." *The Annual of the Society of Christian Ethics* (1992): 19–41.

Pseudo-Dionysius. *Pseudo-Dionysius: The Complete Works*. New York: Paulist Press, 1987.

Ricoeur, Paul. *Essays on Biblical Interpretation*. Edited by Lewis Seymour Mudge. Philadelphia, PA: Fortress Press, 1985.

——. *The Symbolism of Evil*. Translated by Emerson Buchanan. Boston, MA: Beacon Press, 1967.

Rosin, H. H. *"Missio Dei": An Examination of the Origin, Contents and Function of the Term in Protestant Missiological Discussion*. Leiden: Interuniversity Institute for Missiological and Ecumenical Research, Department of Missiology, 1972.

Rowe, Christopher Kavin. "Reading World Upside Down: A Response to Matthew Sleeman and John Barclay." *Journal for the Study of the New Testament* 33, no. 3 (2011): 335–46.

——. *World Upside Down: Reading Acts in the Graeco-Roman Age*. Oxford: Oxford University Press, 2009.

Ryle, Gilbert. *The Concept of Mind*. London: Hutchinson, 1969.

Sanneh, Lamin O. *Disciples of All Nations: Pillars of World Christianity*. Oxford, UK: Oxford University Press, 2008.

——. *Translating the Message: The Missionary Impact on Culture*. Maryknoll, NY: Orbis Books, 1989.

Sargent, John. *A Memoir of Rev. Henry Martyn*. Boston: Perkins and Marvin, 1831.

Sokolowski, Robert. *The God of Faith and Reason: Foundations of Christian Theology*. Notre Dame, IN: University of Notre Dame Press, 1982.

Sunquist, Scott W. *Understanding Christian Mission: Participation in Suffering and Glory*. Grand Rapids: Baker Publishing Group, 2013.

Tanner, Kathryn. *God and Creation in Christian Theology: Tyranny or Empowerment*. Minneapolis, MN: Fortress Press, 2005.

——. *Theories of Culture: A New Agenda for Theology*. Minneapolis, MN: Fortress Press, 1997.

Taylor, Charles. *Human Agency and Language*. Vol. 1, *Philosophical Papers*. Cambridge: Cambridge University Press, 1985.

——. *A Secular Age*. Cambridge, MA: Harvard University Press, 2007.

Tillard, J.-M.R. *Church of Churches: The Ecclesiology of Communion*. Collegeville, MN: Liturgical Press, 1992.

Tippett, Alan Richard. "Conversion as a Dynamic Process in Christian Mission." *Missiology* 5, no. 2 (1977): 203–21.

Toulmin, Stephen Edelston. *The Uses of Argument*. Updated Edition.

Cambridge, UK: Cambridge University Press, 2003.

Vanhoozer, Kevin J. *The Drama of Doctrine: A Canonical-Linguistic Approach to Christian Theology.* Louisville, KY: Westminster John Knox Press, 2005.

———. *Is There a Meaning in This Text?: The Bible, the Reader, and the Morality of Literary Knowledge.* Grand Rapids: Zondervan, 1998.

Vicedom, Georg F. *The Mission of God: An Introduction to a Theology of Mission.* Translated by Gilbert A. Thiele and Dennis Hilgendorf. Saint Louis, MO: Concordia Publishing House, 1965.

Walls, Andrew F. *The Cross-Cultural Process in Christian History: Studies in the Transmission and Appropriation of Faith.* Maryknoll, NY: Orbis Books, 2002.

———. *The Missionary Movement in Christian History: Studies in the Transmission of Faith.* Maryknoll, NY: Orbis Books, 2009.

Ward, Kevin. "Africa." In *A World History of Christianity*, edited by Adrian Hastings, 192–238. Grand Rapids: Eerdmans, 2000.

Weaver, Darlene Fozard. *The Acting Person and Christian Moral Life.* Washington, DC: Georgetown University Press, 2011.

Webster, John. *Barth.* London: Continuum, 2000.

Wetzel, James. *Augustine and the Limits of Virtue.* New York: Cambridge University Press, 2008.

Whately, Richard. *Elements of Rhetoric: Comprising an Analysis of the Laws of Moral Evidence and of Persuasion, with Rules for Argumentative Composition and Elocution.* Carbondale, IL: Southern Illinois University Press, 2010.

Wheatley, Margaret J. *Leadership and the New Science: Discovering Order in a Chaotic World.* San Francisco, CA: Berrett-Koehler Publishers, 1999.

Wiebe, Donald. "Before and after Dialogue: Is There a Significant Difference? A Response to John Cobb's 'Beyond Dialogue.'" *Buddhist-Christian Studies* 6 (1986): 145–49.

Wittgenstein, Ludwig. *Philosophical Investigations.* Translated by G. E. M. Anscombe. Oxford: Basil Blackwell, 1958.

Woodworth-Eller, Maria Beulah. "Sermon on Visions and Trances." In *Reader in Pentecostal Theology: Voices from the First Generation*, edited by Douglas Jacobsen, 26–28. Bloomington, IN: Indiana University Press, 2006.

Young, Frances Margaret. *Biblical Exegesis and the Formation of Christian Culture*. Cambridge: Cambridge University Press, 2007.

Zago, Marcello Abp. "The New Millennium and the Emerging Religious Encounters." *Missiology* 28, no. 1 (2000): 5–18.

Zarefsky, David. *Rhetorical Perspectives on Argumentation: Selected Essays*. Cham, Switzerland: Springer International Press, 2014.

SUBJECT INDEX

—

A

39 Articles, 112, 206
Aagaard, Johannes, 16, 27
Acts, Book of, 92, 144-46, 155-56, 174-75, 193, 195-96, 200-3
actualism, 24-25
adaptation, 91, 181-87
Afanasiev, Nicholas, 195, 226-27
agency, 3, 7, 18-26, 110-12, 173n38, 238-39
agency, missionary agency, 19-22, 67-68
agency, of missionary recipient, 22-24, 64-66, 88-91, 163, 187-90
agency, relationship between human and divine, 30-36, 120-22, 155, 253
agnosticism, 76n17
Allen, Roland, 212, 223, 229-33, 240, 242n71, 251
analogy, principle of, 33, 121
Ananias, 174n39
Anderson, Gerald, 14n7
Annas, Julia, 124n39, 141, 141n83
Anscome, G. E. M, 66n58
antecedant probabilities, 159, 161-62, 180n59, 183, 187
anthropology, 14, 76-78, 82-83, 90-91
apprentice, 140-41, 231, 246
Aquinas, Thomas, 25, 30, 110-11, 114, 117-37, 147-56, 161n7, 180n56, 198, 248, 252-53, 259
Aristotle, 52, 96n64, 97-99, 104, 124n39, 125n42, 129n56, 170, 179

Augustine, 23n30, 119n23, 132, 133n67, 148, 153, 167-69, 170n29, 171n32, 256
Austen, Jane, 148-49
Austin, J. L., 181
authority, 24, 36, 131-32, 185, 201, 206-7, 217, 223-41, 266

B

Balthasar, Hans Urs von, 24-26
baptism, 212, 226-27, 242-43
Barnabas, 94-95, 189n77
Barth, Karl, 5n3, 14-16, 20-26, 28-33, 31n55, 129n57, 251
beauty, 114, 192, 224, 260
Bevans, 13, 23, 116n19, 157, 168-69, 182n61, 247
Bible, 206, 214-23
Bible, Biblical Construals, 59-60
Bible, Canon, 114n5, 115, 216-17
Bible, Fittingness, 112-16, 155, 203
Bible, Interpretation, 112-16, 216
Bitzer, Lloyd, 169
Bonhoeffer, Dietrich, 233-34
Booth, Wayne, 218-19
Bosch, David, 13, 15-16, 26-27, 29, 35, 38, 247
Bria, Ion, 243
Brockriede, Wayne, 104
Brontë, Charlotte, 257, 262-63
Brown, Raymond, 133
Buber, Martin, 101, 214
Burke, Kenneth, 101, 172, 221n46

SCRIPTURE INDEX

—